Contents

About the series

Macmillan Books for Teachers

Welcome to **Macmillan Books for Teachers.** The titles are written by acknowledged and innovative leaders in each field to help you develop your teaching repertoire, practical skill and theoretical knowledge.

Suited to both newer and to more experienced teachers, the series combines the best of classic teaching methodology with recent, cutting-edge developments. Insights from academic research are combined with hands-on experience to create books with focus on real-world teaching solutions.

We hope you will find the ideas in them a source of inspiration in your own teaching and enjoyment in your professional learning.

Adrian Underhill

Titles in the series

500 Activities for the Primary Classroom
Carol Read

700 Classroom Activities
David Seymour & Maria Popova

An A–Z of ELT
Scott Thornbury

Blended Learning
Pete Sharma & Barney Barrett

Beyond the Sentence
Scott Thornbury

Children Learning English
Jayne Moon

Discover English
Rod Bolitho & Brian Tomlinson

Learning Teaching
Jim Scrivener

Sound Foundations
Adrian Underhill

Teaching Practice
Roger Gower, Diane Phillips & Steve Walters

Teaching English Grammar
Jim Scrivener

Teaching Reading Skills
Christine Nuttall

Uncovering CLIL
Peeter Mehisto, David Marsh & Maria Jesus Frigols

Uncovering EAP
Sam McCarter & Phil Jakes

Uncovering Grammar
Scott Thornbury

400 IDEAS FOR INTERACTIVE WHITEBOARDS

Instant Activities using Technology

Pete Sharma, Barney Barrett and Francis Jones

MACMILLAN

Macmillan Education
4 Crinan Street
London N1 9XW
A division of Macmillan Publishers Limited
Companies and representatives throughout the world

ISBN 978-0-230-41764-9

Series design by Mike Brain
Typography by Greg Sweetnam
Page layout by MPS Limited, a Macmillan Company
Cover design by Andrew Oliver
Cover photograph by Alamy/John Terence Turner
Illustrated by MPS Limited, a Macmillan Company

The publishers would like to thank Graham Stanley for his thoughtful insights and recommendations when reviewing the manuscript, Sandra Attard-Montalto, Agata Biernat, James Dunbar, Vilson Coimbra Oliveira Filho, Brian Finch, Kirsty Greig, Sarah Milligan, Adam Ramejkis, Anita Strasser and Jo Timerick for kindly contributing ideas and Barbara Gardner for coordinating them, Elaine Allender, Samantha Birkett and Dita Phillips at British Study Centres and Victoria Pradas for allowing their lessons to be observed and Julia Glass, Miranda Hamilton and Jamie Keddie for sharing views, opinions and ideas on how technology should be used in class.

Authors' acknowledgements
Many thanks to everyone at Macmillan Education for their wonderful hard work and

Printed and bound in Thailand

2018 2017 2016
9 8 7 6 5 4

dedication to this project, and to our Series Editor, Adrian Underhill; this book is truly a team effort.

Pete Sharma
Thanks to the staff in the Teaching Grid, Warwick University, UK for their help in running the lesson which provided the inspiration for the *Experimental Teaching Space* case study. Thanks to Anne Laws and her work on cultural awareness training which informs the activity *The Ideal Colleague*. Thanks to author Vaughan Jones for providing the inspiration behind 'toggling' between publisher-produced materials and materials from the Internet and also to Claudio Franco for his ideas on using a wiki for peer correction. Thanks to María and Jade, for their love, patience and support.

Barney Barrett
Thanks to Steve Lowe, Louise Raven and all the teaching staff at marcus evans Linguarama in Stratford-upon-Avon whose classroom experience and teaching ideas provided the basis or inspiration for many of the activities. Thanks also to John and Mary Barrett for their love and support.

Francis Jones
Many thanks to Pete S for the training and for fixing that first gig in Madrid all those years ago. Thanks also to Norman Harrison for IT support in times of crisis and to Mary Rebelo for her assistance and good advice. Thanks to Steve Chapman at Dragonfly Training for introducing me to IWBs and for his continued support, help and friendship. Finally, biggest thanks of all to Nicole, Eva and Harri for their love, support and unending patience.

The author and publishers would like to thank the following for permission to reproduce their photographs:

Macmillan/FANCY p219(tl), Macmillan/ImageSource p219(tr).

About the authors

Pete Sharma

Pete started his EFL career as a Business English teacher in Madrid, moving to Finland before returning to the UK. Variety is the spice of life, and the quest for variety has driven his work as a teacher, teacher trainer, Director of Studies and school manager. He became the training and development manager for Linguarama, a Business English organisation, and has inspected schools, taught writing seminars in the Middle and Far East, and helped create trainer training courses. Changing from ESP to EAP, he currently divides his time between lecturing at universities and writing. He is a self-confessed conference addict, presenting regularly at IATEFL and BESIG. The use of technology in language teaching really 'lights his fire', although spending six years to complete a Masters in Educational Technology and ELT may be stretching the point. Pete is the co-founder and co-director of Pete Sharma Associates, a training organisation: http://www.psa.eu.com. He regularly blogs and tweets on technology.

Barney Barrett

Barney has worked as a business English teacher since the mid-1990s. After a brief stint working in-company in Spain, he returned to the UK and settled down as a member of the core teaching team at the marcus evans Linguarama school in Stratford-upon-Avon. It was here that he met Pete. Their mutual interest in computer-based language learning resulted in two co-authored books for language teachers: *The Internet and Business English* (Summertown, 2003) and *Blended Learning* (Macmillan, 2007). With and without Pete, he also writes teaching materials for interactive and online products as well as for more traditional formats. When not trying to figure out the pedagogical possibilities of digital technologies, he is more likely than not to be found out on his mountain bike.

Francis Jones

Francis began his EFL career working for Linguarama in Canterbury before taking up a post in Madrid where he spent two years before moving to Italy. Back in the UK for over a decade, he has a keen interest in media formats and IT. He has written for and produced a great number of television and radio programmes in the UK, whilst also developing and delivering training programmes across a range of areas. He was one of the first IWB trainers to specialise in EFL when he started delivering courses in the subject for the training consultancy Dragonfly Training some years ago, and has also delivered his own media training courses for pupils and teachers at secondary schools across the UK. These include film-making and video and radio production courses.

Foreword

It seems that the Interactive Whiteboard has the potential to change English Language Teaching classrooms around the world, and perhaps more thoroughly than previous technological developments. And as the price in real terms falls and publishers bring out coursebooks fully-designed for IWBs, we are likely to see them spread at an even greater rate. The speed and competence with which teachers have learnt to exploit the IWB to enhance their own teaching style is remarkable, indicating a stronger and more positive response than to many previous technological advances. The heads-up, participatory nature of IWBs will mean that with good training there will be further moves away from teacher-dominated presentational activities towards active student engagement and participation not possible with conventional boards.

This handbook is designed to help you get up to speed smartly and quickly, based on the experience of countless teachers, brought together and presented by the authors, all of them trainers in ELT technology. More experienced IWB users will find ideas here to expand and increase their repertoire.

If you are new to the IWB then the first of the four chapters *Using regular programs* enables you to get off to a quick start by using the IWB as a giant class computer screen, on which you can display any of the software you usually use on your computer. You could display an activity you have designed instead of photocopying it, or an Internet page or photos. Then using pen, finger or virtual onscreen keyboard, you and your students can immediately interact with that material by writing on the IWB over or beside the text or picture, editing, highlighting, pasting, directly on the interactive board. There is an immediate kinaesthetic connection between class, material and language activity. And at the click of a button all this can be saved to revise later.

In the second chapter *Using the whiteboard software*, the capabilities of the inbuilt IWB software are explored. These enable you to drag, cover, colour, resize and store, use dice, quizzes, and make use of a wide range of ready-made lesson activities into which you simply drop the language data you want to practise. Some dedicated activities for individual brands of whiteboards are also included and in these cases there are usually similar tools on the other brands.

The third chapter *Using published materials* enables you to exploit the IWB functionality alongside the new generation of published materials designed around IWB applications. You can display heads-up versions of texts, pictures, dialogues, questions, all of which can be clicked to reveal further activities, sound files or videos. Thus you no longer need to hunt down the books, tapes, CDs or CD player before the lesson. None of this is necessary in the all-in-one package displayed on the interactive screen.

Chapter four, entitled *Creating and adapting your own materials,* helps you master the basic skills you need to create or enhance any of your self-designed and adapted materials. Apart from being attractive, colourful and tactile, the IWB immediately opens up the opportunity for a more heads-up, interactive and cooperative learning community.

The activities in this handbook are designed to serve as springboards for the new forms of creativity that the IWB brings, and to inspire teachers to exploit what amounts to a paradigm shift in classroom potential.

Adrian Underhill Series Editor

Introduction

1.1 What is an interactive whiteboard?

An interactive whiteboard (IWB) is a large interactive display that connects to a computer and projector. The data projector projects the image of the computer screen onto the surface of the whiteboard. Users then control the computer and software through this tactile interface using either a special e-pen, or their finger.

This introduction to using IWBs offers an overview of the main options and choices to be made before using one in the language classroom. It then describes the features, benefits and challenges of using an IWB. If you have already installed the IWB, or already have experience of using it, you can skip this introduction.

1.2 Practicalities

Hardware

There are a number of makes of IWB. Market leaders include Smart and Promethean. The software included with all makes of IWBs has a number of core features, such as drawing tools, and on-screen keyboard and character-recognition. Users of SmartBoards interact with the board with their finger, or pens; users of Promethean Activboard use a special e-pen. Other well-known makes include the Hitachi Starboard. All these products come with an indispensable user manual from the manufacturer, and training is usually provided. Product websites contain a huge range of information, support material, online training modules, ready-made lessons and lesson ideas.

Size

Interactive whiteboards come in a range of sizes, from fairly small and portable to the larger wall-mounted IWBs for use with full-size classes. A smaller board could sit on a table and be viewed comfortably by a small group of students. A standard screen size is 48"-77"; a wider screen format is 87"-94".

Mobility

One of the first choices to make is whether to have a mobile set-up, so the board can be moved from room to room, or a static set-up in which the board is permanently mounted on the wall.

The advantage to having a mobile board is that it allows a school to purchase just one IWB and then use it in a number of classrooms. Moving it usually involves pushing the IWB on a trolley with wheels. There are a number of disadvantages to moving the IWB around, such as having to disconnect and reconnect cables each time you do this, the possibility of tripping over cables and the regular need to re-calibrate the board with the projector.

An ideal solution for a school would be to have an IWB in each room although this obviously has a cost implication! If the board is fixed, then everything is already set up and in place when teachers come into the classroom.

Electronic data projectors

There are a number of options for setting up the projector. In the mobile board set-up, the projector can simply sit on the table next to the computer. In classrooms with a permanent IWB set-up, the projector is often ceiling mounted and the teacher uses an infra-red remote control to turn it on and off. The current trend is to have a built-in projector above the IWB. This is known as a 'short-throw' projector and this eliminates problems such as users staring into the beam of light, or casting a shadow across the screen.

Portable alternatives to IWBs

There are a number of portable alternatives to using a full-sized IWB. The mimio is one such device which can be temporarily fixed to a hard surface, such as a normal whiteboard, using the small suckers on the reverse of the device. Like the IWB, the mimio requires connecting to a projector. The mimio is positioned next to an image of a computer screen from the data projector, and it is this image which then becomes interactive. Users interact with the image with a special e-pen. This device could be a boon for those seeking a low-cost way to try out IWB functionality with small groups, or for freelance teachers who teach in a number of sites.

Another alternative is the ebeam, a circular device which is similar in functionality to a mimio. It is also 'stuck' onto the whiteboard, and like the mimio, needs to be connected to an electronic data projector. Ingenious teachers have even explored low-cost alternatives, such as the use of a common Wii remote control. While providing some of the benefits of using a full-size IWB, there are limitations, such as the lack of proprietary software.

Setting up

To get up and running, the data projector needs to be connected to the computer as usual with a single cable. The whiteboard is connected with a USB cable to the USB port on the computer. The installation of the IWB hardware, followed by the loading of proprietary software (such as Smart software and Promethean Activinspire) is usually taken care of by the manufacturer or the re-seller.

When the teacher prepares the classroom for a lesson, the sequence of turning on the IWB is fairly straightforward:

1 Turn on the computer.

2 Turn on the data projector.

3 The IWB should then display the computer screen.

The manual contains all the relevant information for setting up the whiteboard, as well as FAQs (frequently-asked questions) and tips for trouble-shooting.

The teacher needs to learn the sequence for calibrating the IWB. On a SmartBoard, click the *Orient* symbol in the Control panel. There are a number of points displayed on the screen; simply click on these points to calibrate the board. Boards need calibrating at regular intervals.

1.3 Features

There are a number of exciting features on an IWB.

Annotation

When you write on the surface of the IWB, you can save your annotations. When you click to close a flipchart you are working on, an on-screen message appears asking you if you want to 'Save annotations'. If you click *yes*, then you should save this as a file with a new name.

Zoom tool

The *marquee zoom* allows teachers to use the zoom tool to crop any part of a picture or page and enlarge it.

Screen reveal

This allows teachers to cover part of the screen and reveal it bit by bit. It is similar to the spotlight tool, which comprises a circle which you can move across the board to reveal any part of the surface.

Screen capture

You can take a snapshot of the IWB screen and save this as a picture.

On-screen keyboard

The on-screen keyboard allows users to enter text on the IWB as an alternative to the computer keyboard.

Handwriting recognition

You can write text with the pen, mouse over this and change it to editable text.

Learner response systems

Learner response systems, or personal response systems, allow students to vote on a particular topic. Students are given a small, hand-held device which allows them to press an option (A, B or C, for example) and vote on a subject. After voting, the results are displayed on screen.

Text-input devices allow students to type in characters, rather like texting, so they can spell words, for example. The students' answers are sent wirelessly to the IWB.

Slates

The teacher can use a slate, or tablet, to work on the IWB from a distance. This allows the teacher to walk around the room, perhaps behind the students, as opposed to having to be standing next to the whiteboard. It also means they can hand the slate to the learners, who can pass it to other students.

1.4 The benefits of using an IWB

There are a number of ways using an IWB can enrich a language lesson.

Using multimedia

An IWB allows teachers and students to benefit from the full range of multimedia in their language classrooms. This includes video, DVD, pictures, audio, and the Internet. Using the Internet includes not only websites but also social networking sites, blogs, wikis and Virtual Learning Environments. Previously, much digital learning material such as CD-ROMs were largely consigned to individual use in the self access centre, rather than being integrated into lessons.

Memorable lesson lead-ins

The teacher can reveal a photograph bit by bit to generate interest in a topic. Video clips, animations and photographs can all be used to create memorable lesson lead-ins.

Involving learners

Language practice can be physical, fun and motivating, with students coming out to the front to manipulate objects on the whiteboard and engage in awareness raising activities. This can be beneficial for the kinaesthetic learner. The integration of pictures, photographs, animations and video using the IWB can benefit visual learners, while the integration of audio clips and the discussion stimulated by challenging tasks can benefit auditory learners.

Reviewing language

Reviewing language has never been easier, with teachers able to access all the digital flipcharts they have created during a language lesson. Teachers can create a handout during the lesson and then save it to the school's computer network to print out later, post it to the students' learning platform or email it to individual learners.

Personalised content

The teacher can create a personalised course to seamlessly support their coursebook syllabus. Teachers and students can use photographs connected with their own lives, or taken in the lesson.

Saving lessons

After annotating pages, the teacher can save them for use in a follow-up lesson, or for use with another group. A complete course can be saved or customised and then re-used, saving preparation time.

Heads-up learning

Teachers can encourage what is known as 'heads-up' learning: students do the follow-up work on an exercise they have done in their books by looking at the whiteboard. Instead of being (perhaps) on the wrong page, or getting left behind, the teacher can keep students together by controlling what the students see on the whiteboard, as well as the pace of the lesson. In terms of giving feedback on exercises, the teacher can instantly reveal the answers to only the question(s) the students got right, allowing them to do follow-up work on problem areas.

Audio transcripts

The audio transcript can be displayed and specific sections of the script can be played at will. This option was simply not possible with an audio cassette or CD. Video can be played with or without subtitles, with or without sound and even with or without pictures, opening up opportunities for different language activities.

1.5 Challenges

There are a number of challenges when using an IWB. The teacher has to bear in mind that no technology is 100% reliable. Things go wrong, and having a contingency plan is always advisable. When using an IWB, there are more things to think about when setting up a class, and allowing extra time for this is a good idea.

It can be tempting to run classes 'from the front' and simply use the IWB as a powerful presentation tool. This could see a return to highly teacher-centred approaches which may not always be in the learner's best interests. It is normal to over-use the IWB at first. Later, it is easier to integrate it into a lesson as and when it provides the most benefit, such as to provide memorable warmers or effective review.

The IWB has been described as a 'tool'. It is not the IWB itself which can transform lessons, but how it is used by the language teacher to enrich the learning experience.

1.6 Focus on the future

Technology continues to change at an impressive speed. In terms of hardware, there are exciting developments in areas such as touch-screen IWBs, and new ELT software is coming onto the market constantly. In order to keep abreast with these continuing developments, check www.macmillanenglish.com/methodology, which will provide further, practical teaching ideas for using IWBs as well as suggestions for further reading and a glossary of terms.

1 USING REGULAR PROGRAMS

INTRODUCTION

The activities in this section all use software which is probably already on your computer or can be downloaded from the Internet, and several well-known and reliable websites. If you and your students are new to using an IWB then this familiarity should allow you to focus on the process of teaching and learning English without having to first learn a new interface or set of commands.

You can continue to employ many of the same pieces of software you are already familiar with but run through your interactive whiteboard. This means you can start using this piece of equipment quickly but using your finger or IWB pen to move around the board and to click on buttons and menus instead of reaching for the mouse.

Instead of relying on printed handouts, you can display and edit documents through the board. You can run your existing presentations via your IWB. You and your students can instantly highlight text and select images from different sources and copy and paste them into documents and presentations. You can use programs such as Google Earth, media players; online services such as search engines like Google and Yahoo! photo websites like Flickr, and Internet encyclopedias like Wikipedia; and Internet learning resources like those from the BBC and other providers. If you have a CD-ROM dictionary installed on your computer, you can keep it open and minimised in the background ready to jump to the fore when you need a definition or pronunciation model. Until you become used to using the software that comes with your IWB, you can use some of these programs to do the sort of ordering and dragging and dropping that are common IWB activities.

You can use any of these pieces of software in conjunction with the IWB software, allowing you and your students to stand at the board and use the IWB pen to draw and write on those programs. You can then save those annotations for future reference. This is a very different interaction to sitting in front of a monitor and using a mouse. Drawing on and labelling a photograph of their town is often the kind of kinaesthetic experience some students require to help keep them interested and motivated.

GRAMMAR

G1 Daily routine jigsaw

Level beginner to elementary
Interaction whole class
Aim To sort pictures of a daily routine into a chronological sequence and describe that routine.
Language focus present simple for routines
Technology presentation software

Before the class

Use the image function of a search engine to find photographs representing the stages in a daily routine. Depending on the age of your students these might include: *getting up, taking a shower, having breakfast, going to school, having lessons, having lunch, going home, doing homework, having dinner (with your family), going to the cinema, going to bed.*

Paste the photographs into presentation software, one per slide, but mix up the order.

Procedure

1   Run the presentation. Elicit from the students what activity is described in each photograph. For lower level students, you can write the key vocabulary, eg the main verb, onto the slide with an IWB pen.

2   Set the presentation into edit mode, ie with all the slides displayed on the left of the screen.

3   Ask the students which of the photographs should come first. Invite a student to come to the board and drag that slide to the correct position in the list.

4   Repeat step 3 until all the slides are in the correct order.

5   Run the presentation again. Ask a student 'What time do you get up?'. Write the answer on the slide. Continue through the slides asking a different student each time.

6   Invite a student to come to the board to run through the presentation, explaining their daily routine.

7   Ask the students to practise in pairs.

Follow up

Keep the re-ordered and annotated presentation to use in a subsequent lesson for review.

Variation

If your students have access to digital cameras, ask them to create a similar presentation by taking their own photographs.

G2 Comparing with pictures

Level elementary
Interaction whole class
Aim To use pictures to introduce or practise comparatives.
Language focus *In the example:* adjectives to describe people
Alternatives: adjectives to describe towns, cars
Technology presentation software and a photosharing website

Before the class

Use the photosharing website to choose a pair of photographs. Each photo should feature a single person and the two people should be as different from each other as possible. Paste each photo into a slide in the presentation software then add a third slide with the two photos side-by-side.

Procedure

1 Brainstorm pairs of adjectives to describe people, eg *tall / short, old / young, fat / thin, beautiful / ugly, long hair / short hair* etc.

2 Display the first photograph. Ask the students to suggest the person's name, nationality, age, and job. Invite students to make sentences describing the person, using the words brainstormed in stage 1. Repeat for the person in the second photo.

3 Display the third slide with the two photos together and elicit comparisons between the two people, eg *Mario is older than Jennifer.*

4 Model a question, eg *Who is younger, Mario or Jennifer?* Invite students to ask each other questions about the two people.

Follow up

Put students in pairs to write sentences as a review.

Variation

Add a third photograph to introduce superlatives.

G3 Correcting a text

Level elementary
Interaction pairs, whole class
Aim To identify and correct mistakes in a short text.
Language focus *In the example:* present simple vs. present continuous
Alternatives: past simple vs. present perfect, *going to* vs. *will*
Technology word-processing software reviewing tool

Before the class

Type this text into a word-processing document:

My name is Klaus. I am coming from Germany. In Germany, I am living in a small town near Kassel. I am married. My wife's name is Suzanne. We are having three children. My children are going to school in Kassel. They all learn English which is very important. At the moment, I visit Ireland. I stay in Dublin for four weeks. I study English at a language school. I am having lots of problems with English grammar. I am needing English for my job.

Print copies to distribute. If necessary, you may want to pre-teach some of the vocabulary in the text since the activity is principally about recognising structure.

Make sure the reviewing tool on your word-processing software is switched on.

Procedure

1 Display the text on the board. Give the class a few minutes to read it then ask them what they think might be wrong with it.

2 Once the grammar point has been identified, divide the class into pairs and ask them to find and count the number of mistakes in the text. Ask the pairs to report back on how many mistakes they have found and invite them out to annotate the text.

3 Distribute the handout and ask the pairs to work together to correct the mistakes.

4   Invite a student from one pair to come to the board and correct the first mistake. If all the pairs agree, invite another student to correct the next mistake and so on to the end of the text.

Follow up

Use this activity as a review of this grammar point, to give you an idea of how much extra teaching is necessary.

Answer

There are nine mistakes:

*My name is Klaus. I **come** from Germany. In Germany, I **live** in a small town near Kassel. I am married. My wife's name is Suzanne. We **have** three children. My children **go** to school in Kassel. They **are** all **learning** English which is very important. At the moment, I **am visiting** Ireland. I **am staying** in Dublin for four weeks. I **am studying** English at a language school. I am having lots of problems with English grammar. I **need** English for my job.*

G4   What's happening?

Level elementary
Interaction pairs
Aim To use photographs of street scenes to practise talking about what's happening at the time of speaking.
Language focus present continuous
Technology image function of a search engine and presentation software

Before the class

Find an image of a street scene with lots of activity and paste it into a slide. Depending on the size of your class or how long you want to do this activity for, you may want to have several pictures, each one on a different slide.

Procedure

1   Display the (first) photograph on the board. Tell the class what they are looking at, eg 'This is 42nd Street in New York' or 'This is the centre of Mumbai' and ask them to describe the picture with a partner.

2   Point to a person in the photograph who is engaged in some activity, eg walking down the street, talking to another person, etc and ask 'What's s/he doing?'.

3   Repeat step 2 for other people in the photograph(s). If your students do not know the verb necessary to describe the action, write it onto the photograph with the IWB pen.

4   Continue with further questions about the people in the photographs, eg *What are they talking about? Where are they going? Who are they going to visit? Why are they (doing that)?*

Variation

This activity can also be combined with one practising future forms. For example, after *Where are they going?* you could ask *What are they going to do there?* or *What do you think will happen next?*

G5 Unscrambling sentences

Level elementary
Interaction whole class, pairs
Aim To identify parts of speech and parts of sentence and put them into the correct order.
Language focus *In the example:* present simple and past simple sentences
Alternatives: question forms
Technology website for word cloud creation, eg Wordle™ or WordItOut

Before the class

Create a word cloud for each of these sentences:

London is a big crowded city. Maria plays the piano every day. Philip usually cycles to school. Naomi reads quietly in the library after school. Graham bought some new shoes in London last week.

Save the word clouds or output them as pdfs.

Procedure

1 Display the first word cloud. Ask the students to identify the parts of speech, ie which word is the verb, which ones are nouns, adjectives and so on. As each one is correctly identified, label them using an IWB pen.

2 Ask which word they think is the subject of the sentence.

3 Give the students two minutes to work in pairs to unscramble the words into the correct order. Ask for a volunteer to write their answer on the board. Invite other suggestions if this not correct.

4 Repeat steps 1–3 with the other word clouds. Note that the time references, *every day, after school, last week* could go at the beginning as well as the end of the sentence.

5 Students can create and save similar word clouds to test the rest of the group.

Variation

With longer or more complicated sentences, a timer could be used to add a competitive element to the pair work stage.

G6 Digital storytelling

Level pre-intermediate
Interaction groups, whole class
Aim To use narrative tenses to tell a story in the past.
Language focus past simple and past continuous tenses
Technology IWB software

Before the class

Open a flipchart page and import six pictures selected at random, either by copying pictures from a website or by using your own pictures. Include a few pictures of people. Copy the flipchart page several times, once per group.

Procedure

1 Divide the students into small groups. Open the flipchart and ask students to look at the six photographs. Elicit descriptions of each photograph and deal with any unknown vocabulary. Tell students to work in their groups and create a story from these six pictures. They can change the order of the pictures, depending on their story.

2 When the groups have finished, allow each group to go to the IWB and re-order their pictures chronologically.

3 Students from each group stand up in turn and deliver their story to the class. Monitor the activity and record any important language mistakes.

4 Give students feedback, particularly focusing on their use of the past tenses.

G7 What has changed?

Level pre-intermediate
Interaction pairs, whole class
Aim To discuss changes to a place between a point in the past and today.
Language focus present perfect
Technology presentation software and a photosharing website

Before the class

There are a couple of ways of obtaining pictures for this activity. One is to use a search engine to search for *'then and now'* photographs. You can also add the name of a city, eg *Paris* to your search criteria. Another source of pictures are specific groups dedicated to comparing old pictures to current ones often found on photosharing websites.

Create a presentation with three slides. The picture of *then* goes on the first slide, *now* on the second and both on the third.

Procedure

1 Display the first picture. If it is a place that might be familiar to your students, ask if they recognise where it is. Ask the students to describe what they see in the picture. Help with vocabulary if necessary.

2 Repeat step 1 with the second picture. Make sure the students are aware that the pictures show the same place.

3 Now ask *What has changed?* Give students five minutes to work in pairs and write from memory as many changes as they can remember. Use the third slide to confirm how well they have remembered.

Follow up

Students can work in pairs to discuss what has changed where they live during their lifetimes or an agreed period.

G8 Collocation checker

Level intermediate
Interaction whole class
Aim To use a feature of a search engine to check common collocation mistakes.

Language focus common collocation mistakes
Technology Internet search engine

Before the class

Prepare a word-processing document or screen with your IWB software which contains this list:

I am agree / I agree, make mistakes / do mistakes, it depends of / it depends on, take the train / drive by train, it is the same as / it is the same like.

Procedure

1 Display the list of collocations.

2 Ask the students to discuss in pairs which phrase in each pair of collocations they think is correct. Ask the students to vote on their choice. Use the IWB pen to record the number of votes for each collocation.

3 Enter the first collocation into the search engine but inside double quotation marks, ie *"I am agree"* and draw the students' attention to the number of results (this is shown on the results page). For *"I am agree"* it should be less than a million. Now do the same for *"I agree"* and note that the number of results is over 50 million.

4 Repeat step 3 with the other pairs of collocations. In each case the correct collocation will have a considerably higher number of results than the incorrect one.

Variation

This process is useful for technical collocations in the ESP classroom, especially if you are unfamiliar with the terms used and they are not listed in general dictionaries.

G9 Comparing facts and figures

Level intermediate
Interaction whole class
Aim To compare detailed data about different countries.
Language focus comparatives and superlatives
Technology online encyclopedia

Before the class

Visit an online encyclopedia and find lists comparing countries. For example, search for *list of countries by population.*

Procedure

1 Ask the students to choose four countries from anywhere in the world. If you have a mixed nationality group, then use their home countries.

2 Ask the students to try and guess the population, land area, GDP per capita (per person) and average life expectancy for each country. Use the IWB software to write the range of answers on the board.

3 Use the online encyclopedia to look up the actual answers. Give credit to those students whose answers were the closest.

4 Write up the actual figures and use them to drill comparatives and superlatives. Challenge the students to use as many forms as possible to make the comparisons, eg *The population of China is bigger than the population of India. More people live in China than in India. India's population is not as big as China's. India's population is nearly as big as China's. China has the biggest population in the world.*

Follow up

Students can use the website for homework to create questions for the rest of the class. For example, *Which is bigger, Japan or the UK?*

Variation

You can select alternative or additional facts depending on the type of class. For example, in a CLIL classroom you might be focusing on geographic or demographic facts, a business English class may prefer to look at economic facts and figures.

G10 Missing articles

Level intermediate and above
Interaction pairs, whole class
Aim To decide which articles (*a / an, the*) are used in a text.
Language focus articles
Technology word-processing software

Before the class

Cut and paste the content of a text suitable for your students into a word-processing file. Delete any articles and print copies for students. Paste the edited text and the original into the digital flipchart.

Procedure

1 Display the first text and elicit the article that is missing from the first gap.

2 Divide the class into pairs and ask them to decide what the missing articles are. Monitor and help as necessary.

3 Invite the students to come out in turn and using the pen tool, write in the missing articles in the first sentence. Check the class agrees with the suggested answer. When another student disagrees, ask that student to add their suggestion using a different colour. Draw a red question mark next to the different suggestions.

4 Continue until students have finished annotating the text. Click to the next flipchart page to compare the group's attempt with the original. Clarify and explain as necessary. Remember that sometimes, there may be more than one possibility.

Follow up

Ask students to make any corrections on their original sheet. You may need to do more in-class work on this area if students have a lot of problems with this exercise.

G11 Dictogloss

Level upper intermediate and above
Interaction pairs or small groups, whole class
Aim To reconstruct a short text after hearing it read out loud.
Language focus *In the example:* mixed tenses, ie present simple, present continuous, present perfect, past simple
Alternatives: any grammar point or lexical set you wish to review
Technology word-processing software

Before the class

Type this text into a word-processing document:

I was born in India but, when I was about ten years old, my family moved to the United States. My father worked at a university in California for eight years. That is why I speak English with an American accent. After a year back in India, I started university in the UK. I studied computer engineering at Cambridge University. After I graduated, I came home again and got married. I have lived in Mumbai since 2002. Six years ago, I set up a software company with my older sister. She is an expert in marketing. The company has grown quickly. At the moment, we are working with several big clients in California.

The vocabulary in this example is deliberately simple as the focus is on the grammatical structures.

Procedure

1 Divide the class into pairs or small groups.

2 Explain that you are going to read a short text and that the students should take notes as you read in order to try and reconstruct the text as accurately as possible.

3 Read the text at a slow but natural pace while the students take their notes. Allow the students to compare notes before reading it once more only.

4 Ask the pairs or small groups to compare their notes and try and reconstruct the text.

5 Nominate a scribe to type and a person to moderate the discussion. The moderator invites the pairs or groups to give their version of the first sentence. The scribe types this into the word processor. This is then discussed by the class until a consensus is reached. If there are any obvious grammatical errors in the text, draw the students' attention to these and give them the opportunity to make changes. The discussion then continues to the next sentence and so on until the class is happy with the text displayed on the board.

6 Open the word-processing document with the original text and compare with the class's version.

Follow up

Highlight any major discrepancies and discuss the reason for them. This may form the basis for further grammar lessons or reviews.

G12 Project presentation

Level upper intermediate and above
Interaction small class
Aim To give a short presentation on a current project.
Language focus mixed tenses
Technology presentation software
This activity works well with business English classes.

Before the class

Create a presentation with the following slides:

1   *My Project*
    - *The background*
    - *The current situation*
    - *Our plans*
    - *The outcome*

2   *The background*

3   *The current situation*

4   *Our plans*

5   *The outcome*

Procedure

1   Show the students slide 1 and explain that they are going to prepare a short presentation about a current project. It could be something at work or a personal project.

2   Show slide 2. Ask what sort of questions would need to be answered to explain the background of the project, eg *When did the project start? What were the objectives? Have they changed? What has been done so far? What problems have there been?*. Add these to the slide.

3   Show the remaining slides and ask questions, eg 'What is happening at the moment? What problems do you have? What are you doing to solve these problems?'

4   Give the students 30 minutes to think about and prepare their presentations.

5   Each student uses slides to give their presentation on the IWB. Encourage the other students to ask questions.

Variation

With intermediate students, add the questions to the slides at the preparation stage and set the bullet points to fly in as you discuss the questions.

G13 Predicting the content of a news article

Level upper intermediate and above
Interaction whole class, pairs
Aim To use headlines displayed in an RSS reader to speculate on and predict the content of the news report.
Language focus the language of prediction
Technology RSS reader software

Before the class

Subscribe to the RSS feed of an online newspaper or news service. For example, BBC news, Google news or France 24.

Set your RSS reader to display the headlines only, ie not the summary information.

Procedure

1 Display a list of headlines from the RSS feed. Ask the class to choose two headlines.

2 Divide the class into pairs. Ask them to discuss the headlines and predict the content of the articles.

3 Starting with the first headline, ask each pair to report their predictions.

4 Click on the headline to show the complete article. Ask students to skim read the opening paragraphs to see how close they were in their predictions.

Follow up

Focus more closely on one of the stories. See G14 *Analysing a news article*.

G14 Analysing a news article

Level upper intermediate and above
Interaction whole class, pairs
Aim To identify and analyse the grammar used in a news article.
Language focus mixed tenses
Technology newspaper or news service website

Before the class

Choose an appropriate article from the website. It should be short, display a range of grammatical forms and be interesting and relevant to your students. Make a note of the URL. You could also pre-teach any vocabulary you think necessary. This gives students a hint about the content and makes step 1 more productive.

Procedure

1 Display the headline of the article and ask the students to predict the content.

2 Display the entire text and give the students time to read.

3 Ask the class to identify which parts of the article talk about past or present events or are statements about the future. Invite students to highlight these in three different colours.

4 Divide the class into pairs. Ask them to create a timeline and order the events described in the article chronologically.

5 Draw a timeline on the board and invite students to the board to annotate it until the class is agreed on the order of the events from the article.

Follow up

Use the entire activity as a model for students to choose an article themselves, re-order the events chronologically, then present the story to the group. A writing task could be added as a further stage in which the pairs produce a summary of the article.

VOCABULARY

V1 Brainstorm around a topic

Level beginner to intermediate
Interaction whole class
Aim To brainstorm vocabulary and use word clouds to record it.
Language focus *In the example:* weather
Alternatives: any lexical set you wish to review
Technology website for word cloud creation, eg Wordle™ or WordItOut

Procedure

1 Write the vocabulary topic on the whiteboard, ie *weather*.

2 Divide the students into pairs. Give the pairs ten minutes to brainstorm as many words or collocations related to weather as possible (lower levels may require more time or just until they run out of ideas).

3 Ask each pair to read out their list. Type the words for each list into a single word-processing document or appoint a scribe from each pair to do this. Use the spell-checker.

4 Copy the entire list and paste it into the website text box to create your word cloud. The size of the words in the cloud depends on how often they appeared in the list.

5 Save the results and distribute the hyperlink to the class.

V2 Crossword

Level beginner
Interaction pairs, whole class
Aim To complete a crossword created using an online crossword creator.
Language focus *In the example:* places you find around a town
Alternatives: any set of words you wish to review
Technology online crossword creator

Before the class

There are many crossword creator programs online. Some can be bought and downloaded for a small sum while others are free, these include puzzlemaker.com and crosswordpuzzlegames.com.

Enter these words and clues into the table: *railway station – where you go to catch a train; bank – where you keep your money; post office – where you buy stamps; butchers – where you buy meat; bakers – where you get bread; supermarket – where you can buy all types of food; bus station – where you catch a bus; pool – where you can go swimming; restaurant – where you can go for dinner; cinema – where you go to see a film; theatre – where you go to see a musical; museum – where you can see things from the past.*

Use these words and hints to make the crossword, then take and save a screengrab to use in the lesson.

Procedure

1 Display the screengrab of the crossword and elicit the answers for one of the clues.

2 Divide the class into pairs. Ask half the pairs to think about the *across* clues and half the *down* clues. Give them time to discuss and make notes.

3 Invite a pair to choose a clue to answer and to come out to use the IWB pen to write in the word.

4 Repeat step 3. If an answer does not fit invite another pair to try.

5 Once the crossword is complete, take another screengrab to print or save.

Follow up

Recycle some or all of the vocabulary in a fluency exercise, eg a role play giving directions.

Variation

This activity can be done as an auction game in which the pairs bid for the clues they want to answer then score points for being correct.

V3 Labelling photos

Level beginner
Interaction whole class
Aim To teach / review vocabulary by labelling an image.
Language focus vocabulary
Technology presentation software

Before the class

Use the image function of a search engine to find a picture / photograph that illustrates the vocabulary you plan to focus on (eg an office scene, interior of a house, street scene, airport, cut-away diagram). The bigger the image file the better; this gives you better resolution. Copy and paste the image into two consecutive slides so that it fills each slide completely.

Procedure

1 Display the first slide on the whiteboard. Invite students to come up and label it using a pen. The class can say whether or not they agree with the words used.

2 Erase any mistakes and invite students to correct any spelling mistakes.

3 Save a copy of the presentation with the annotations.

4 Later in the class return to the original, unlabelled slide.

5 Ask the students in pairs to write down as many words as they remember but without checking their notes or a dictionary.

V4 Vocabulary groups word cloud

Level elementary
Interaction pairs, whole class
Aim To identify groups of words from within a larger group.
Language focus *In the example:* furniture vocabulary
Alternatives: fruit, vegetables, fish, meat
Technology website for word cloud creation, eg Wordle™ or WordItOut

Before the class

Create a word cloud using the following list of words (NB the ~ symbol is used to link words so that they appear together in the word cloud):

double~bed, single~bed, wardrobe, bedside~table, dressing~table, sofa, armchair, coffee~table, television~table, bookcase, dining~table, chair, cabinet, footstool, desk, stool, cupboard, three-piece~suite.

Procedure

1   Display the word cloud on the board. Ask the students what all the words have in common, ie they are all items of furniture.

2   Divide the class into pairs. Ask them to divide the words into smaller groups based on the room they would expect to find the furniture in and write down their answers.

3   Invite a student to come to the board and use an IWB pen to draw a line around one group of words then name the room. Figure 1.1 shows an example for *bedroom*.

Figure 1.1 Furniture word cloud with one group of words already marked

4   Repeat step 3 with a different colour pen until all the words have been included in a group. Some words may fall into more than one group, eg, *bookcase* could go in *living room* as well as *office*.

V5 Company organigram

Level pre-intermediate
Interaction whole class
Aim To complete a blank company organigram.
Language focus language for describing the structure of a company or organisation
Technology word-processing software organigram tool

Before the class

Create the following blank organigram using word-processing software.

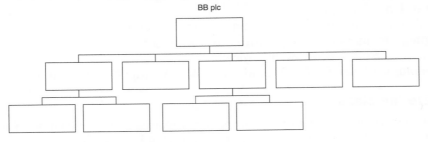

Figure 1.2 Blank organigram

Print enough copies to distribute to each pair in your class.

Also create a completed version like the one in the answer below.

Procedure

1   Divide the group into pairs and distribute the organigram. Tell the students that you are going to explain the structure of BB plc and they have to complete the organigram.

2   Explain the company structure to the class. Pause after each sentence to allow the pairs to discuss and fill in the organigram. Encourage the students to ask you to repeat information and to spell the names.

Karen Macmillan is the CEO and she is responsible for the whole company. She has five managers under her. Gunter Herring is in charge of sales. Michael Rosling is head of UK sales. He reports to Gunter. Angie Fleming is responsible for overseas sales. She also answers to Gunter. Rachel Goldberg is head of marketing. Yukihiro Ono is the production manager. His department is divided into two sections. Antonio Sanchez heads up production in Spain. Zhan Qixiong is in charge of the factory in China. They are both responsible to Yukihiro. Jean-Claude Lafitte is in charge of logistics. And, finally, Amanda Sochum is the finance manager.

3   Ask for a volunteer to fill in the blank organigram on the board using an IWB pen.

Answer

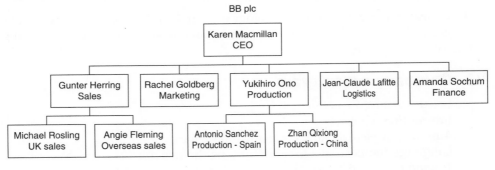

Figure 1.3 BB organigram

V6 Wordsearch race

Level pre-intermediate
Interaction small groups and whole class
Aim To complete a wordsearch created using an online wordsearch creator.
Language focus *In the example:* words linked to money
Alternatives: any set of words you wish to review
Technology online wordsearch creator

Before the class

There are a number of online wordsearch creators which are easy to find.

Use this list of words to make a wordsearch: *coin, note, cash, bank, borrow, lend, save, earn, currency, poor, account, rich, withdraw, pay, ATM.*

Procedure

1 Divide the class into three groups: A, B and C. Give each group five of the words from the list and ask them to use dictionaries to check the meaning of any words they do not know.

2 Ask the groups to write a definition in their own words for each of their five words.

3 Display the wordsearch on the board. Explain the rules of the game to the students. Group A reads the definition of their first word to the other two groups. Those groups then discuss what the word is and where it is on the wordsearch. When they think they know, the group sends a member to use an IWB pen to mark the word on the wordsearch. The group which marks the word correctly first gets a point.

4 Group B now reads their first definition and the game continues until all the words have been found. The group with the most points is the winner.

Follow up

Recycle some or all of the vocabulary in a discussion about how the students manage their money or a role play based on a visit to a bank.

Variation

A quicker version involves you preparing definitions for the words. Read these to the groups of students. The first group which thinks they know the word and where it is on the wordsearch sends a member to mark it on the board. The scoring works in the same way.

V7 Saying big numbers

Level pre-intermediate
Interaction pairs or whole class
Aim To use data from an online encyclopedia to practise saying large numbers.
Language focus large numbers
Technology online encyclopedia

Before the class

Search the online encyclopedia to find a list of countries by GDP (nominal) per capita and list of countries by population.

Procedure

1 Write this number on the board: *141,927,297*. Tell the class that this is the population of Russia. Invite a student to say the number. Give assistance if necessary.

2 Ask the students to brainstorm a list of roughly 20 countries and write these names on the board.

3 Display the list of countries by population.

4 Invite one student to ask another about one of the countries on the class's list, ie 'What is the population of Germany?'. The second student goes to the board, finds the figure and reads it out. That student then asks another about the next country on the list, etc.

5 Repeat step 4 using the list of countries by GDP.

Follow up

These numbers can be used as the basis for an exercise comparing the countries on the class's list of 20.

Variation

This can also be done for decimal numbers by using currency exchange rates.

V8 Saying approximate numbers

Level pre-intermediate to intermediate
Interaction whole class
Aim To introduce and practise saying approximate numbers.
Language focus *roughly, about, approximately, just over, just under*
Technology interactive map of western Europe on the Internet

Before the class

This activity can be done using one of several interactive map websites that give driving directions. Choose the one you want to use and familiarise yourself with its operation. Check and, if necessary change the preferences of the website so that the distances are given in kilometres.

Procedure

1 Ask 'Does anyone know how far it is from Paris to Berlin?' If nobody knows, ask whether they think it is more than 500 kilometres or more than 1,000 kilometres.

2 Display the website and invite a student to enter the city names and read out the distance given once the directions have been calculated. They will say something like 1,048.5 kilometres. Ask for other ways of saying this, ie, 'about 1,050 km', 'roughly 1,050 km', 'approximately 1,050 km', 'just under 1,055 km'.

3 Invite a student to ask another the 'how far' question for two other cities. The second student comes to the board, enters the names of those cities and gives an approximate answer. Continue around the class.

Follow up

If all your students are from the same place, you can extend this activity by getting directions between places the students are familiar with. Introduce the question *How long does it take to get to . . . ?*

Variation

Some of these websites include a measurement tool which allows you to pick out a route directly on the map. This is a more kinaesthetic activity and will be more enjoyable for younger learners.

V9 Creating a restaurant menu

Level intermediate
Interaction pairs then whole class
Aim To create a three-course menu.
Language focus vocabulary for food and dishes
Technology word-processing or presentation software

Before the class

Create a document or presentation slides with the following headings: *Starters, Main courses, Desserts*. Each one should be followed by three empty bullet points.

Procedure

1 Elicit the main headings of courses on a restaurant menu. Display the document or presentation and explain that the group is going to create a menu.

2 Students work in pairs and choose three dishes for each course. Encourage them to use dictionaries if necessary. Provide about 20 minutes for this.

3 Ask each pair to report back on their three starters, explaining what the dishes are if necessary. Write all the starters on the board. The class votes on each starter. Each pair has three votes per course but they cannot vote for their own dishes. The three with the most votes are added to the menu.

4 Repeat step 3 for the main course and desserts.

Follow up

Use this menu for a restaurant role play.

Variation

For lower levels, provide a list of 12 to 15 dishes. First the students have to sort the dishes into the correct course before they vote on which should be added to the menu.

V10 Mind-mapping phrasal verbs

Level intermediate to upper intermediate
Interaction small groups, whole class
Aim To create a vocabulary mind-map of common phrasal verbs.
Language focus phrasal verbs with *get, put, come* and *look*
Technology mind-mapping software

Before the class

Download and install mind-mapping freeware (see V11). Create the following mind-map.

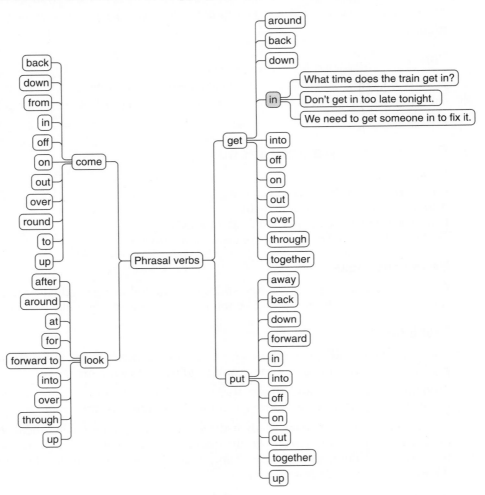

Figure 1.4 Phrasal verb mind-map

Procedure

1 Display the mind-map on the board but with all the particles hidden, ie so that only *come, look, get* and *put* are visible. You do this by clicking once on the nodes with the verbs.

2 Divide the class into four groups. Allocate one verb per group and ask them to brainstorm as many phrasal verbs as they can. Do not allow them to use a dictionary at this stage.

3 Ask the groups to report back by sending a volunteer to the board to make a note of the particles. Reveal the particles in the mind-map and add in any extra that the groups suggest.

4   Draw attention to the example sentences for *get in*. Ask the groups to produce example sentences for each phrasal verb. They can use the examples in the dictionary as a starting point but the sentences should be relevant to them and their lives. Remind them that many common phrasal verbs have several meanings and so will require more than one sentence.

5   Students come up to the board to add each example sentence as they write it. This way you can monitor and make corrections as the mind-map grows.

Variation

A similar activity can be done using common collocations such as nouns that go with *make* and *do*.

V11   Mind-mapping vocabulary

Level intermediate to upper intermediate
Interaction small groups, whole class
Aim To create a vocabulary mind-map on the topic of computers and the Internet.
Language focus *In the example:* vocabulary for computers and the Internet
Alternatives: travel, clothing and fashion, jobs and work
Technology mind-mapping software

Before the class

Search the Internet for mind-mapping freeware, download and install. These are straightforward to use but you should spend a little time familiarising yourself. One way is to create an example mind-map to illustrate the concept to your students.

Procedure

1   Ask the students if they know what mind-mapping is. If you have created an example as suggested above, display this on the board.

2   Explain that the class is going to create a mind-map of vocabulary related to computers and the Internet. Open a new mind-map and enter *Computers and the Internet* as the central topic. Brainstorm with the class what the next node topics could be, ie *hardware, software, email, social networking, Internet terms*.

3   Divide the class into as many small groups as you have nodes, allocate one topic per group and give them about ten minutes to brainstorm words that fit their topic. Encourage them to think of verbs as well as nouns and collocations, eg *click on a link, download a file*.

4   Each group reports back and a volunteer from each group adds their words to the mind-map and explains any new terms to the rest of the class. Encourage the other groups to contribute if they think something has been missed out or does not fit the topic.

Follow up

Use this vocabulary in a discussion about the role of the computer and the Internet in society, especially the effects (positive and negative) of social networking.

Variation

Mind-maps can be used for any vocabulary topic. For lower levels, you can prepare a mind-map with the basic node topics already added then distribute a printed copy along with a jumbled list of vocabulary. The students work in pairs to decide which words go in which topic before completing the mind-map on the board.

V12 Gapping the Academic Word List

Level intermediate and above
Interaction individual, groups
Aim To introduce students to a web program which will raise awareness of the Academic Word List.
Language focus academic vocabulary
Technology the website: http://www.nottingham.ac.uk/~alzsh3/acvocab/index.htm

Before the class

The Academic Word List Gapmaker is a web-based program which will create a gap-fill exercise, using the Academic Word List. Students can paste in their own text, and it will be returned with gaps. By completing the gaps students can practise and expand their core academic vocabulary.

Check the above URL and the web program work. Cut and paste the URL into a flipchart. Select a text you wish your learners to work with. The text should be available in electronic format, eg a word document or a text from the Internet.

Procedure

1   Open the website. Click on the button *AWL Gapmaker* in the menu on the left.

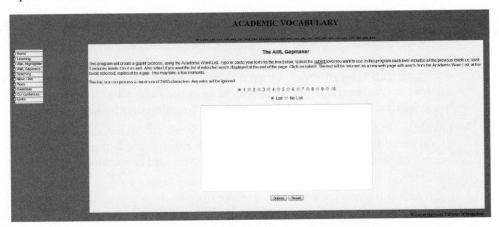

Figure 1.5 The AWL Gapmaker, University of Nottingham

2   Copy and paste the text into the box.

3   Click on the frequency level (1–10) you wish to use. Level 10 will gap the most words and is therefore the most difficult.

4   Invite students out to the whiteboard to complete the gap-fill. The 'deleted' words are at the bottom of the page. Students use the pen tool to fill the gaps.

Follow up

Tell students that they can visit the site and check their own writing to see which words from the AWL they have included by clicking on *Academic Highlighter*. They can generate self-study exercises.

Variation

Students can bring in their own pieces of writing on a memory stick. Cut and paste their text into the AWL gap-fill creator and proceed as above.

V13 Prefixes (opposites)

Level intermediate and above
Interaction small groups then whole class
Aim To brainstorm and test opposites created by adding prefixes to words.
Language focus words and opposites
Technology word-processing software and CD-ROM dictionary quickfinder tool

Before the class

Create the following table:

de-	dis-	im-	in-	ir-	non-	un-

Procedure

1 Write these words on the board: *activate, agree, polite, regular, stick, employed*. Ask the students what prefix can be added to each word to create its opposite, ie *deactivate, disagree, impolite, incorrect, irregular, non-stick, unemployed*.

2 Display the table and add the words from step 1 in the correct columns.

3 Divide the class into small groups. Tell the students they have ten minutes to think of as many words as they can that go in each column. Explain there is a scoring system: they get one point per word in the first six columns but only half a point per word in the final column because words beginning with *un-* are so common, however they lose five points for any columns they leave empty.

4 Assign each group a prefix and ask a volunteer to come up to the board and report back by entering the words into the table. Ask the students to report back. Enter the words into the table.

5 Use the quickfinder tool on your CD-ROM dictionary to check any words that the students are not sure are correct. Award points as explained in step 3. Save the document and distribute to the students.

Variation

This can also be done with suffixes, eg *-ment, -able, -ly* or other types of prefixes, eg *extra-, mega-, multi-*.

V14 Visual Thesaurus

Level upper intermediate

Interaction pairs, whole class

Aim To expand vocabulary by working on a lexical set based around the concept of insurance.

Language focus *In the example:* words related to insurance

Alternatives: keywords suited to your group needs, such as business or finance

Technology the website: http://www.visualthesaurus.com

Procedure

1   Remind students what a thesaurus is. As an introduction, ask students to think of five words related to the word *insurance*. Write them on the flipchart.

2   Open the Visual Thesaurus and search for *insurance*. The results will show a number of keywords such as: *policy, protection, security* and *idemnity*. Compare the results to the students' list.

3   Invite students to come out to the whiteboard to click on any words they don't know. Encourage one of the students to explore the visual display, or click on the audio symbol.

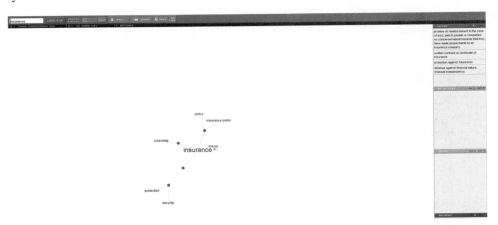

Figure 1.6 Image from the Visual Thesaurus, http://www.visualthesaurus.com, Copyright © 2011 Thinkmap, Inc. All rights reserved

Follow up

Students transfer any new words and collocations, with useful example sentences illustrating meaning, to a page in their lexical notebooks. If possible, send the students to the Visual Thesaurus site to explore key words for them. They can note down five new collocations or synonyms and include them in a word-map. Students come out to the whiteboard and present their findings to the class.

V15 Word frequency

Level upper intermediate
Interaction pairs
Aim To decide how frequent words are through the star system in the Macmillan English Dictionary.
Language focus *In the example:* business vocabulary
Alternatives: any lexical set you wish to review
Technology learner voting devices

Before the class

Check you know how to operate the learner voting devices and that you have one per student. Write a series of six flipchart pages as follows:

Page 1: *Word frequency scale*

1 = extremely common words (Red, 3-star); 2 = common words (Red, 2-star); 3 = fairly common words (Red, 1-star); 4 = less common (Black, no star)

Decide how frequent the following are: *audit* / *takeover* / *payment* / *profit* / *reinsurance*

Page 2: *audit*	1	2	3	4
Page 3: *takeover (n)*	1	2	3	4
Page 4: *payment*	1	2	3	4
Page 5: *profit (n)*	1	2	3	4
Page 6: *reinsurance*	1	2	3	4

Page 7: *final answer*

Procedure

1 Remind students that it is important to know how frequent a word is.

2 Show the first flipchart and present or review the Macmillan word-frequency star-system. If a dictionary entry is red, you will want it to be part of your productive vocabulary (7,500 words); if it is black, you may wish to use it, or simply recognise it as part of your receptive vocabulary.

3 Explain the 1–4 scale: 1 = red 3-star word; 2 = red 2-star; 3 = red 1-star; 4 = black. Tell them to work in pairs and guess the frequency of the five words. Point out that this list includes *at least one* word from each category.

4 Issue students with their learner voting devices. Check they know how to use them. Go to page 2 and ask students to press their option. After the students have voted, click the mouse in order to display the answer. Continue though pages 3–6.

5 Show the correct answer (page 7) and discuss the implications that this has for storing vocabulary.

Variation

Do the above without learner voting devices by writing students' guesses on each flipchart.

Answers

audit (Red 1-star) / takeover (Red 2-star) / payment (Red 3-star) / profit (Red 3-star) / reinsurance (Black)

LISTENING

L1 An introduction to podcasting

Level intermediate and above
Interaction pairs or small groups, whole class, individual
Aim To introduce students to podcasting.
Language focus developing listening skills
Technology podcasts

Before the class

Prepare a flipchart with the following questions:

1 *What is a podcast?*
2 *What kinds of podcasts are there?*
3 *List three benefits of listening to podcasts.*

Embed links to three podcasts for students to listen to, such as a BBC News podcast.

Procedure

1 Display the questions and ask students to work together to discuss the questions.

2 After five minutes, ask a student to come out and write their answer to the first question on the page. See if the other students approve, or wish to add or refine the answer in any way.

3 Move through the other questions in the same way.

4 When all three questions have been answered, click on the various links. Ask students a global question, such as *What is this item about?* Play a section again and demonstrate that you have the ability to pause and play a section as many times as you wish to catch a specific vocabulary item.

Follow up

If possible, ask students to listen to a podcast online. Encourage them to take notes in order to summarise the content for a partner.

Answers

1 An audio file, usually of a programme, that is made available on the Internet for download and playback using a computer.

2 Authentic – news / academic / comedy programmes / long (30 mins) and short (5 mins), podcasts made for language learners, academic podcasts, teacher-made podcasts.

3 Portable – you can listen to them anywhere, good for intensive listening – you can pause and re-listen to sections as many times as you like, good for background listening, eg mp3 players / in the car.

L2 Authentic presentations

Level upper-intermediate to advanced
Interaction individual
Aim To listen to presentations and take notes.
Language focus vocabulary arising from the chosen presentation
Technology presentations website such as ted.com

Before the class

Browse the Internet and find a website which contains presentations which you think will be of interest to your students, ie ted.com. Many presentations posted on line are supported by interactive transcripts and subtitles that can be switched on and off.

Procedure

1   If the presenter is well-known internationally, eg Bill Gates or Al Gore, put their name on the whiteboard and ask the students what they know about this individual and what they think the presentation may be about. If the presenter is not well known, tell the students something about them. Write the title of the presentation on the whiteboard and ask the students what they think the presentation may be about.

2   The result of step 1 may produce some relevant vocabulary. Add to this the words and phrases that you noted before the class. Divide these amongst the students to look up in a dictionary and feed back the meanings to the group.

3   Provide any other culturally relevant information, eg products' names, places and people that your students may not be familiar with.

4   Tell the students that they should take notes on the main points of the presentation. Emphasise that they are listening for gist and that the notes made during their first viewing should be brief but coherent. Play the video full-screen. You may want to play the presentation with subtitles.

5   Divide the students into small groups. Ask them to compare notes and prepare short summaries.

6   Ask the groups to report back. Put the main points onto presentation slides.

7   Use the transcript to focus on areas of the presentation where the students' summaries are confused. The students can amend or add to the presentation slides prepared in step 6.

Follow up

Nominate one of the groups to take the presentation slides from step 6 and use them to prepare a presentation to give in a subsequent class. This works well if this activity is repeated with different presentations so that every member of the class has an opportunity to participate.

L3 Noticing accents

Level upper intermediate to advanced
Interaction whole class
Aim To raise awareness of different accents.
Language focus English spoken with a number of accents
Technology International Dialects of English Archive website and Audacity

Before the class

Go to the IDEA website: http://web.ku.edu/~idea/index.htm and click on *Europe* in the menu on the right.

Now click on *Hungary* in the menu. Listen to the recordings. Choose one you would like to use and download it by following the instructions in red on the webpage.

Do the same for India, Scotland and Spain.

Rename the files, eg, *Recording 1*, *Recording 2* etc.

The sound files are in mp3 format and will play through any software. However, the reason for using Audacity is that each recording begins with an introduction which identifies the nationality of the speaker. You can open several different audio files in separate Audacity windows, each one cued up to play in the position you want, ie after this introduction.

Procedure

1 Ask the students if they think they can tell what sort of accent a person has when they hear them speak English. Clarify that accent and dialect are not the same thing. Explain that accent is pronunciation that depends on a person's geographical origins and, sometimes, their social background. Dialect is a regional variation of a language that has words and features of grammar particular to that region as well as accent.

2 Tell the students they are going to hear short excerpts from four speakers. Explain that all four speakers are reading the same short story. Display the text on the board but tell the students that they should focus on the sound of the speakers' voices and consider the question: Do they have the same, similar or different accents?

3 Play about 45–60 seconds of each recording and elicit the students' response to the question in step 2.

4 Now ask students if they think the speakers are native or non-native speakers of English. Play a portion of the audio and collect responses. At this stage, do not provide any feedback on whether the students are correct or not.

5 Tell the students that the four speakers are from Scotland, India, Spain and Hungary. Play the audio for a third time and ask which speaker is from which country.

6 Explain that understanding accents is not really a question of how difficult the accent is but to what degree you are familiar with it, and that regular exposure to an accent is the best way to improve your understanding of people with that accent.

Follow up

Show the students the IDEA website and explain how to use it. Encourage them to visit it and to download and listen to recordings of people with accents they need to be more familiar with.

Variation

With more advanced students or those with wider international experience, you can turn this into a quiz. You provide a list of countries and the objective is to match the accents to the countries. The students can work as individuals, pairs or in teams.

READING

R1 Re-ordering paragraphs

Level intermediate
Interaction pairs, whole class
Aim To skim read a jumbled text and put the paragraphs into the correct order.
Language focus understanding the main ideas of a text
Technology word-processing software

Before the class

Type this text into a word-processing document but arrange the paragraphs in a different order:

It may be hard to believe that such a quick and convenient procedure could change your life. However, that is exactly what can happen with SuperLaser vision correction. Can you imagine having perfect 20:20 vision? Many of our satisfied customers are now able to see with natural, unaided eyesight for the first time in their lives. After laser eye treatment, you will be able to drive, read, go to the movies, go swimming and play sports without stopping to worry about glasses or contact lenses.

We are the oldest established laser eye company in Europe. We opened our first clinic in 1990. Since then we have carried out over a quarter of million treatments. As well as using the very latest technology, we are experts in preparing people for their treatment and providing aftercare.

Every one of our laser surgeons has been certified by the European Association of Ophthalmologists. We have helped to set the standards for our industry and we meet those standards with every treatment we perform. Our reputation in the industry is the one by which all other laser eye surgery providers measure themselves.

So, when you come to make a major decision like laser vision correction, you want to be sure you are in the hands of the best people in the field. Those people are SuperLaser. Book now for a free consultation and see how we can change your life.

Procedure

1 Explain that you are going to show the students a short text about laser eye surgery but with the paragraphs jumbled up. Brainstorm what they know about the subject and what sort of words they think might appear. Explain that they should only skim read, ie glance quickly through to get the main idea of each paragraph.

2 Open the document to display the text. Give the students three minutes to skim read and write down the numbers of the paragraphs in the correct order before you minimise the document window again.

3 Divide the class into pairs and ask them to compare their answers. Ask the pairs to report back their answers.

4 Display the text again to check the answer. Cut and paste it into the correct order.

5 Discuss why this is the correct order, ie how did the students reach their conclusion?

6 Ask students to suggest a headline for the article.

R2 Matching headings to paragraphs

Level intermediate
Interaction pairs, whole class
Aim To skim read a text and match headlines to the correct paragraphs.
Language focus understanding the main ideas of a text
Technology word-processing software

Before the class

Use the text from R1 and the headings below and type them into a word-processing document. (Note: You should avoid using the text to do both activities in the same lesson.)

A Our successes; B Time for a decision; C A simple treatment could change your life; D Our reputation

Number the paragraphs 1–4 and print copies to use as handouts.

Before you start the activity, highlight the main text and click on *cut*. You can then reveal the text at the appropriate stage by clicking on *paste*.

Procedure

1 Divide the class into pairs. Display the headings. Ask the pairs to read them and discuss what they think the article is about and the possible content of each part of the article.

2 Tell the students they will have a short time to skim read a text and decide which headline goes with which paragraph. Reveal the text by clicking on *paste*. Give the students two minutes and then minimise the word processor window.

3 Give the pairs time to discuss then ask them to report back their answers.

4 Display the text again to check the answer. Invite a student to cut and paste the headlines into the correct position.

5 Discuss why this is the correct order, ie how did the students reach their conclusion?

Answer

1 C   2 A   3 D   4 B

R3 Inserting sentences

Level intermediate
Interaction pairs, whole class
Aim To skim read a text and insert sentences into the correct places in a text.
Language focus reading about a historical site
Technology word-processing software

Before the class

Type these four sentences and the following text into a word-processing document.

1 *This generated important income for the country.*

2 *The urban part has 140 structures.*

3   *Now it is one of the most popular tourist destinations in South America.*

4   *However, the Spanish conquistadors who destroyed most Inca cities never discovered Machu Picchu.*

THE LOST CITY OF THE INCAS

*Today, almost everyone knows the name Machu Picchu, the ruined Inca castle in the south of Peru. However, it only became known to the outside world about 100 years ago. In 1911, Hiram Bingham, an American historian, conducted archaeological digs and helped to make Machu Picchu world famous as 'The Lost City of the Incas'. In 1983, it became a UNESCO World Heritage Site. **(a)***

*No one knows exactly why Machu Picchu was built. The archaeological evidence shows that it was built in 1450 AD and inhabited for about 100 years. Cusco, the capital of the Inca Empire, is only 80 kilometres away. **(b)** The jungle grew up and hid it until it was 're-discovered' in the twentieth century.*

*Machu Picchu sits on the top of a mountain 2,450 metres above sea level. **(c)** These include the residence of the Inca Emperor, the houses for the ordinary people who worked in the fields, and temples to the gods of the Incas. The agriculture was done on terraces on the slopes below the main part of the settlement. The structures are all made from large stones and designed to withstand earthquakes which are common in Peru.*

*Machu Picchu today is in the middle of a fight between the tourist industry and the archaeologists and historians and the ordinary people of Peru. In 2003, over 400,000 tourists visited the site. **(d)** On the other hand, this number of people is causing a lot of damage to the site. However, the people who want to protect Machu Picchu are winning. Construction plans to improve access to the site have been cancelled and it is illegal to fly over the area. Hopefully, these and other measures will help to preserve Machu Picchu for future generations.*

Before you start the activity, highlight the text and click on *cut*. You can then reveal the text at the appropriate stage by clicking on *paste*.

Procedure

1   Divide the class into pairs. Display sentences 1–4. Ask the pairs to read them and discuss what they think the article is about and whether they come from the beginning, middle or end of the article.

2   Tell the students they will have a short time to skim read the text and decide where the sentences should go in the text. Reveal the text by clicking on *paste*. Give the students two minutes then minimise the word processor window.

3   Give the pairs time to discuss then ask them to report back their answers.

4   Display the text again to check the answers. Cut and paste the sentences into the correct positions.

Follow up

You can use this text for activity R4. If your students are interested in this topic, ask them to do some research on the web and report back their findings to the class.

Answer

(a) 3   (b) 4   (c) 2   (d) 1

R4 Scanning a text for specific information

Level intermediate
Interaction pairs, whole class
Aim To scan a text in order to identify specific, requested items of information.
Language focus reading about facts and figures
Technology word-processing software

Before the class

Use the text from activity R3 and the questions below. Type them into a word-processing document.

1   *When did Machu Picchu become known to the outside world?*

2   *When was Machu Picchu built?*

3   *How many buildings are there at Machu Picchu?*

4   *How many people visited Machu Picchu in 2003?*

Before you start the activity, highlight the text and click on *cut*. You can then reveal the text at the appropriate stage by clicking on *paste*.

Procedure

1   Divide the class into pairs. Display the questions. Ask the pairs to read them and discuss what they think the article is about. Explain that they are going to see the text for only two minutes and they will have to scan it, ie look through quickly, to find information to answer the questions.

2   Distribute the handouts with the questions. Give the students time to read the questions, then reveal the entire text. Give them two minutes to scan the text, then minimise the word processor window.

3   Give the pairs time to discuss then ask them to report back their answers.

4   Display the text again to check the answer. Invite students to come to the board and use an IWB pen to highlight the parts of the text that provided them with the answers.

Variation

Here is a more difficult set of questions for higher level students. These can be used for a second scan of the text after the first set have been answered.

1   *Where did the name 'The Lost City of the Incas' come from?*

2   *Approximately when did the Incas stop living at Machu Picchu?*

3   *What is special about the buildings at Machu Picchu?*

4   *What are you not allowed to do near Machu Picchu?*

Answers

1 1911   2 1450 AD   3 140   4 Over 400,000   5 It was coined by Hiram Bingham
6 Around 1550 AD   7 They are designed to withstand earthquakes   8 It is illegal to fly over the site.

R5 Matching definitions

Level intermediate
Interaction pairs, whole class
Aim To scan a text in order to identify words that match a set of definitions.
Language focus reading about a historical site
Technology word-processing software and CD-ROM dictionary

Before the class

Use the text from activity R3 and the list of definitions below and type them into a word-processing document. (NB You should avoid using the text to do both activities in the same lesson.)

1 *Someone or something that a lot of people have heard of.*

2 *When an activity, place or thing is liked by many people.*

3 *Facts or physical signs that help to prove something.*

4 *Found something that was not known before.*

5 *Relating to towns or cities.*

6 *A sudden shaking of the ground.*

7 *Make something better.*

8 *Not allowed by law.*

Before you start the activity, highlight the text and click on *cut*. You can then reveal the text at the appropriate stage by clicking on *paste*.

Procedure

1 Divide the class into pairs. Display the title of the article. Ask the students to read it and discuss what they think the article is about. Explain that they are going to see the text for only two minutes and they will have to scan it, ie look through quickly, to find words that match a number of definitions.

2 Distribute the handouts with the definitions. Give the students time to read them then reveal the entire text. Give them two minutes to scan the text then minimise the word processor window.

3 Give the students time to discuss then ask them to report back their answers.

4 Display the text again to check the answers. Invite students to come to the board and use an IWB pen to highlight the words that match the definitions.

5 Use a CD-ROM dictionary to confirm the answers.

Variation

You can also use synonyms instead of definitions, eg phrasal verbs and latinates.

Answers

1 famous   2 popular   3 evidence   4 discovered   5 urban   6 earthquake   7 improve
8 illegal

R6 In the news

Level intermediate and above
Interaction groups
Aim To introduce students to authentic texts; to practise reading skills; to lead in to a
    fluency lesson.
Language focus reading; fluency and discussion
Technology the Internet

Before the class

Select six current newspaper articles which will be of interest to your students.
Number the texts 1–6. Print out copies of the articles.

Open a flipchart and write a selection of six headlines from the texts you wish to use.

Make three more copies of the flipchart page and add a title to each one, as follows:
1 *Vocabulary*, 2 *Background*, 3 *Predictions* and 4 *Questions*.

Procedure

1 As an introduction to the lesson, ask students to brainstorm some stories which are
    currently in the news. When they have finished, invite students to come out to the
    whiteboard and write up the topics of their stories.

2 Tell students that one way to process a text is to follow these four steps: (1) check you
    know the words in the headline; (2) consider what (if anything) you know about the
    cultural background; (3) predict the content; (4) ask specific 'questions' and check if
    these questions are answered.

3 Move to the digital flipchart and tell students to read the headlines. Put students into
    pairs to discuss each of the four points from step 2. Allow students to use dictionaries.

4 Open the first flipchart page, *Vocabulary*, and ask students to come out and write
    definitions next to any new words in each headline.

5 Continue as above with flipchart pages 2–4.

6 Divide the students into discussion groups. Ask students in each group to select a text
    they would like to read. Issue the texts and set a ten-minute limit for the reading task.

Follow up

Put the students into discussion groups. They should summarise their article and find out
the other students' reactions and thoughts about the story. Keep language notes and give
feedback at the end of the lesson on any major language mistakes.

Variation

Use the IWB pens to show how to rewrite the first headline as normal text by adding
missing words, eg *200 die alleges PR man; 200 people have died, Public Relations
man alleges.*

Comment

This series of activities (pre-reading + reading + fluency) provides a framework for students
to get to grips with authentic texts.

R7 QuickFinder

Level intermediate and above (NB Most of the dictionaries with this feature are advanced learner's dictionaries)
Interaction pairs, whole class
Aim To demonstrate the *QuickFind* feature of a CD / DVD-ROM learner's dictionary using a webpage.
Language focus key vocabulary from a reading text
Technology CD-ROM dictionary

Before the class

Open the dictionary program you intend to use (some require you to have the disc in the computer) and choose a piece of text from a website for your demonstration. This could be an article from an online newspaper or a blog. Prepare a short summary of the text.

Check that the *QuickFind* feature integrates with your web browser.

Procedure

1 Display the website page on the whiteboard and divide the students into pairs. Give the pairs one minute to skim read the text for the main idea and then minimise the browser window.

2 Ask the pairs to write a three-sentence summary of the text.

3 When they have all finished, ask a couple of volunteers to read out their summaries. Ask the other students to listen and note any discrepancies between the summaries.

4 Display the text again and give the students longer to look. Ask them to identify any unknown words that prevented them from giving an accurate summary.

5 Use the *QuickFind* feature to automatically look up those words and then ask the students to amend their summaries as necessary.

6 Finally, display your summary so that the students can compare it to their own.

SPEAKING

S1 Charting the results of a survey

Level pre-intermediate
Interaction pairs, whole class
Aim To prepare and conduct a survey then collate the results in pie charts.
Language focus language for talking about types of books, films, computer games, music and sports
Technology presentation software

Before the class

Prepare a presentation with five slides headed *books, films, computer games, music, sports*.

Procedure

1 Show the class the presentation with the five headings. Divide the group into pairs and ask them to brainstorm different types for each category, eg

books: fact, romance, adventure, science fiction, historical

films: action, comedy, romance, animation

computer games: shooting, sports, brain games

music: rock, pop, classical

sports: team, water, athletics.

2 Ask the pairs to report back with their different types. Agree five or six for each category. Add them to the appropriate slide on the presentation.

3 Re-organise the pairs and ask them to find out from each other what their favourite type is on each category and, if there is time, why.

4 Ask the pairs to report back on their partner's favourites. Use the chart function in the software to create a pie chart on each page of the presentation. Record the results of each survey question in the appropriate pie chart, or appoint a student to do this.

5 Run the presentation. Comment on which type is the most and least popular in the book category. Find a student who gave the most popular as their favourite and invite them to explain why. If possible do the same with the least popular type. Repeat for the other four categories.

Variation

This activity can be used for any sort of topic which allows for multiple-choice questions. Business English students could produce market research surveys; students at an educational institute could produce a survey about that institute, its facilities and what could be done to improve them.

S2 Telephone jigsaw dialogue

Level pre-intermediate
Interaction whole class, pairs
Aim To re-order a short business telephone conversation into the correct sequence.
Language focus telephone language for answering the phone and taking and leaving a short message
Technology presentation software

Before the class

Create a presentation with one line of this jumbled telephone conversation on each slide or use a screen from your IWB software. The numbers given in brackets indicate the correct order of the lines, and should not be included in the presentation.

A: *Good morning, Ellie's Electronics. How can I help you?*	(1)
B: *Yes please. My number's 0745 069 6231.*	(10)
A: *Sure, go ahead.*	(7)
B: *OK, can I leave a message?*	(6)

A: *Certainly.Would you like her to call you?* (9)

B: *That's right. Thanks for your help.* (12)

A: *Hold the line, please . . . I'm afraid she's not here at the moment, Dougal.* (5)

B: *This is Dougal from the delivery company.* (4)

A: *Thank you. Goodbye.* (13)

B: *Good morning. I'd like to speak to Ellie please.* (2)

A: *So, that's 0745 069 6231.* (11)

B: *Can you tell her there's a problem with the delivery.* (8)

A: *Who's calling?* (3)

B: *Goodbye.* (14)

Procedure

1 Show the presentation in edit mode, ie with all the slides displayed on the left of the screen. You may need to scroll down the list of slides so that your students can see all the lines of the dialogue.

2 Divide the students into pairs and ask them to decide the correct order. Tell them that the first and last sentences are in the correct position.

3 Ask the students which line of the dialogue should come next after *Good morning, Ellie's Electronics. How can I help you?*. Invite a student to come to the board and drag that slide to the correct position in the list.

4 Repeat step 3 until all the slides are in the correct order.

5 Choose two students to play the role and ask them to read their parts as you click through the presentation.

6 Ask the students to practise in pairs.

Follow up

When the students practise in pairs, they can personalise the dialogue by inserting their names, company names and a message appropriate to their own situation.

S3 Internet quiz

Level pre-intermediate to intermediate
Interaction small groups, whole class
Aim To create and do a quiz using information from the Internet.
Language focus *In the example:* asking and answering questions about people's lives and achievements
Alternatives: asking and answering questions about places, countries, films
Technology online encyclopedia

Before the class

This activity requires students to do research in small groups so you will need as many computers with internet access as you have groups.

Procedure

1 Ask the students who their heroes are, eg historical figures, pop stars, sports people etc. Make a list of names on the board. Explain to the students that the class is going to choose one person to research and prepare a quiz for the rest of the group. Ask the students to vote for the person they are going to research.

2 Divide the students into two or three small groups. Tell the students they need to skim through an online encyclopedia entry and create five questions about the subject. Suggest that they avoid the obvious questions, eg *When was she born? When did he die?* etc. Allocate a computer to each group and give them 30 minutes to read and prepare questions. Remind them that they will need to be ready to answer each other's questions so they should look through the entire article.

3 Reorganise the students into small groups containing one student from each of the research groups. The students ask each other their questions and award each other points for correct answers from what they remember reading in the article.

4 Invite each group to check the answers to their questions by displaying the article on the IWB and using the IWB pens to highlight the relevant information. Record the scores on the board.

Follow up

Ask the students to write a brief summary of the person's life based on the answers to the questions.

S4 Scrolling dialogue

Level pre-intermediate to intermediate
Interaction pairs, whole class
Aim To build and practise a typical dialogue for checking in at a hotel.
Language focus *In the example:* language for checking in at a hotel
Alternatives: buying a train ticket, checking in for a flight, leaving a message on the telephone
Technology word-processing software

Before the class

Create a document showing a hotel receptionist's half of a checking in dialogue as follows:

Receptionist: Good afternoon. Can I help you?

1

Receptionist: Could I have your name, please?

2

Receptionist: Could you spell your surname, please?

3

Receptionist: Thank you. You have booked a double room for two nights. Is that correct?

4

Receptionist: Could you fill in this registration card, please?

5

Receptionist: Did you come by car?

6

Receptionist: OK. May I take a copy of your credit card, please?

7

Receptionist: Thank you very much. This is your key card. Your room number is 349. Take the lift to the third floor and turn left.

8

Receptionist: Is there anything else I can help you with?

9

Receptionist: Breakfast is from 7 to 9 o'clock.

10

Receptionist: You're welcome. Enjoy your stay.

Procedure

1 Ask the students how often they stay in hotels. Brainstorm the sort of information they usually have to give when they check in at the reception desk.

2 Display the receptionist's half of the dialogue. Divide the class into pairs and ask them to discuss what the guest would say at each stage in the dialogue.

3 Ask the pairs to report back and fill in the guest's part with the most appropriate responses.

4 Reduce the size of the word processor window so that only the receptionist's first line is visible. Choose one student to be the receptionist and ask for a volunteer to be the guest. The receptionist reads their line and the guest has to remember theirs. Scroll the document up so that the guest's line is revealed in the window. If they are right, scroll again to the next line for the receptionist. Continue with the remainder of the dialogue.

5 Repeat step 4 with two more volunteers until the student playing the guest is getting most of the lines correct.

Follow up

Ask the students to role play the entire dialogue in pairs. Build a similar dialogue for checking out of the hotel.

Answer

This is a sample of the kind of things the guest might say. The main variation is the last question from the receptionist.

1 Good afternoon. I have a reservation.

2 Yes, it's Marcel Sladkowska.

3 Yes, it's S-L-A-D-K-O-W-S-K-A.

4 Yes, that's right.

5 Certainly.

6 No, I arrived by taxi.

7 *Yes, here you are.*

8 *Thank you very much.*

9 *What time is breakfast?*

10 *Thank you very much.*

S5 Record and edit role play

Level intermediate
Interaction pairs, whole class
Aim To record and refine a dialogue.
Language focus shopping language, vocabulary to describe mobile phones
Technology recording software, such as Audacity®

Before the class

Use your IWB or word-processing software to prepare a screen to display these dialogue prompts:

Buyer	*Seller*
want to buy a phone	
	budget?
give budget	
	features: camera, web?
camera but not web	
	suggest product
ask price	
	give price
too expensive	
	offer cheaper product
be interested	
	offer monthly contract
ask for pay-as-you-go	
	give total price
agree, ask to pay by credit card	

Procedure

1 Ask if anyone in the group has bought a new mobile phone recently. What factors did they have to consider: price, features, contract or not, payment?

2 Display the dialogue prompts. Divide students into pairs. Ask them to role play the situation. Monitor and assist with vocabulary.

3 Ask for two volunteers to be recorded. Make one the buyer and the other the seller.

4 Ask the class to tell the buyer what to say for the first prompt. Record the agreed phrases. Re-record if necessary.

5 Repeat step 4 for each stage in the dialogue and ask for feedback from the rest of the group.

6 Play back the completed dialogue.

7 Ask for two more volunteers and record another version.

Variation

This also works well with telephone role plays, eg leaving a message, asking for information, or situations such as ordering in a restaurant.

S6 Restaurant audio jigsaw dialogue

Level intermediate
Interaction whole class, pairs
Aim To re-order a recorded dialogue between a waiter and customer in a restaurant into the correct sequence.
Language focus language for ordering food in a restaurant
Technology recording software, such as Audacity®

Before the class

Record the following jumbled dialogue with a colleague. Make sure you leave about two seconds between each line so that it is easy to see where one line ends and another begins when the recording is displayed. The numbers given in brackets indicate the correct order of the lines, and should not be included in the recording.

A: *Good evening madam. Are you ready to order?*	(1)
B: *Medium rare, thank you.*	(8)
A: *Today it's watercress and potato.*	(3)
B: *I'll have a steak please.*	(6)
A: *Would you like anything else to drink?*	(11)
B: *I'll have a salad please.*	(10)
A: *And would you like any side dishes with your steak?*	(9)
B: *That sounds good. I'll have that for my starter.*	(4)
A: *And for the main course?*	(5)
B: *Yes please. What is the soup of the day?*	(2)
A: *How would you like that?*	(7)
B: *I'll have another glass of sparkling water please.*	(12)

Procedure

1 Play the jumbled dialogue. Ask the students what they think the situation is.

2 Ask the students which line of the dialogue should come next after *Good evening madam. Are you ready to order?*. Play the recording until they identify a suitable line.

3 Invite a student to come to the board to highlight that part of the recording, and cut and paste it into the correct place.

4 Repeat steps 2 and 3 until all the lines are in the correct order.

5 Play the entire recording again to confirm that it makes sense.

6 Ask the students to practise in pairs.

Follow up

This speaking activity can be repeated using larger teams of students, ie one waiter and several diners, using menus created as part of activity V9.

S7 Digital mind-mapping

Level intermediate and above
Interaction small groups, whole class
Aim To produce a class mind-map on the topic of reading.
Language focus speaking
Technology mind-mapping software

Before the class

Ensure you have mind-mapping software installed on your computer (see: V11, *Mind-mapping vocabulary*).

Open the mind-mapping software. Type *Reading* in the oval in the middle as this is going to be the central topic. Add the node topics *What? Why? Types? Problems?* and *Strategies?*

Procedure

1   Display the mind-map and elicit an example for each of the nodes from the class (eg *What? – newspapers; Why? – for pleasure; Types? – skimming; Problems? – there are too many unknown words; Strategies? – try to guess an unknown word from context*).

2   Divide the class into five groups and give each group one of the node topics to discuss. Ask each group to brainstorm ideas for their topic area for three minutes.

3   Elicit feedback from the first group. One person from the group can present their points while another person types into the mind-map software. When the group has finished, ask for any other contributions from the class. Add these to the mind-map.

4   Continue as in step 4 for the other four node topics.

5   Sum up by summarising the key points on the mind-map. Tell students that mind-maps are good for brainstorming ideas and making notes.

S8 Powerful presentations

Level intermediate and above
Interaction whole class, pairs or small groups
Aim To introduce the class to the skills needed to prepare and deliver an effective presentation.
Language focus business skills
Technology presentation software

Before the class

Prepare a slide with the details below, including the mistakes:

Any presentation needs to be three things: accuracy, fluency and efficient.

The ideal font size for text is 12pt.

Never spill check your slides.

ALWAYS USE UPPER CASE.

The 8 × 8 rule states there should be no more than eight lines on each slide and no more than eight words to a line.

The best colours to use are blue on a purple background; other colour combinations which work well are purple and orange.

Remember, always read your slides aloud.

Use key words only.

Whistles and bells, especially animations, should be used at all costs.

Do not use pictures; text is always better.

Procedure

1 Tell the students you are going to give them a presentation but unfortunately, some of the words on the board are wrong. They will therefore need to help you to correct the presentation.

2 Give the presentation using the bullet points on the prepared slide. Students listen and decide which parts of the presentation are inaccurate.

3 Students work in pairs to discuss the presentation and decide what should be changed.

4 Invite students to come out and annotate the text using the IWB pen. They should get whole-class approval for their changes. Monitor the activity.

5 Summarise by delivering the corrected presentation.

Suggested answers

Any presentation needs to be *accurate*, *fluent* and *effective*.

The ideal font size is *40pt*.

Always spell check your slides.

Only use upper case *rarely,* eg for headings.

6 × 6 rule / no more than *six lines on each slide* / no more than *six words to a line*

The best colours to use are *white on a black background;* other colour combinations which work well are *blue and yellow, red and black.*

Never read your slides aloud.

Don't use too many bells and whistles: *avoid* animations.

Do not use too much text; use graphics where possible.

S9 Shrinking topics list

Level intermediate and above
Interaction pairs
Aim To initiate and sustain a small-talk style conversation on a specific topic.
Language focus small-talk topics
Technology website for word cloud creation, eg Wordle™ or WordItOut

Before the class

Use the website to prepare a word cloud with these topics (NB the ~ symbol is used to link words so that they appear together in the word cloud):

weather, in~my~free~time, travel, my~town, music, food~and~drink, sport, current~affairs, fashion, cars, gadgets.

Procedure

1 Tell the students the three key rules of making and sustaining small talk:

1 Always give a little more information than the question asked for.

2 Turn the question round, ie *And what about you?*

3 Show interest.

Elicit ways of showing interest, eg *Uh-huh, I see, Really, That's interesting,* etc.

2 Display the word cloud and divide the class into pairs. Invite one of the students to choose a subject. Ask the pairs to have a conversation on that topic, eg sport – 'Did you see the match last night?' Use an IWB pen to cross the word off the list.

3 Allow the conversation to run for roughly five minutes then ask another student to select a topic and re-start the conversation using that topic.

4 Continue until the list is exhausted. Usually the students will choose the more straightforward topics first so that it becomes more challenging as the list shrinks.

Follow up

Make a note of the topics the students found more difficult to talk about and prepare a future lesson to brainstorm vocabulary for this topic.

Variation

Allow students to choose the topics at the beginning. Number them on the board, then after each five-minute period the student responsible for the next topic has to find a suitable way of changing the direction of the conversation.

S10 Controversial issues

Level upper intermediate
Interaction individual, group, whole class
Aim To discuss controversial issues, and to see which arguments can change people's opinions.
Language focus speaking
Technology learner voting devices (LVDs)

Before the class

Check that you have a learner voting device for all students. Choose the option where students can vote: 1 / 2 / 3 / 4 / 5.

Prepare a digital flipchart and write a number of controversial statements on the whiteboard, eg *People should be able to choose when they want to retire. Downloading music for free from the Internet without paying is stealing.*

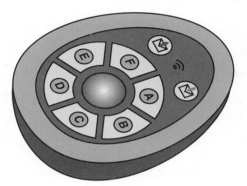

Figure 1.7 Voting device

Procedure

1 Introduce the following scale to learners, using the IWB screen:

1 = strongly disagree   2 = disagree   3 = not sure   4 = agree   5 = strongly agree

Issue students with individual LVDs. Test the devices by making a controversial statement, such as 'Grammar is not important', and asking students to vote. The result of the voting is displayed on the whiteboard as a graph.

2 Tell the students they are going to discuss controversial issues and see which arguments can change people's opinions. Reveal the first topic you wish to discuss on the whiteboard and ask students to vote. Tell them the voting is 'blind' and make a note of the results.

3 Divide the students into small groups in order to discuss the statement and prepare arguments for and against the statement.

4 Ask two people from each group to present their arguments.

5 At the end of the talks, ask the students to vote again and make a note of the results, before moving on to the next statement for discussion.

6 After the discussion, debrief the activity. Tell students whether the initial voting was different from the final vote. Look back over the lesson and decide which arguments they thought were best, specifically which ones convinced anyone to change their minds.

Variation

This activity can be extended into a formal debate with a chair, and a final vote for or against a motion. Voting can be used in a wide number of activities, including a quiz, a grammar review class and a fluency lesson.

S11 Breaking the rules of effective presentations

Level upper intermediate and above
Interaction whole class, pairs or small groups
Aim To present the idea of 'breaking the rules' when giving presentations.

Language focus speaking; business skills
Technology presentation software and presentations website

Before the class

Prepare two flipchart pages. The first contains five or six presentation tips:

Use graphics	*6 × 6 rule*	*Use signposting language*
Don't read aloud	*Use prompt cards*	*Maintain eye-contact*

On the second, add a link to a stimulating presentation which you believe will interest the group, from an online presentation website.

Procedure

1   Tell students to work in pairs and to read the presentation tips, deciding which three are the most important.

2   Ask a pair to come out to the whiteboard and drag their selections to the right of the whiteboard and justify their choices. Invite students to come out and add any further tips.

3   Tell students they will now watch a presentation. Open the presentation. Ask the students to keep a note of which rules the presenter followed. Click on the presentation and play it.

4   When the presentation has ended, ask the students to evaluate it in pairs. Was the presentation successful? How far did the presenter follow or break the rules?

Follow up

Ask students if watching this clip will affect their next presentation. Students prepare and deliver a presentation in which they consciously 'break the rules', eg read a text / use no visuals / use no signposting language. The other students watch and try to identify which of the rules was broken.

Comment

Many effective presenters in the real world don't use many of the rules taught on presentation skills courses.

WRITING

W1 Spell checker

Level pre-intermediate
Interaction pairs, whole class
Aim To identify and correct spelling mistakes in a letter.
Language focus typical spelling mistakes
Technology word-processing software

Before the class

Enter this text into a word-processing document. Make sure you include the mistakes.

Dear Maria

Thank you for your leter. I recieved it yesterday. I am sorry I didn't write before but I had to change my adress in Febuary so some of my post got lost.

Luckily, I quickly found some new accomodation. My new apartment is in a very beatiful nieghbourhood. I am sharing it with a freind. She works at a langauge school and she is helping me with my grammer.

The other good news is I now have a new, permanant job at a company that sells advertisments.

Pleese write again soon.

Yours truley

Alexandra

Make sure the software is set to hide spelling errors.

Procedure

1   Display the letter on the board. Ask the students what type of writing it is, what the relationship between the two people is, and why Alexandra is writing to Maria. Ask the students what they think is wrong with the letter.

2   Once they have determined that it contains spelling mistakes, divide the class into pairs and distribute the handout. Ask the students to count how many spelling mistakes there are (14).

3   Invite a student to come to the board and use an IWB pen to underline the words they think are misspelt. Ask the class if they agree. Make any changes then switch off 'hide spelling errors' to confirm the choice.

4   Give the pairs 10 to 15 minutes to discuss and correct the mistakes.

5   Appoint a student to operate the mouse. Invite a student to say what the correct spelling of *letter* is. If the whole class agrees, the student with the mouse can right-click on the word and make the correction. Continue with all the mistakes.

Follow up

If your group does a lot of writing, collect examples of their spelling mistakes. Create a list of these and proceed in the same way as above.

Variation

A more challenging variation uses words that are not shown up by the spell checker, eg, *write/right, there/their/they're, here/hear etc.*

Answers

letter, received, address, February, accommodation, beautiful, neighbourhood, friend, language, grammar, permanent, advertisements, Please, truly

W2 Email templates

Level intermediate
Interaction small groups
Aim To use templates to produce short business emails.

> **Language focus** email phrases for inviting someone to a meeting, explaining you are not available and proposing an alternative, accepting an invitation
> **Technology** word-processing software

Before the class

Type these email templates into three word-processing documents:

Dear ____

I am writing in reference to ____. I would like to propose a meeting to ____. Are you available on ____?

Please find attached ____.

I look forward to ____.

Best regards

____

Dear ____

Thank you for ____. Unfortunately, I am not able to ____ on ____ because I am ____. I am available on ____ or ____. Which is best for you?

Best regards

____

Dear ____

Thank you for ____. ____ is the best date for me. Can we start at ____?

Please find attached ____. I have made some changes to ____.

I look forward to ____.

Best regards

____

Procedure

1 Display the first template on the board. Ask the students to read it and say what type of email it is, ie an invitation to a meeting.

2 Ask the students to choose two names for the correspondents; fill those into the template. You can do this yourself or appoint a scribe to do the typing.

3 Fill in the gaps in the template, asking the students to propose suitable information.

4 Open the second template, confirm with the group that it is a reply to the first, then repeat the procedure in step 3. Continue with the third template to complete the email exchange.

5 Save and print the resulting emails.

Follow up

Ask the students to write emails to each other using the template. This could be as part of preparation for a role play of the meeting in question.

Variation

As well as a scribe, you could appoint a chairperson to run the discussion in your place.

You can also use colours to highlight the text that has been added or use the reviewing tools to show the changes.

For lower levels, provide phrases to go into the gaps.

Model answer

*Dear **Agneszkia***

*I am writing in reference to **the new marketing campaign**. I would like to propose a meeting to **discuss the schedule and budget**. Are you available on **Tuesday 3 February**?*

*Please find attached **a draft agenda and a copy of the proposed budget**.*

*I look forward to **hearing from you**.*

Best regards

Javier

*Dear **Javier***

*Thank you for **your email**. Unfortunately, I am not able to **attend a meeting** on **Tuesday 3 February** because I am **going to be in Moscow**. I am available on **Friday 6** or **Monday 9**. Which is best for you?*

Best regards

Agneszkia

*Dear **Agneszkia***

*Thank you for **getting back to me**. **Monday 9** is the best date for me. Can we start at **10.30**?*

*Please find attached **the latest version of the budget**. I have made some changes to **the figures for advertising**.*

*I look forward to **seeing you in February**.*

Best regards

Javier

W3 Group writing

Level intermediate
Interaction whole class
Aim To practise using standard phrases to write an email.
Language focus *In the example:* email language for arranging a meeting
Alternatives: email language for inviting, giving directions, requesting information
Technology word-processing software, CD-ROM dictionary

Before the class

This is an activity to review email phrases and so works well as a follow up to the presentation of standard language for opening and closing emails.

Procedure

1 Explain that the group is going to write an email together. Appoint a chairperson to lead the discussion and a scribe to enter the text. (A wireless keyboard is good for this activity as the scribe can face the whiteboard.)

2 Tell the group the email is going to be to arrange a business meeting. Elicit ideas for the identity of the writer and the person receiving the email, the reason for the meeting and when and where it is to be held. Note this information on the whiteboard.

3 The chairperson leads the group in discussing each sentence which is then typed into a word-processing document by the scribe. As the document is displayed on the whiteboard it is easier to make changes or spot mistakes. The group can also use a CD-ROM dictionary to help with spelling and collocations.

4 Monitor and provide feedback during and after the writing stage.

Follow up

Students write a response to the email as homework or this is done as the next group writing task.

W4 Email phrase lottery

Level upper intermediate
Interaction pairs or small groups
Aim To write a business email based around a limited number of standard email phrases.
Language focus business email phrases
Technology word-processing software

Before the class

Enter this list of email phrases into a word-processing document. They do not have to be in any particular order.

Thank you for your email of ... Just a quick note about ... I am writing in regard to ... Could you ... Sorry about ... We regret to inform you that ... I would be grateful if you could ... I'll get back to you ... Do you want me to ... Would you like me to ... Thank you in advance for ... Please find attached ... Do not hesitate to contact me if ... I look forward to ... See you ...

Procedure

1 Display the list on the board. Divide the class into pairs or small groups (a maximum of five students per group) and ask them to decide whether each phrase is formal or informal and the function of each, eg introducing the subject of the email, making a request, etc.

2 Ask the students to report back and clarify any misunderstandings.

3 Tell the students that they are going to choose some of the phrases then write an email using those phrases.

4 Invite the first pair or group to choose a phrase and mark it on the document as taken. Continue round the groups until all the phrases have been taken. Remind them that a good email should not mix formal and informal styles.

5 Give the groups time to write their emails – preferably at a computer. Display each email, ask the other groups to check that the phrases have been used correctly and discuss whether improvements could be made.

Variation

The step in which the groups choose their phrases can be turned into an auction to create a competitive element. The payback comes with the final emails and whether the phrases have been used correctly or not.

This example uses phrases for business emails, however this activity can be performed with any set of phrases or vocabulary that is often used in writing.

W5 UK vs. US spelling

Level upper intermediate
Interaction pairs or small groups
Aim To identify American spelling in a text and find the British equivalent using a dictionary.
Language focus UK vs. US spelling
Technology CD-ROM dictionary *Quickfind* tool

Before the class

Type this text into a word-processing document:

I work in the theater and two months ago I was away traveling. When I got home I saw that my new neighbor had painted his house dark gray from top to bottom. It looked like a battleship! I complained to him about the color. He explained that he had bought 300 liters of paint at a very low price. I didn't want to cause offense so I dropped the matter. Two weeks later he set up an eight-meter satellite dish in the center of his back yard. It affects my cable TV so now I can't receive certain programs. I didn't want to criticize his behavior but I had to say something to him. The problem is, he has no sense of humor and refused to apologize. I didn't mean to antagonize him but then last week, he slashed the tires on my car and now my cat has disappeared. The rest of the neighborhood is organizing a petition against him.

Procedure

1 Display the text on the board, make sure your program's spell checker is turned off. Ask the students to read the story and to answer the question 'What problems is the writer experiencing with his new neighbour?' and 'Is the writer British or American?'.

2 Divide the students into pairs and ask them to identify and count how many words in the text they think are spelt using US spelling rather than UK.

3 Ask the students to report back on the number they have found. Explain that ending words with *-ize* is acceptable in UK English but they should be careful not to use a mixture of *-ize* and *-ise*.

4 Give the pairs time to make the changes to British spelling.

5 Invite students to come to the board and change the spellings and use the Quickfind tool on the dictionary to quickly confirm whether or not they are correct.

Follow up

Ask the students to use the text to work out some of the basic rules for the differences between UK and US spelling.

Variation

If your group is learning US English then use the answer below as the starting text.

For higher levels, this can be done with an authentic text, eg an article from a US newspaper.

Answer

18 differences (14 not including the -ize spellings):

*I work in the **theatre** and two months ago I was away **travelling**. When I got home I saw that my new **neighbour** had painted his house dark **grey** from top to bottom. It looked like a battleship! I complained to him about the **colour**. He explained that he had bought 300 **litres** of paint at a very low price. I didn't want to cause **offence** so I dropped the matter. Two weeks later he set up an eight-**metre** satellite dish in the **centre** of his back yard. It affects my cable TV so now I can't receive certain **programmes**. I didn't want to **criticize/criticise** his **behaviour** but I had to say something to him. The problem is, he has no sense of **humour** and refused to **apologize/apologise**. I didn't mean to **antagonize/antagonise** him but then last week, he slashed the **tyres** on my car and now my cat has disappeared. The rest of the **neighbourhood** is **organizing/organising** a petition against him.*

W6 Changing an email from informal to formal

Level upper intermediate and above
Interaction pairs, whole class
Aim To rewrite a business email to change its style from informal to formal.
Language focus business email phrases
Technology reviewing tools on a word-processing program

Before the class

Type this text into a word-processing document:

Hi Bill

Sorry I haven't got back to you but I've been up to my eyeballs.
Just a short note to check if you can still make it on Tuesday next week.

It's no problem to pick you up from the station in the morning and drop you off at the hotel. I'm sure you remember that the office is just round the corner. The meeting kicks off at 10.30.

Cheers for emailing over your presentation. I've attached a document with a handful of ideas for changes. If you could OK them and get back to me pronto, that would be great. Do you want me to run off some handouts?

I'm not around on Wednesday but I'm back at my desk on Thursday if you need to give me a bell about anything.

See you next week.

All the best

Agatha

Make sure the reviewing tools are switched on so that the changes the students make are displayed.

Procedure

1 Display the text on the board. Ask the students to read the email and say what is the relationship between the writer and the person receiving the email and the reason for the message, ie colleagues or business associates, and to confirm arrangements for a meeting. Now ask them what they think about the style. They should notice that the style is informal but appropriate if Bill and Agatha are close colleagues.

2 Explain that they are going to imagine that Bill is Agatha's client and to rewrite the email in a more appropriate formal style for that situation.

3 Divide the class into pairs and set a time limit. Remind them to include all the information from the first email.

4 Once the time is up, appoint a scribe and a chairperson. The chairperson leads the class in a discussion of what changes to make while the scribe uses the keyboard to enter the new text.

Follow up

Set a homework task to write two emails: one in an informal style and one more formal. The style of the emails should be appropriate to the person they are writing to.

Variation

This example is a higher level text for Business English learners, however, simpler, less business-oriented emails can be used for other classes.

Suggested answers

Dear Bill

I apologise for not contacting you before now.
I am writing to confirm your attendance at the meeting on Tuesday 14 April.
I have made arrangements for a driver to collect you at the railway station and take you to your hotel. It is only a short walk from there to our offices. The meeting starts at 10.30.

Thank you for sending your presentation in advance. Please find attached a document with some proposed amendments. I would be grateful if you could confirm that you are happy with them as soon as possible. Would you like me to print copies of the handouts for you?

I am out of the office on Wednesday. However, if you have questions, do not hesitate to call me on Thursday.

I look forward to seeing you next week.

Best regards

Agatha

W7 Using a class wiki for refutation

Level upper intermediate and above
Interaction groups, whole class
Aim To present and practise the concept of 'refutation' of arguments.

Language focus essay writing; argumentation, specifically refuting arguments
Technology class wiki; presentation software or series of flipcharts

Before the class

Prepare a slide with the following words and phrases on it, typed in individual text boxes and jumbled:

Introduction | Thesis statement | Counter-arguments | Refutation of counter-arguments | Your arguments | Conclusion

In the class wiki, create a new page with the essay title *Capital punishment is a necessary part of the justice system*. Save the page.

On the page, add two headings: *Pro-arguments* and *Counter-arguments*. Make these headings hyperlinks to two new pages – create the two pages and save them.

Procedure

1 Tell students that they will be writing an 'argument' essay, or 'persuasive' essay. Open slide 1 and check students are clear about the idea of 'refutation'. Ask a student to come out and re-order the items on the whiteboard. Invite comments from the class about the suggested answer. Why include counter-arguments? Why would your own arguments come at the end of the essay?

2 Write the essay topic on the whiteboard and divide the class into group 1 (for) and group 2 (against). Ask students to work in their groups and to brainstorm their arguments. Monitor and support.

3 Open the class wiki. Click on the link to open the *Pro-arguments* page. Group 1 go to the keyboard and type in their three strongest arguments. When the group have finished, click on *Save page*.

4 Click on the link to open the *Counter-arguments* page. Group 2 add their arguments. Click on *Save page*.

5 Give students their homework task. During the week, an appointed student from group 1 should visit group 2's page and refute each argument. Group 2 should do the same on group 1's page.

Follow up

In the next class, open up the wiki and go through the counter-arguments. Encourage students to comment on the strength of the argument and the wording. Print off the pages. You may need to input any necessary language, eg *Some people believe that . . ./ Statistics clearly show. . . .* Finally, using the pages, students write their essay, individually or in pairs.

Variation

The activity can be done in class without a wiki. Do steps 1–4 in class using presentation software. Print out the *Pro-arguments* page and the *Counter-arguments* page and issue them to the opposite group. Students work together in their groups to refute the arguments, then come out to the front and add their refutations to the slides on the IWB. Print out and copy the final presentation. Students then write their respective essays for homework.

Comment

Students sometimes have problems seeing the difference between a counter-argument and a refutation. Working away from the class allows students the time to consider their rebuttal and compose it in writing. Using a wiki allows different group members to edit the same text at different times.

PRONUNCIATION

Pron 1 Introduction to the phonetic chart

Level elementary to pre-intermediate
Interaction whole class
Aim To introduce the students to the symbols of the phonetic chart and the sounds they represent.
Language focus phonetic symbols
Technology Macmillan phonetic chart

Before the class

Download the Macmillan phonetic chart from:
http://www.macmillanenglish.com/methodology/phonetic-chart.htm

Procedure

1 Display the chart on the board. Explain to the students that the chart shows 44 sounds that are used in the pronunciation of English words. Explain that the chart is divided into the 12 long and short vowels in the top left, the eight diphthongs in the top right and the 24 consonants in the bottom half of the chart.

2 Click on each symbol so the students can hear the sound and the example word. Do this several times for each symbol, encourage the students to repeat the sound and word.

3 Depending on the native-tongue(s) of your class, you may want to focus on certain pairs of sounds, eg, /iː/ and /ɪ/, or /r/ and /l/.

Follow up

The next stage is usually to show how the phonetic sounds are combined to make words. You can do this using a CD-ROM dictionary to play models and display the phonetics.

Variation

With small classes you can invite the students to come to the board to test the others by choosing a symbol and asking a classmate to make the sound before clicking to hear whether they are correct.

Pron 2 Marking sentence stress

Level elementary to pre-intermediate
Interaction pairs, whole class
Aim To mark the stressed word in a set of sentences.
Language focus sentence stress, in this example around the word *think*
Technology Longman Dictionary of Contemporary English 5th Edition (LDCE) DVD-ROM

Before the class

Look up the word *think* in the LDCE and copy and paste the first set of example sentences into a word-processing document as a handout:

I think that you're being unfair.

I thought I heard something.

He didn't think anyone would believe him.

Do you think I should call him?

For some reason, I keep thinking it's Friday today.

The recession lasted longer than anyone thought it would.

Am I right in thinking that you have a brother?

I can't help thinking that he's made a mistake.

Do you honestly think I would do something so stupid?

Procedure

1 Display the definition of the word *think* and draw the students' attention to the example sentences. Tell them that they are going to listen to each sentence and identify the stressed words. Ask which words are usually stressed in an English sentence, ie the key words or those that help to communicate the main information.

2 Divide the group into pairs and distribute the handout. Click on the symbol to play the first sentence. Ask the pairs to discuss and underline the stressed words on the handout. Play the audio again if necessary. Invite a willing student to the board to use an IWB pen to mark the stress on the sentence. Ask the other students if they agree. Play the audio again to confirm.

3 Repeat with the other sentences.

Follow up

Draw attention to the intonation patterns in the sentences, ie rising on the stressed words but falling at the end of the sentence.

You can go on to record students saying the sentences using the dictionary's record facility or a program such as Audacity®.

Variation

This can be done with any word in the dictionary which is illustrated by several examples.

Answers

I <u>think</u> that you're <u>being unfair</u>.

I thought I <u>heard</u> something.

He <u>didn't</u> think anyone would <u>believe</u> him.

Do you think I should <u>call</u> him?

For <u>some</u> reason, I keep thinking it's <u>Friday</u> <u>today</u>.

The <u>recession</u> lasted <u>longer</u> than anyone thought it <u>would</u>.

Am I <u>right</u> in <u>thinking</u> that you have a <u>brother</u>?

I can't help <u>thinking</u> that he's made a <u>mistake</u>.

Do you <u>honestly think</u> I would do something so <u>stupid</u>?

Pron 3 Recording homophones

Level pre-intermediate
Interaction pairs, whole class
Aim To listen to and identify which of a pair of homophones is being said.
Language focus homophones
Technology recording software, such as Audacity®

Before the class

Use Audacity® to make a recording of the following sentences:

When you get there, give me a call. When you get their answer, call me.

The last time I ate strawberries I was quite ill. We have eight strawberries left, do you want them?

I'm over here by the door, where are you? I can't hear you; someone close the door.

I don't know what you mean. I have no idea what you mean.

No, they aren't part of my family. They brought my aunt with the rest of the family.

Can you write your address here, please? Is that the right address?

I can see the ocean from my hotel window. I watched the sea from my hotel window.

What's the time? Our clock has stopped. We have another hour before we stop.

Make sure you pause for a second before the second sentence in each pair, and for two to three seconds between each pair.

Also prepare an IWB page with this list:

their / there, eight / ate, here / hear, know / no, aunt / aren't, right / write, see / sea, our / hour

Procedure

1 Show the students the list of words and ask them why they think the words have been paired in this way, ie they are homophones: they have the same sound but different spellings and meanings. Invite students to say the pairs of words to confirm this, if necessary use a CD-ROM dictionary to provide models.

2 Divide the class into pairs and distribute the handout. Explain that they are going to listen to pairs of sentences and have to identify which word in each pair is said in which sentence. Play the recording but pause after each pair of sentences to allow time for the students to discuss and decide.

3 Conduct feedback by inviting students up to the board to highlight the word from each pair they heard.

4 Play the recording again and encourage the students to repeat the sentences.

Follow up

Provide students with a list of homophones (there are plenty on the Internet) and ask them to create pairs of sentences that demonstrate the difference in meanings.

Pron 4 Recording minimal pairs

Level pre-intermediate
Interaction pairs, whole class
Aim To listen to and identify words in a set of minimal pairs.
Language focus minimal pairs
Technology recording software, such as Audacity® and Macmillan phonetic chart

Before the class

Use Audacity® to make a recording of the following pairs of words:

ship | sheep, chair | share, dead | dad, lunch | launch, three | tree, cat | cut

Enunciate them as clearly as possible and leave two or three seconds silence between each pair.

Prepare a page on the IWB using the list above.

Download the Macmillan phonetic chart from: http://www.macmillanenglish.com/methodology/phonetic-chart.htm

Procedure

1   Play the recording to the students. Ask them whether the words in each pair are the same or different.

2   Divide the class into pairs and show the page. Explain that they have to identify which word in each pair is said first. Play the recording again but pause between each pair to allow time for the students to discuss and decide.

3   Conduct feedback by getting students up to the board to identify which of the pairs they heard.

4   Play the recording again and encourage the students to repeat the words.

5   Display the phonetic chart. Invite students to the board to indicate the sounds that were different in each pair.

Variation

You could create a similar exercise using pronunciation mistakes collected from your own students.

Sometimes it is possible to use Audacity's® visual display of the recording to demonstrate the differences between the sounds. This is clearest with long and short vowels, eg *sheep* and *ship*.

Answers

sheep /iː/	*ship* /ɪ/	*chair* /tʃ/	*share* /ʃ/
dead /e/	*dad* /æ/	*launch* /ɔː/	*lunch* /ʌ/
tree /t/	*three* /θ/	*cat* /æ/	*cut* /ʌ/

Pron 5 UK vs. US pronunciation

Level pre-intermediate
Interaction pairs, whole class
Aim To highlight some differences between British and American pronunciation.
Language focus UK and US pronunciation differences
Technology Longman Dictionary of Contemporary English 5th Edition (LDCE)
DVD-ROM

Before the class

Create a page with this list of words:

dictate, fragile, centre, class, secretary, laboratory, lieutenant

Procedure

1 Display the list on the board and ask the students what might be significant about this list, ie the words are pronounced differently in the UK and the US.

2 Elicit the pronunciation of each word from the students. If a student gives the British pronunciation, ask whether anyone knows what the American version is.

3 Use the dictionary to confirm the differences (American pronunciation is given first, followed by a $ symbol, then British pronunciation).

4 Search for *dictate* in the dictionary. Click on the symbol to play an example sentence. Ask the students whether they heard the British or American pronunciation. Note that the LDCE does not indicate whether the speaker is British or American and the accents are distributed randomly.

5 Repeat for the other words in the list. Some of the words only have British accents in the example; *lieutenant* has no examples linked to it.

Pron 6 The schwa in unstressed syllables

Level intermediate
Interaction pairs, whole class
Aim To draw attention to the frequent use of the schwa in unstressed syllables.
Language focus the schwa /ə/
Technology Macmillan English Dictionary (MED) CD-ROM *Sound search* tool

Before the class

Display the following words on the IWB:

attention, environment, appointment, comfortable, reasonable, accommodation, disagreement, impossible, politician.

Procedure

1 Display the MED's *Sound search* tool on the board and indicate the vowels to the students. Ask them which vowel sound they think is the most common in English, ie the schwa /ə/. Click on the symbol to hear the sound and word. Explain that the schwa is never part of a stressed syllable within a word.

2 In the main window of the dictionary look up the word *announcement* and show how, because the second syllable is stressed, the first and last vowel sounds become the

schwa rather than /æ/ or /e/. Play the pronunciation recording again and encourage the students to repeat it.

3   Divide the group into pairs and show the flipchart. Ask the pairs to discuss each word and identify the stressed syllable and count the number of schwas used.

4   Ask the pairs to report back. Use the dictionary to check their answers.

5   Ask the students if they can see any pattern from the words, ie the three types of endings illustrated are never stressed so always use the schwa, eg

atten*tion* /ʃən/ environ*ment* /mənt/ comfor*table* /əbəl/

6   Open the MED's *Sound search* tool again and enter ⋆/ʃən/ and show the students that this sound occurs at the end of nearly 1,000 words in the dictionary. Repeat with the other two suffixes.

Follow up

Working on separate computers, the students in pairs can use the MED's *Sound search* tool to take words from the three sets of search results in step 5 to create a similar pronunciation quiz for the others in the group.

Answers

attention (2), en**vir**onment (3), a**ppoint**ment (2), **com**fortable (2), **reas**onable (2–3), accommo**da**tion (3), disa**gree**ment (2), im**poss**ible (2), poli**tic**ian (2)

Pron 7   Who says what?

Level intermediate and above
Interaction pairs, whole class
Aim To explore the alternative ways in which a set of words are pronounced.
Language focus common words with more than one pronunciation
Technology learner voting devices, pronunciation preference polls, Longman
    Pronunciation Dictionary 3rd Edition CD-ROM

Before the class

Prepare a series of eight flipchart pages, each containing one of the words / letters below with alternative pronunciations:

	A	*B*
absurd	əbˈsɜː(r)d	əbˈzɜː(r)d
ate	et	eɪt
controversy	kənˈtrɒvə(r)si	ˈkɒntrəvɜː(r)si
economic	ekəˈnɒmɪk	iːkəˈnɒmɪk
H	eɪtʃ	heɪtʃ
kilometre	ˈkɪləmiːtə(r)	kɪˈlɒmɪtə(r)
often	ˈɒft(ə)n	ˈɒfən
zebra	ˈzebrə	ˈziːbrə

Open the CD-ROM and go to the *Pronunciation preference polls* section. Minimise the page.

Procedure

1 Issue the voting devices. Check students are familiar with how to use them.

2 Open the flipchart to show the words you have selected. Tell students that there are often two (or more ways) to pronounce a word. Ask students to read the words / letter and decide which alternative they think is the most common with native speakers. Ask students to vote on each word.

3 Click to display their answers as a bar chart. Toggle to the *Pronunciation preference polls*. Click on each word in turn in the index, then click on the graph to show the correct answer.

4 Continue as above for the other seven words.

Follow up

If possible, students explore other words in the *Pronunciation preference polls*. They can also find graphs showing how the younger generation pronounce words differently.

Answers

absurd	əbˈsɜː(r)d 77%	əbˈzɜː(r)d 23%
ate	et 55%	eɪt 45%
controversy	kənˈtrɒvə(r)si 60%	ˈkɒntrəvɜː(r)si 40%
economic	ekəˈnɒmɪk 38%	iːkəˈnɒmɪk 62%
H	eɪtʃ 84%	heɪtʃ 16%
kilometre	ˈkɪləmiːtə(r) 37%	kɪˈlɒmɪtə(r) 63%
often	ˈɒft(ə)n 27%	ˈɒfən 73%
zebra	ˈzebrə 83%	ˈziːbrə 17%

LEARNING TO LEARN

L2L1 Needs analysis

Level elementary
Interaction individual, group
Aims To do a whole-class needs analysis.
Language focus needs analysis
Technology Macmillan *Global* eWorkbook

Before the class

Go to the *Portfolio* and click on *Global Needs Analysis*. Print out copies of the Needs Analysis for students.

Procedure

1   Issue the Needs analysis forms and ask students to complete them individually.

Needs analysis

English is important for me because

_____

_____

_____

I need English (or I will need English in the future) to

_____

_____

_____

Tick the boxes to show how important these things are for you now or in the near future.

	Not important	Quite important	Very important
Describe people's character and behaviour			
Narrate a series of events			
Express opinions and discuss topics			
Participate in meetings			
Understand and make presentations			
Negotiate			
Succeed in job interviews			
Socialise in English			
Make travel arrangements			
Adapt language for different situations			
Describe products and processes			
Read for enjoyment			
Work with complex texts (for example scientific, historical, business-related)			
Make telephone calls with confidence			
Use the internet productively			
Understand films and TV programmes			
Be aware of different writing styles, use of humour etc.			
Write and read notes and emails			
Write and read business and personal letters			
Pass an exam			

Which three are your priorities? Mark them with an asterisk (*).

Figure 1.8   Needs analysis (Macmillan *Global* eWorkbook)

2   Put students into pairs to compare and discuss their answers.

3   Bring up the pdf on-screen. Elicit responses for the first question: *English is important for me because* . . . Ask some students to come out and write their answer on the whiteboard.

4   Do the same for the second question: *I will need English in the future because* . . .

5   Invite all the students out in turn to tick their three priorities on-screen. (See Figure 1.11.) Sum up by telling students that they will work on the most popular areas during the course.

Follow up

Revisit the Needs analysis flipchart at regular intervals during the course, to see if the students' priorities have changed. Revisit the Needs analysis at the end of the course in order to check that the key areas were covered.

L2L2 Ready made collocation lists in dictionaries

Level elementary

Interaction pairs, whole class

Aim To predict which verbs collocate with a set of common nouns then check the
result with a dictionary.

Language focus *In the example: bed, school* and *game*

Alternatives: bus, lunch and *table*

Technology Longman Dictionary of Contemporary English 5th Edition (LDCE)
DVD-ROM

Before the class

Prepare a way to display the three nouns: *bed, school* and *game.* You can use a word-
processing document, your IWB software or mind-mapping software.

Procedure

1 Write *email* on the board and elicit some verbs that usually go with it, eg *read, write,
send, delete.* Explain to students that these are collocations, ie pairs or groups of words
which go together.

2 Divide the class into pairs. Tell the students that they will have ten minutes to discuss
and think of as many verbs as they can that collocate with the three nouns you are
going to give them.

3 Display the nouns *bed, school* and *game* and give the pairs time to discuss.

4 Ask the pairs to report back with their lists and invite them to write them on
the board.

5 Look each of the nouns up in the LDCE and click on the *Collocations from this entry*
link on the left of screen.

6 Add any extra verbs from the dictionary to the students' lists. Query any verbs from
the students that were not in the dictionary list. If it is agreed they do not collocate,
then remove them. Save the lists and distribute to the class.

Follow up

The students can use the collocations to create gap-fill exercises for each other in which
they have to choose the correct verbs to complete the sentences.

Variation

A higher level variation can focus on a very specific area of vocabulary, eg verbs that
collocate with *pollution, environment, damage,* as a warmer to a discussion.

Answer

bed: *go to, get into/get out of, climb into, crawl into, jump into/out of, stay, make the, change a,
put somebody to;*

school: *go to, attend, start, leave, send somebody to;*

a game: *play, see, watch, have, win, lose, tie, draw*

L2L3 Storing vocabulary on Macmillan English Campus (MEC)

Level pre-intermediate and above
Interaction groups
Aim To demonstrate how to use *My Word Lists* on Macmillan English Campus.
Language focus vocabulary
Technology Macmillan English Campus

Before the class

You will have already created some word categories. Go to the Macmillan English Campus. Click on *Work Area* and *My Word Lists*.

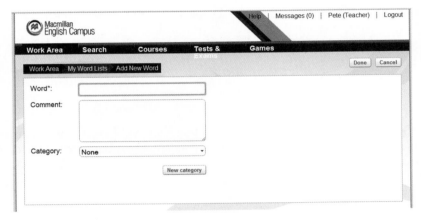

Figure 1.9 Screen shot from MEC

Procedure

1 Ask students how they store vocabulary and suggest that they can store their vocabulary in their *Word Lists* on the Campus. One feature of this is that you can create different categories to store words, such as *verbs / nouns / adjectives,* or topics: *fruit / school subjects / business* etc.

2 Demonstrate adding vocabulary. Click on *Add New.* Type in the new word, eg *abstract.* Type in the meaning. Click on *Select a category.* From the drop-down menu, choose the appropriate category from those you have created. In this example, EAP. Click on *Done.*

3 Invite a student to come out and add another word. Monitor and guide as necessary.

4 Demonstrate other features: how to review words by category / how to cut and paste a definition from Macmillan English Dictionary Online.

Follow up

If students are able to log in to Macmillan English Campus or their MPO (Macmillan Practice Online) then ask them to start their word list and add some new words from the last lesson. This is a good exercise to begin a session on how to store vocabulary.

L2L4 Building vocabulary lists with the dictionary

Level intermediate
Interaction small groups, whole class
Aim To use a dictionary's list feature to demonstrate how to create a vocabulary list.
Language focus hotel vocabulary
Technology Dictionary CD-ROM and word-processing software

Before the class

Familiarise yourself with the operation of the *My Lists* function.

Procedure

1 Explain that you are going to use a CD-ROM dictionary to build a vocabulary list around the topic of hotels.

2 Divide the class into small groups and give them ten minutes to brainstorm as many words as they can think of connected to hotels.

3 Ask the small groups to report back with their lists. Get volunteers from each group to write their words on the board and use a tally to keep track of how many times a word is included on a list. Delete any words that appear in every list. Explain that the target is to focus on words the students need to learn, not the ones they already know. Also delete any words that do not fit the topic.

4 Create a new list in a word-processing document called *Hotels*. Look up each word that only appeared once in the class's list and add it to this list. The process of looking up words often reminds people of other words they had not previously thought of, so encourage the students to make suggestions during this process. Ask the class whether each word should be included or not.

5 Copy the list and distribute to the students.

Follow up

Ask the students to study the list as homework, then practise the vocabulary in a subsequent class with hotel situation role plays, eg checking in and out, and complaining.

Variation

If you introduce this idea at the beginning of a course then several lists can be set on the first day. At the end of each day, decide which words from that day's lessons should be added to the lists. The lists can be copied and pasted into word-processing documents and distributed at regular points during the course, eg daily or weekly.

L2L5 Words with multiple meanings

Level intermediate
Interaction pairs, whole class
Aim To focus on examples of words with multiple meanings and how often the words are used with those meanings.
Language focus *In the example: change, close* and *return*
Alternatives: interest, place and *part*
Technology Macmillan English Dictionary (MED) CD-ROM or website:
http://www.macmillandictionary.com

Before the class

Put this list of meanings into a word-processing document or a screen of your IWB software:

replace someone | something, exchange money, reduce distance, shut, put on different clothes, put | send | take something back, get on a different vehicle, stop doing business, stop computer program, go | come back, become | make different, produce profit, stop use of road etc., hit ball back, elect someone to position, start something new, end | finish, do | say something similar back.

Procedure

1   Use the MED to look up the word *feel* and display the result on the board. Highlight that the dictionary definition lists seven different basic meanings for the word. Ask students if they know how that order is determined, ie on the basis of frequency of use with the most commonly listed first etc.

2   Write *change, close* and *return* on the board. Tell the students that these are three more very common words which have several different meanings.

3   Divide the class into pairs and show the list you prepared. Explain that the list contains 18 meanings; six per word. Ask them to match the meanings to the words on the board.

4   Invite the pairs to report back with their lists and write them on the board.

5   Ask the pairs to look at the list again and put the meanings into order based on frequency with the most common first etc.

6   Ask the pairs to report back with their lists and modify the order on the board.

7   Look each word up in the MED and check the order of the meanings against the class's lists. Note that the MED lists 12 meanings for *close* but only six have been included in this activity.

Follow up

Decide how important each meaning is for your students, ie are they likely to need to know and use all the meanings listed? Ask the pairs to make a choice and create example sentences for each meaning of each word to help them learn and remember them.

Answer

change	close	return
1 become / make different	1 shut	1 go / come back
2 start something new	2 stop doing business	2 put / send / take something back
3 replace someone/ something	3 stop use of road etc	3 do / say something similar back
4 exchange money	4 end / finish	4 produce profit
5 put on different clothes	5 stop computer program	5 hit ball back
6 get on a different vehicle	6 reduce distance	6 elect someone to position

L2L6 Thesaurus top ten

Level intermediate to upper intermediate
Interaction small groups, whole class
Aim To use a thesaurus to identify the most common synonyms or
  near-synonyms.
Language focus *In the example:* basic adjectives
Alternatives: noun and verb combinations
Technology Macmillan English Dictionary (MED) CD-ROM

Before the class

Put the following list onto your IWB:

big, small, happy, important, good, difficult

Procedure

1 Load the MED CD and show the students the definition of the adjective *hot*.
  Indicate the thesaurus button. Ask whether anyone in the class can explain
  what a thesaurus is, ie a book that categorises words by meanings and use rather
  than alphabetically like a dictionary. Explain that the MED CD-ROM can give
  a long list of words in the same category or just the top ten. Brainstorm with
  the class what words they think are in the top ten for *hot*. Click on the button
  to check.

2 Divide the class into small groups and show the screen you have created. Assign a
  word to each group and ask them to list as many words as they can that are synonyms
  or near-synonyms.

3 Ask for a volunteer to report back with their list. Invite them to the board to
  write up their synonyms and to check how many of their words appear in the
  top ten.

L2L7 Continuing to learn

Level intermediate and above
Interaction groups
Aim To provide a range of ideas for autonomous post-course study.
Language focus all aspects of language study
Technology presentation or IWB software / language learning software such as
  CD-ROMs / Internet

Before the class

Prepare a presentation with the following text set out as mind-maps on six slides. Use
the example mind-map given for slide1 as a model for slides 2–6.

Slide 1: Continuing to learn

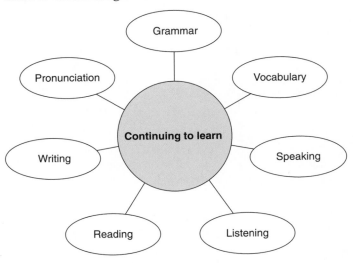

Figure 1.10 Mind-map

Slide 2: Grammar

- Grammar reference book
- Interactive exercises (eg e-workbook / CD-ROM practice / online grammar exercises / mobile devices)
- Grammar exercises on a CD-ROM dictionary

Slide 3: Vocabulary

- Review items in lexical notebook
- Exercises on CD-ROM / DVD ROM dictionary
- Review and self-test activities on DVD-ROM / Smartphone
- Storing new words electronically (eg Macmillan Practice Online)
- Use an Internet dictionary

Slide 4: Speaking and listening

Speaking

- Fluency / conversation classes

Listening

- News (eg BBC) – use pause and repeat
- Films on DVD (with subtitles in English)
- Podcasts (eg subscribe to iTunesU / mp3 player)
- EAP – ease (Essential Academic Skills in English) on the Internet

Slide 5: Reading and writing

Reading

- Graded readers
- Journals / magazines

Writing

- Oxford iWriter (OALD)
- Guides (eg Macmillan English Dictionary)

Slide 6: Pronunciation

- Download the phonemic chart from the Internet
- CD-ROM dictionary – listen and repeat

Customise the presentation to the needs of your own group; add hyperlinks to recommended online practice materials; check you have relevant CD-ROMs loaded.

Procedure

1 State the aims of the presentation: to provide ideas for continued study in the language. Click on the overview slide (1). Divide the students into small groups. Give each group a topic area (grammar / vocabulary etc). Ask each group to brainstorm three ideas for their topic.

2 Invite a student out from each group in turn to present their ideas to the group. Students can write up their ideas on a blank flipchart page or slide.

3 As each student finishes, flip to your original slide to provide further ideas.

Follow up

Print out the presentation as a handout with several slides per page, or upload it to the students' VLE so they can access it. Students can develop their own future learning plans.

L2L8   Interpreting a dictionary entry

Level intermediate and above
Interaction individual, groups
Aim To label the sections of an entry in a monolingual learner's dictionary.
Language focus vocabulary
Technology CD-ROM / DVD-ROM dictionary

Before the class

Open a CD-ROM dictionary and find the entry you wish to use. Take a screen shot of the entry and paste it into a digital flipchart. Type the following words into the flipchart around the screen shot.

headword / definition / pronunciation / stress / examples

Customise this list, depending on the dictionary you use and the entry you select.

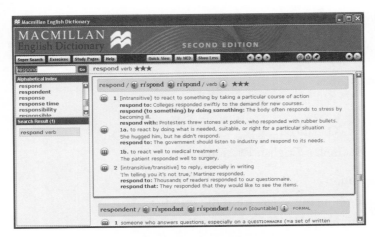

Figure 1.11 Entry from Macmillan English Dictionary

Procedure

1   Open the flipchart. Tell students to look at the words around the edge of the picture.

2   Ask some students to come out in turn and using the pen, circle a word and link it to the correct place on the dictionary entry. Encourage students to work out the more difficult items (eg the mark ' to show word stress).

3   Ask each student to come out in turn and annotate any symbols used.

Follow up

Students look up new words in their monolingual dictionaries in advance of the next activity.

Variation

1   Copy several dictionary entries to the flipchart in order to illustrate a wider range of symbols.

2   Use the 'clip-board' on the CD-ROM to cut and paste the word into a word-processing document. Print out a hard copy for students to annotate before moving to step 2.

L2L9   Learning how to listen

Level intermediate and above
Interaction groups, whole class
Aim To introduce students to the skill (and sub-skills) of listening.
Language focus listening
Technology presentation software

Before the class

Prepare a presentation as follows. On slide 2, embed some website links to suitable sites which students can use to improve listening.

Slide 1:

speed / accent / unknown vocabulary / slang / idiom / contractions / sounds change in connected speech / humour / irony / puns / cultural knowledge

Slide 2:

Watch the news – pictures and diagrams as visual clues / watch again on the Internet and print out a support text

Listen and read – listen first, then listen and read, eg a graded reader

Films on DVD + subtitles

Listen to fast speech, eg on the Internet, and use the pause (podcasts / presentation websites)

Listen to English songs and read the lyrics

Do extra listening using course materials (CD-ROM / Internet)

Prepare for a listening by making a lists of words you expect to come up

Procedure

1 As an introduction to the lesson, brainstorm the kinds of things we listen to in English. Invite students to come out and write their ideas on the IWB (films / the news on TV / documentaries / TV programmes / the weather / radio programmes / music / other people / lectures).

2 Present two questions on the IWB. *Why is listening to English sometimes so difficult?* and *What strategies can students use to improve their listening?* Divide the class into two groups. Group A work together to answer the first question, group B work together to answer the second question.

3 Ask students from group A to come out and write up their answers in key-words / phrases on the IWB. Ask the other group to see if they can add anything. Show your answer on slide 1 and draw attention to any additional points.

4 Follow the same procedure with group B and slide 2. Demonstrate some examples of useful listening strategies.

Follow up

Print out the flipcharts as a handout, or upload it to the students' VLE.

L2L10 Ranking the qualities of a good language learner

Level intermediate and above
Interaction pairs, whole class
Aim To discuss and then rank a list of qualities required to be a good language learner at the beginning of a course.
Language focus what makes a good language learner
Technology word-processing software

Before the class

Type this list into a word-processing document or onto a page of your IWB:

Good learners are:

– aware of their learning style and preferences

– well-organised

– inquisitive about the language they are learning

– realistic about the time and effort required to learn a new language

— *willing to take risks and be creative*

— *able to use their mistakes as opportunities to develop and improve*

— *self-critical about their strengths and weaknesses*

— *good guessers*

— *able to study and learn independently*

— *able to watch not only what words and sentences mean but also how they are put together*

— *able to accept the new language as a separate system*

— *tolerant of the differences between their language and the one they are learning*

— *able to use contextual clues to help them understand*

— *able to create their own opportunities to practise*

Procedure

1   Ask the students what qualities they think are required to be a good language learner. Write them on the board.

2   Display the list you created before the class and compare with the one created in step 1. If the class list contains anything that is not in the original list, add it at the bottom.

3   Divide the class into pairs and ask the students to discuss the list and rank the items in order of importance with 1 the most important, and so on.

4   Ask the pairs to report back with their rankings. If the class agree, type in the number and a space in front of the item in question.

5   When the entire list has been ranked, highlight the text and use the *Sort* tool to re-arrange the list in numerical order. Save and print the list and distribute to the class.

L2L11 Self assessment using CEF checklist

Level intermediate and above
Interaction individual, group
Aims To match Common European Framework (CEF) descriptors to levels and identify which level students' listening skills are.
Language focus *In the example:* CEF mapping for listening skills
Alternatives: reading, speaking, writing
Technology chart of CEF levels

Before the class

Choose the language skill area you wish to focus on, eg listening. Access or produce a chart of CEF levels A1 to C2 with the appropriate descriptors (slide 2). Then produce a second slide (slide 1) with descriptors A1 and C2 in the correct place, and A2 to C1 jumbled up.

Procedure

1   Open slide 1 and ask students to read the descriptors. Tell students that they must match the descriptors to each level.

2   Ask a student to come out and drag one of the descriptors to the appropriate level. See if all the students agree. Go with the majority. Tell students you will check at the end.

3   Continue until all the descriptors are in place.

4   In order to check, open slide 2 with the correct chart.

5   Ask students to work in pairs and decide on what level they think they have reached in their listening skills. Invite students to come out and tick the appropriate level. Sum up by saying that these descriptors are guidelines, and only focus on one skill (listening). They are useful in setting personal targets.

L2L12   Course introduction

Level all
Interaction groups
Aim To introduce the class to the range of material available on their language course.
Language focus all areas: grammar / vocabulary / language skills / pronunciation
Technology presentation software, language course components

Before the class

Prepare two slides with the two checklists below, containing hyperlinks to any online support material. Check you have any relevant CD-ROMs loaded and open, so you can simply click on the tab to access the material in class.

Check you have any necessary passwords for your students. If there is a language lab available, book this as a follow up to the lesson.

Checklist 1 – Course components

coursebook

workbook

CD-ROM / multi-ROM / DVD ROM

eWorkbook

Web 2.0 tools: class blog / class wiki

online learning platform: VLE / password

online practice material or tests / access code

Checklist 2 – Practical tips

How to log in to your e-learning environment: password

How to use your e-learning environment

How to record vocabulary in your online notebook

How to access the mp3 files on your course CD-ROM to listen to before or after the lesson

How to transfer a listening file from your eWorkbook to a mobile device

Procedure

1   Tell students which components of their course they will receive. Tell them they can access this material 24/7. Show them any eWorkbooks or CD-ROMS which accompany their materials so that they can look at the material before a class,

or use it to consolidate a lesson and do further practice. Show the content of some of the sections you want them to look at in step 3.

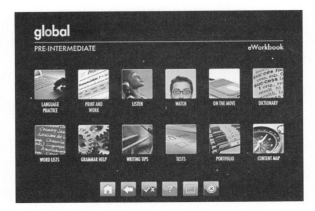

Figure 1.12 eWorkbook for Macmillan's *Global* course: Pre-intermediate Contents page

2   Demonstrate any materials selected and any useful features so that students are aware of them and will be able to use them in their own time.

Figure 1.13 *Global* eWorkbook: Saving a video file to a Smartphone

3   Give the students a hands-on opportunity to explore their digital support material. Use computer facilities if appropriate and possible. Help the students access their online materials using their passwords.

Comment

Many students on a language course do not take advantage of some of the core course components, such as the CD-ROM at the back of their coursebook. One major reason for this is that there is no formal introduction to these materials. This re-usable and customisable activity can help kick-start a blended approach to a language course.

PROJECTS

Proj 1   Planning a holiday webquest

Level pre-intermediate to upper intermediate
Interaction small groups, whole class
Aim To research information from the Internet then use that information to plan a holiday.
Language focus reviewing language for talking about maps, sightseeing, food and restaurants, hotels, transport, and planning
Technology presentation software

Before the class

This activity requires students to work in groups and research information on the Internet. You will need at least five computers with Internet access for them to achieve this. Because both the research and discussion stages require quite a lot of time, you might want to run this activity over more than one lesson.

Prepare a presentation with six slides headed *Where to stay, What to see, Where to eat, What to buy, How to get around* and *Schedule.*

Create a handout with addresses of websites where students will be able to find information on the city they are researching.

Procedure

1   Divide the class into five small groups. Ask them to brainstorm the sort of things they would need to consider when planning a holiday. Ask the groups to report back ideas. Write them on the board.

2   Tell the students to imagine that they are all going on holiday together to London. Explain that they are going to research different areas of information that they will need, then work together to make a plan which they will present to the rest of the group.

3   Distribute the handout and allocate one of the areas to each group. Send each group to work on a separate computer to research their area. Ask them to save their results onto memory sticks. This research step will require at least 30 to 40 minutes.

4   After they have completed their research the groups transfer their results to the computer linked to the IWB.

5   Appoint a chairperson to run the discussion. Open the presentation. The chairperson invites the group responsible for accommodation to present their results and the entire class discuss which hotel they will choose. The discussion continues through the rest of the slides, culminating with a discussion of the schedule for the holiday. During this step, provide whatever support you think necessary.

Follow up

Save the completed presentation. Ask the students to write about a past or future holiday as a homework task.

Proj 2 Peer correction with a class wiki

Level intermediate and above
Interaction groups, whole class
Aim To encourage students to peer correct.
Language focus essay writing
Technology class wiki

Before the class

Set up a class wiki. The wiki provides your students with an opportunity to practise their writing away from the classroom.

Procedure

1   Present the wiki and its functions in the lesson and check the students are happy using it. Give the students their essay title for homework, eg *Describe the advantages and disadvantages of telecommuting.* Ask them to each post their essay on the class wiki.

2   When the deadline for the homework has passed, put students into pairs and ask each student to open their classmate's essay before the next lesson and make between three and five corrections. Tell them not to forget to click *Save changes.*

3   In the next lesson, open the wiki and look at a selection of corrected essays. Ask the students who made the corrections to come out to the IWB and explain their corrections to the whole group. Monitor and evaluate. You can use the *History* button at any time to access the original text.

Follow up

Mark all the essays as usual. In the next lesson, provide group feedback.

Variation

In the second lesson, ask all the students to visit everyone else's essays and make one change to each one if necessary.

Comment

This activity carries over more than one lesson. Discuss with the group first if they would like their writing to be read by their peers before the teacher corrects them. Encourage the group to agree to this extra stage.

Proj 3 Dictionary project

Level intermediate and above
Interaction pairs, groups
Aim To produce a short report with recommendations about which dictionary the language school should buy.
Language focus all four language skills
Technology presentation and word-processing software, flipchart

Before the class

Prepare a flipchart as below, with the stages of a report, in a jumbled order.

Title | Contents page | Introduction [Background | Who for | Scope | Aims] | Method | Data | Findings | Recommendations | References

Customise and photocopy the following email:

To: Mark Summers [School Principal]
From: Jane Reed
Re: Dictionary class sets

Dear Mark

Thanks for your email.

I am really pleased that we now have budget approval to provide all students on our language courses next year with their own dictionary as part of their course materials.

I asked Jack, one of our core teachers, and Wang Li, the class rep, what they thought. Here are their replies:

Jack: 'I think we should get monolingual dictionaries, but I'm not sure which one. They all have CD-ROMs in the back. I can ask the teachers what they prefer.'

Wang Li: 'I think the students can bring their own electronic dictionaries to class. Also, there are free dictionaries on the Internet. Maybe the college can save this money and use it for another purpose? I can ask the students what they prefer.'

There seems to be a lot of disagreement. I will get back to you soonest with a short report and recommendations.

Best wishes
Jane Reed
Director of Studies

Procedure

Session one

1   As an introduction to the lesson, write the word *Report* on the whiteboard and ask students to think about the different kinds of report. Write students' ideas on the whiteboard, eg *school report | police report | medical report | scientific report*. Find out if they have ever written a report, and if so, what it was about. Did the report have different sections?

2   Open the prepared flipchart. Ask a student to come out and drag the phases of a report into the correct order. Get whole-class agreement. Run through the sections of the report and explain any terms (eg *scope*) and give advice and clarification as necessary (eg data is objective / two or three bullet-pointed recommendations / consulting more than one group of people is encouraged).

3   Tell students that they will be writing a short report. Issue copies of the email and let students read it. Check understanding by asking questions: 'What's happened? What does the Director of Studies think?' Divide students into groups.

4   Tell students they should use 'primary data' ie a questionnaire. The rest of this project session is spent creating the questions for the questionnaire. Students should finish this task for homework, print copies and bring to the next session.

Session two

1   Students issue their questionnaire to others in the group and any other people who are willing and available, such as the teacher.

2   Students collate the feedback and discuss the findings and decide their final recommendations. They should create any visuals they wish to use in their report.

3 Tell the groups to allocate the various sections of the report to individual students and begin drafting them. For homework students can finish drafting their part of the report.

Session three

1 Students work together to produce their report. If possible, this should be word-processed.

2 Students prepare a short presentation of their report (eg using presentation software) containing the data, findings and recommendations sections.

3 Each group comes out to the IWB to deliver their presentations. Ask the audience to take notes on the recommendations, and be ready to ask any questions at the end.

Follow up

Compare the results of the reports. Why were the results similar / different? Give any language feedback necessary. Take in the reports and give written feedback.

Variation

Higher level groups can be more ambitious in comparing two or three sources of data, such as recorded interviews; they can also use in-text references and produce a short bibliography.

Case study: First time user

Eve is a teacher at a private business English school. She has been using computers with her students throughout her teaching career. She employs them to access the Internet and use EFL software such as CD-ROM dictionaries and other programs. With small groups of only two or three students they gathered round the monitor of the computer. When she had larger groups, she used a data projector to display the computer screen.

Six months ago the school installed IWBs in several of the classrooms and promised the teachers extensive training on how to use the software bundled with the boards. However, there was no definite date for this training. Eve decided not to wait but to try and adapt her existing use of digital technology to the IWB.

She discovered that some things were very straightforward. The two easiest things were manoeuvring around websites where a mouse click to activate a link was replaced by tapping the board, and running slide presentations. What proved more awkward was anything that involved entering text. With the CD-ROM dictionaries and search engines, she could use the virtual keyboard displayed on the board. However, if she wanted to enter longer pieces of text such as example sentences in a grammar lesson or for email writing activities, she had to retreat to the computer in the corner and use the keyboard. After several days of this she acquired a wireless keyboard and mouse which reduced the amount of walking back and forth she had to do.

Something she quickly discovered, and now makes regular use of, was an automatic feature of the IWB software. This allows her to use an IWB pen to write over any program she is using, then save a grab of that screen with the annotations that she and her students had made. These screen grabs increasingly appeared as part of periodic and end-of-course reviews.

At first, the novelty of the board caused her to spend a lot of time standing and teaching from the front of the room. When this was highlighted in the feedback from an observed lesson, she responded by handing control of the board and the pens to her students as much as she could. This initially brought up the issue of students finding the unfamiliar technology difficult to control. They had to learn to stand so that they did not throw a shadow over the board. Many found it difficult to judge how much pressure they had to exert to manipulate things on the board and everyone struggled with the virtual keyboard. However, Eve persisted and the students supported each other until everyone who did a course with Eve was comfortable with the IWB as part of furniture and tools of their language learning classroom.

Case study: e-vocabulary notebooks

Jessica teaches in a large language school in a major city. She has several groups of students who meet, on average, once a week. Her classroom is equipped with an IWB which she has now been using for about a year.

At the beginning, she regularly printed copies of her IWB screens and distributed them as handouts after the lessons. She encountered two problems with this. Her less well organised students often lost these pieces of paper which put them at a disadvantage when she asked them to review earlier lessons and the management of the school expressed a concern about the quantity of paper she was consuming.

Jessica decided to set up electronic vocabulary notebooks for each of her groups. These were computer folders which contained all the documents, images and screen grabs from each of her lessons. The school did not allow students access to their network so she established these e-vocabulary notebooks on the classroom computer. After every lesson the group's notebook was updated and added to. Most of her students already had memory sticks or knew how to save data on their phones or mp3 players and the others quickly acquired some sort of portable memory device. At the end of each lesson or, in the case of some courses, each week, they took a copy of their latest version of their e-vocabulary notebook.

Initially there was some confusion about what this resource was, who had access to it and what the students were supposed to do with it. In response to this, Jessica gave over part of a lesson to introduce the idea systematically and for each group of students to discuss what should be stored in the e-vocabulary notebook, how the content should be organised, and who should be allowed to edit it. The groups came to the same conclusions: pretty much everything from the board should be stored; it should be organised into a simple set of sub-folders, although the names of these sub-folders varied from group to group; and that, other than the teacher, no one should edit the original copy on the classroom computer without the agreement of the group.

Shortly after, there was a near disaster when one student believed he had accidentally deleted his group's notebook. A copy was quickly recovered from another student's memory stick. After that, Jessica always took her own back-up copy before the students.

In the same way as before the e-vocabulary notebook was introduced, how the material was used depended on the individual student. Some were thrilled to have easy access to everything studied during the course. Others printed the material themselves and some never looked at it. Jessica made an effort to remind the groups what had been added and increasingly referred the students to the materials in the notebook as part of their homework and as preparation for tests.

Eventually, Jessica's students started to share their e-vocabulary notebooks with students from other groups. At this point, it was decided to try a school-wide trial of the idea.

2 USING THE WHITEBOARD SOFTWARE

INTRODUCTION

In this chapter you will find activities that can be made using software found exclusively in individual software packages. These activities do not use the general tools familiar to all interactive board programs but extra features included by the manufacturers which can only be found in their own packages. Please note that while these instructions are specific to the described activities they are not intended to act as an IWB user's guide.

In some cases, these features are readymade lesson activities which can be used simply by clicking or dragging the thumbnail onto the page. In these cases you will find some explanation as to how you might organise the activities so that you can maximise the level of student participation.

In other cases, activities use the range of templates and flash activities that require your input and which give you literally thousands of options to tailor-make activities to meet your students' needs.

The majority of the activities and ideas in this chapter use the Smart Lesson Activity Toolkit 2 facility, though there are also activities from the Promethean Resource Browser. However, users of all boards should read the activities as many can be adapted so that they can use regular interactive whiteboard tools.

GRAMMAR

G1 *I come from...*

Level beginner
Interaction individual
Aim To give basic information about the countries students come from.
Language focus present simple
Technology Smart Gallery, Promethean Resource Library

Before the class

Drag an appropriate continental map onto the page. This can be found in the Gallery / Browser / Library. With classes of students from multiple continents, find out where students come from and, if necessary, store each continental map on a different page.

Procedure

1 Ask a volunteer student to come to the front, and point at the part of the map where they come from.

2 Ask them to locate the graphic of the country from the Gallery / Resource Library and drag it into the right place.

3 Ask them to say the name of the country and the name of the city where they come from. You can also ask them to name the capital city or any other points of interest. Any other information they can give (which countries neighbour their own, what the climate is like etc) is also encouraged.

G2 Comparing countries

Level beginner to pre-intermediate
Interaction individual
Aim To talk about countries using comparatives and superlatives.
Language focus comparative and superlative adjectives
Technology Smart Gallery or Promethean Resource Browser

Before the class

In the Gallery / Browser / Library find *Maps* and then *continents* and drag a continent onto a page. The continent map will fix as a background.

Next, find a minimum of ten country shapes that you can drag onto the page and fit into place over the country outline on the map. Write the name of the country on the country shape and group the name and the shape together.

Write a list of adjectives in a clear space on the page: *hot, cold, big, small, dry, wet, green, arid, flat, mountainous.*

Procedure

1 Ask students to give you one sentence comparing two countries you have labelled, eg *Russia is bigger than Italy.*

2 Divide the class into pairs. Ask students to write down four or five sentences using the board for ideas.

Variation

Use other images from the gallery: animals, vehicles etc.

G3 Daily routine time-line

Level elementary
Interaction individual, pairs
Aim To describe daily routines.
Language focus present simple, linking words
Technology timelines

Before the class

Create a timeline using your IWB software with a number of appropriate times and activities for your typical day: eg *7.15 am: wake up, 7.30 am shower, 8.00 am breakfast* etc.

Click *ok* and the times will appear on the timeline.

Procedure

1 Show the timeline without the activities to the students and ask them to discuss in pairs what they think you do at each time. Monitor as they do this.

2 Ask students to come up to the board to write answers in chronological order, eg *wake up, have a shower* etc above and below the times.

3 When you have worked through the list, erase the annotations and call up the real answers by tapping on the circles on the timeline.

4 Ask students to use the language to write about their own daily routines.

Variation

As only one piece of information can be revealed at any one time, students can ask you to reveal pieces of information they might have forgotten. Only accept properly formed questions: *'Excuse me, what do you do at 11 am?'*

G4 Daily routine verb filler

Level elementary
Interaction pairs
Aim To write correct verb forms in a gap-fill exercise.
Language focus present simple tense
Technology Smart Version 10

Before the class

Type in the following text.

Yesterday I woke up at 7.30 am. My brother, James, usually wakes up ten minutes before me but yesterday he overslept. We both usually have breakfast at around 7.45 am but as James was running late he left for work without having any. I ate some cereal and then left the house at 8 o' clock. I ran to the bus stop and caught the bus at ten past eight. I arrived at school at twenty to nine.

Underneath the text write the infinitive forms of the verbs / phrasal verbs: *wake up, oversleep, have, be, leave, have, eat, leave, run, catch, arrive.*

Place rectangles from the *shapes* tool of the IWB over each of the underlined words, adjusting them when necessary so that they cover all of the word. Set each of the shapes so that they fade out when clicked.

Procedure

1 Tell the students about your daily routine, perhaps using *Daily routine track line.*

2 Display the text and ask students to work in pairs and to discuss the correct forms of the words that they think are hidden under the rectangle shapes.

3 Ask students to volunteer answers. Click on the rectangles to reveal the answers.

4 When all the answers have been revealed, cover up the text and put students into pairs to see how much they can remember.

Variation

If you want to make it easier, write the verbs in the order they appear in the passage, making sure you repeat the verbs that appear more than once. For a more challenging task, write them once only in a random order.

G5 Questions to answers using the screen shade

Level elementary
Interaction pairs
Aim To write questions to match responses.
Language focus question forms
Technology Smart screen shade or Promethean Revealer

Before the class

Type the following responses and questions so that the responses are on the left-hand side of the screen and the questions are aligned on the right:

'Very well, thanks.'	*'How are you?'*
'I work in a bank.'	*'Where do you work?'*
'I'm twenty five years old.'	*'How old are you?'*
'It's going to rain.'	*'What's the weather forecast?'*
'No thanks, I've just eaten.'	*'Would you like something to eat?'*
'I'm a teacher.'	*'What do you do?'*
'I like playing the guitar and reading.'	*'What are your hobbies?'*
'We're spending two weeks in Girona.'	*'Where are you going for your holidays?'*
'Yes, I'll have a coffee, please.'	*'Would you like a drink?'*
'Yes, I've got a rabbit and a cat.'	*'Have you got any pets?'*

Pull the screen shade across to cover the questions.

Take note that the Promethean Revealer can only move either horizontally or vertically and can't move in both directions simultaneously. If using this, type the questions so that they come under each answer, otherwise you will reveal all of them at the same time.

Procedure

1 Look at the first example and elicit a correct question to fit the answer.

2 Put the students into pairs. Ask them to look at the ten responses on the board and to write down the question for each of the answers.

3 Conduct feedback and award a point for the correct question, a point for correct spelling and a point for correct punctuation. Reveal your own questions on the board as you check each item.

4 In many cases there will be more than one answer so if a student comes up with an alternative, but equally correct question, award another point for fun. This will encourage them to be creative but do remember that the question must be a good fit for the answer.

Variation

This can be done as a sorting exercise with two lists printed side by side, out of order. Students can connect the two parts by drawing lines.

G6 Superlative crossword challenge

Level elementary
Interaction individual, pairs
Aim To compile a crossword puzzle based on superlative forms.
Language focus *In the example:* superlatives
Alternative: irregular past forms
Technology Smart LAT 2

Before the class

Follow the path *LAT 2, Games, Crossword* and either double-click the thumbnail or drag it on to the page.

Click *Edit* and then input *Biggest* in the first box in the WORD column and *Big*, next to it in the CLUE column. Next, input the following superlatives followed by the adjectives:

*2 Largest – Large   3 Slowest – Slow   4 Prettiest – Pretty   5 Most Handsome – Handsome
6 Fastest – Fast   7 Happiest – Happy   8 Wisest – Wise   9 Thinnest – Thin
10 Gentlest – Gentle*

Click on *Generate*. In a few seconds the crossword will appear on the screen. Clues are accessed by pulling the tab from the right-hand side of the screen and then clicking on the appropriate number. You can write the clues down the right-hand side of the page, if you like, as in this instance they are short 'cues'. This will allow students to complete the crossword in their own time. If you prefer them to complete one clue at a time then use the clue tab. Print off the crossword.

Procedure

1   Hand out the printed crosswords, one to each student.

2   Ask the students to complete the crossword using one of the methods above. If you'd prefer to go through the exercise one clue at a time, ask the students to call out the numbers they wish to input. Note that you can input the letters either by hand or via the keyboard by choosing the *Input method* feature at the right-hand side.

G7   Word types pelmanism

Level elementary
Interaction teams
Aim To match a set of words to their word class.
Language focus *In the example:* word classes
Alternatives: past and present verb forms, verb / noun collocations
Technology Smart LAT / all other whiteboard software for manual creation

Before the class

Smart users: Follow the path *LAT 2, Activities, Pairs*. Double left-click on the thumbnail or drag it on to the page. Click *Edit* and then, in the box at the top right, next to *No of pairs*, select *8*. Then type in the following pairs: *see – verb, jacket – noun, quickly – adverb, it – pronoun, she – personal pronoun, nice – adjective, but – conjunction, outside – preposition.*

When using the *Flash* activity in the Smart LAT, the media randomises each time it is opened, making it more of a challenge to find the words with repeated playing.

Non Smart users can create this pairs game by creating boxes using the shapes tool.

Procedure

1   Show the first item to the students and ask them to identify the word class.

2   Divide the class into two teams and explain the game to them.

3   Ask a student from one team to call out a number and then ask another member from the same team to call out another number. The aim is to match the word with the

word type. If the team find the correct word class, they score a point and have another turn. If they don't find it, play passes to the other team.

4   Alternate between teams, keeping score as you go. Continue until the activity has been completed.

G8   Countable / Uncountable images

Level elementary to pre-intermediate
Interaction individual, whole class
Aim To get students to categorise images.
Language focus *In the example:* countable and uncountable nouns
Alternatives: regular and irregular verbs
Technology Smart LAT 2 – all other IWBs without checking / marking tool

Before the class

Smart users: Go to *LAT 2, Activities, Category sort – image.* Click *Edit* and then bring in images of bread, sugar, milk, rain, snow, water, rice, butter (uncountable nouns) and man, boy, ball, house, dish, bus, car, cat (countable nouns).

In the windows on the page you will see the term *Drag Image Here.*

Look up the images you need in the *Gallery* search window. Press *okay* when you have filled the squares, adding or subtracting the number you need.

Non Smart users: Draw a straight line down the middle of the page and a horizontal line across the bottom which leaves room to store your images. Drag in the images from the Gallery / Browser / Library and store them at the bottom of the screen. Write the terms *Countable* and *Uncountable* either side of the vertical line at the top of the page.

Procedure

1   Display the page on the screen. Ask the students to write the words for the images.

2   Pick an example and ask if it is uncountable or countable. Divide the students into pairs and then ask them to write a *C* or a *U* after the words.

3   Check the answers, one by one, asking the students to tell you which words they have used for each image, just in case there are irregularities.

4   After checking answers, ask students to come out and drag the images into the right place.

G9   Question words dice

Level elementary to pre-intermediate
Interaction whole class
Aim To practise *wh-* question formation.
Language focus *wh-* question words
Technology SMART Notebook – Lesson Activity Toolkit 2.0 – Keyword dice

Before the class

Smart users: In the Lesson Activity Toolkit 2.0, click on the folder called *Tools* and drag the *Keyword – dice* onto a page. Click on the *Edit* symbol and enter the following words:

what, when, where, who, why, how.

Procedure

1 Start with an empty whiteboard page. Elicit the *wh-* question words and write them on the board.

2 Now display the page with the dice. Click on the dice and ask a student a question beginning with that word, eg *where* – 'Where are you from?'.

3 Invite a volunteer to the board. The student clicks on the dice and uses it for a question directed to another student. That student then has to come to the board and do the same thing. Continue until every student has asked and answered at least one question. Provide feedback and correction as you go along.

Variation

Divide the class into pairs. Click on the dice ten times. Each time the pairs have to write a question beginning with that word. Pair the students differently and they practise asking and answering the questions.

G10 Irregular verb tables

Level pre-intermediate
Interaction groups
Aim To revise irregular verbs by revealing hidden past forms.
Language focus irregular verbs
Technology Smart Version 10, table shade

Before the class

Create a 3 × 9 table with *infinitive, past simple* and *past participle* as the column headings. Fill in the table using the following verbs:

drink, drank, drunk; give, gave, given; fight, fought, fought; buy, bought, bought; shrink, shrank, shrunk; take, took, taken; bring, brought, brought.

Use the table shade to cover the table.

Input the numbers *1, 2* and *3* as separate items and activate *Infinite clone* for each number. Drag the cloned numbers in a random order into a single pile at the top left of the screen.

Procedure

1 Show a verb from the first column and ask students to tell you what the two past forms of the verb are.

2 Choose a group and then drag a number from the pile at the top of the page. If you drag a number 2 from the pile, click on cell 2 from the next example. The group must now tell you what the other two forms of the verb are.

3 Work through the table.

G11 Active / Passive table activity

Level pre-intermediate to intermediate
Interaction individual
Aim To convert a number of active sentences into the passive voice.
Language focus the passive voice
Technology Smart table, cell shade

Before the class

Create a table with each of the following sentence in a separate row:

My boss called me this morning.

I was called by my boss this morning.

Buck and Mills have taken me on as an underwriter.

I've been taken on by Buck and Mills as an underwriter.

Claire picked up the bill.

The bill was picked up by Claire.

Bob opened the letter.

The letter was opened by Bob.

HR cancelled my contract.

My contract was cancelled by HR.

Mrs Draper fired Dave.

Dave was fired by Mrs Draper.

Everyone here loved him.

He was loved by everyone here.

Place a cell shade over each of the passive sentences, these will disappear when clicked to reveal the answers.

Procedure

1 Present the table to the class and ask them to provide the passive versions of the sentences on paper.

2 Ask students to come to the board, one by one, to volunteer their answers. They tap on the cells to reveal the answers.

Variation

Add a cell shade to the active sentences to focus on the form of these.

G12 Questions to answers

Level pre-intermediate to intermediate
Interaction whole class
Aim To form questions accurately.
Language focus *what, who, where, when etc*
Technology screen shade / Revealer tool

Before the class

Write down around ten details from your life. You could include your date of birth, birthplace, university town, favourite pop group, number of siblings etc.

Write them in different colours if you want to aid clarity. Use the screen shade to hide the answers.

Procedure

1 Reveal the first cue by drawing the shade down.

2 Elicit from the students what they think the question might be. They can do this orally.

3 For lower levels, ask students to write down the questions when all the answers have been revealed. You can turn to the next page to reveal a page where the questions appear above the answers. Make sure you write questions in one colour and answers in another for clarity.

Follow up

Ask one student to come out to the front and do their own version for the rest of the class.

G13 First conditional gap-fill

Level intermediate
Interaction pairs
Aim To drag phrases into place on the board to complete first conditional sentences.
Language focus *In the example:* the first conditional
Alternatives: second conditional, third conditional
Technology Smart table, cell shade

Before the class

Create a 3 × 8 table, with the following sentence beginnings in the first column:

If I work hard

If we go to Madrid

If I see Juan

If I go to London

If we invite Soo

If I don't work

If it is sunny

Leave the second column blank and in the third column type the following sentence endings:

I will pass my exams.

we can visit the Prado.

I will tell him.

I will take a photo of Buckingham Palace.

she will be really pleased.

I won't get paid.

we will take a picnic.

Copy and paste the sentence endings so that they are below the table and arrange them in a random order.

Procedure

1 Show the beginning of the first sentence and elicit the second part from the students. Drag it into place from the bottom of the screen.

2 Ask the students to work in pairs and to match the sentence beginnings to the endings underneath.

3 Drag up the phrases and put them into the boxes the students suggest, asking if anyone disagrees with the suggestions. Continue until all sentences are complete and then reveal the answers at the end, correcting any errors.

G14 Process images

Level intermediate
Interaction individual, pairs
Aim To describe processes using the passive voice.
Language focus passives
Technology Lesson Activity Toolkit 2 (Smart)

Before the class

Find pictures that relate to a process, eg the manufacture, production and selling of a packet of coffee, going to a football match or a concert etc.

Smart users: Copy and paste the images onto a Smart Notebook page and then move all of these images into *My Content* in the *Gallery*.

Access *Image Arrange* from the *Activities* menu in the LAT and after clicking on *Edit*, drag the images into the squares in the right order. When you have finished, click the *No of Images* panel at the top and select the right number, depending on how many images you have inserted. Press *OK*.

Non Smart users: create a similar activity by inserting the images in a random order on a page. In this case, you won't have a checking function, however.

Procedure

1 Students come up, one by one, to move the images into the right order. One student can come up to represent a group, who can call out.

2 When the students have finished, check the answers using the *check* function.

3 Students then describe the process using the passive voice.

Follow up

For further study, students can write down the whole process in their books.

G15 Word type quiz

Level intermediate
Interaction teams
Aim To identify word types by playing a multiple-choice quiz.
Language focus word types
Technology Smart LAT 2

Before the class

Follow the path, *LAT 2, Activities, Multiple Choice*. Double left-click the thumbnail or drag it onto the page and click on *Edit*. In the spaces provided write your question (at the top) and the multiple choices in the boxes labelled *A, B, C,* and *D*. Click in the box next to *Number of questions* and input the number *five*.

Next input the following questions and answers. Capitalise the word you want the students to identify. The correct answers are highlighted below in **bold**.

1 *SHE had a lovely smile. Adverb | **Pronoun** | Verb | Noun*

2 *He spoke **QUIETLY** so that the others would not hear. **Adverb** | Conjunction | Noun | Verb*

3 *The sky was **DARK** blue. Conjunction | Noun | **Adjective** | Verb*

4 *You **ARE** going to be late – get a move on! Noun | **Verb** | Pronoun | Preposition*

5 *I want to be a singer when I'm older **SO** I practise every day. Verb | Noun | Adverb | **Conjunction***

Then make another five-question quiz:

1 *He was working **IN** the house. **Preposition** | Verb | Noun | Adverb*

2 *She was a good musician **BUT** she struggled to play the piano that night. Adjective | Noun | Preposition | **Conjunction***

3 *He found a **WALLET** on the floor and handed it in to the receptionist. Verb | **Noun** | Adverb | Pronoun*

4 *He missed his train by five **MINUTES**. Pronoun | Verb | Conjunction | **Noun***

5 ***JANE** screamed when she saw the face at the window. Noun | Adverb | Adjective | **Proper Noun***

Procedure

1 Divide the class into two teams. Ask for a volunteer to come to the front.

2 Ask the volunteer to tap on what they think is the right answer as they go through the quiz. The other students can call out to help. Note each wrong answer including multiple wrong answers within the same question (ie if someone presses three incorrect answers before hitting the correct one, mark down three errors). Start with a total of 40 marks and deduct one for each error made – you must be quick to spot the errors so just make a mark on a piece of paper.

3 After the first team have taken their turn, call up a volunteer from the other side and follow the same procedure.

4 Add up the scores and announce the winner.

Variation

To help comprehension you can read out the questions that appear, or you can ask a confident student to do this.

G16 Magic table verbs

Level intermediate to upper intermediate
Interaction individual, whole class
Aim To name the past simple form of verbs.
Language focus *In the example:* past simple
Alternative: opposites
Technology Smart Version 10

Before the class

Draw a rectangle using the *shapes* tool. Fill it with colour and double click on the shape to activate a text box. Write the present simple form of a verb, eg *go*, in the box. Press *Return* on the keyboard and then, underneath, write the past simple form, *went*. Now, resize the rectangle until you can only see the top word (*go*). Stretch and move the rectangle so that the word sits in the middle of the space.

Now, click on the *pen* tool and draw a simple dot / full stop underneath the rectangle. Change the properties of the dot so that it is completely transparent. Now group the transparent dot and the rectangle. When you move the rectangle into the large cell at the top of the page, the rectangle will expand, revealing the two words, *go* and *went*.

Continue to input more examples on the board using *infinite clone* to reproduce the rectangles. You don't have to space out the boxes – you can stack them up one behind the other, meaning you can use as many examples as you like.

Procedure

1   Split the class into groups of four. Ask Group A to nominate another group to provide the past simple form of the verb at the top of the pile. If the nominated group get the answer correct, they are awarded two points. If they get it wrong, the nominating team get two points. Play the game until all the examples have been used.

Variation

This can be used for many other areas of teaching, including multiple-choice testing for reading exercises or video lessons.

> **VOCABULARY**

V1 Adding up

Level beginner
Interaction pairs
Aim To identify and add numbers together.
Language focus numbers
Technology Smart Gallery or Promethean Resource Browser. You can also find
    free-to-use virtual dice online.

Before the class

Have the dice ready to use on the screen.

Procedure

1 Review numbers with the students.

2 Show the dice on the IWB and tap them to make them roll. Elicit from the students what the total is.

3 Divide the class into teams and ask for a volunteer from each team to come out to the front. Explain that when you roll the dice the students have to call out the total shown. The person who gets it right first scores a point for their team.

4 The winning team is the first to score ten points.

V2 Animal connecting game

Level beginner
Interaction individual
Aim To connect sounds of animals with the words.
Language focus animals vocabulary
Technology Promethean Active Inspire

Before the class

Open the animal sounds from the shared resources section.

Drag around 15 of the sound thumbnails onto the page and line them up along the bottom. Number them by typing in numbers separately and then placing the numbers by the side of the sound thumbnail. Group the number with the thumbnail.

Then write the names of the animals at the top of the page.

Procedure

1 Tap on sound effect number one. Ask the students to write down the name of the animal that they think makes that sound.

2 When you have done this for all of the sounds, ask students to compare their answers in pairs.

3 Check the answers. Ask students to come to the board, one by one, to tap a sound effect and tell you their answer, before moving it into place.

V3 Image labelling activity

Level beginner
Interaction individual, whole class
Aim To build vocabulary.
Language focus *In the example:* animals vocabulary
Alternatives: any lexical group
Technology LAT (Smart)

Before the class

Open the Image select activity from the Activities menu and drag a number of images of different animals that you want to focus on. The images will flash up on screen when you activate the tool. Write the names of the animals underneath the boxes.

This activity is best used to review vocabulary.

Procedure

1 Tell students that they are going to see a number of images of animals and when they think they know the name they should come up to the front and touch the board.

2 Display the first picture.

3 When the first student comes up to the board, ask them what they think the name is and invite them to tap the box to reveal the correct answer.

V4 Picture stories

Level beginner to pre-intermediate
Interaction individual, whole class
Aim To identify and name pictures – in this example, of food.
Language focus food vocabulary
Technology Smart LAT 2

Before the class

Open the dice tool and activate the *image* tool so that you can apply images to each face of the dice. Insert images of the vocabulary area you want to practise. Note that you can drag images from the Smart Gallery but that any other pictures must first be installed into *My content* in the Gallery.

Procedure

1 Display the page and click through the dice, leading a drill of the vocabulary.

2 Once students are familiar with the items split them into small groups and explain that they are going to write a dialogue containing the items in a specific order.

3 Roll through the dice for each group, they should each receive a slightly different order.

4 When the groups are finished ask for a pair of volunteers from each group to perform theirs for the class.

Variation

For more abstract items, put words on the dice faces and conduct a drill before putting students into groups.

V5 Animated answers

Level elementary
Interaction individual, whole class
Aim To guess the occupation from a written clue.
Language focus job vocabulary
Technology Smart LAT, can adapt to any IWB software

Before the class

Open the Gallery and drag a number of pictures of occupations to the top of the page. Write the name of the job under each picture and then place a rectangle over both. Set the box so that it will fade out when it is clicked. Above each of the rectangles type a short definition, eg *You buy bread from this person.*

Procedure

1 Show the pages, one by one and ask students to work in pairs, and to name the pictures.

2 Ask students to come to the board to click on the squares. When they are clicked they will fade out to reveal the picture and job title.

V6 Time telling

Level elementary
Interaction teams
Aim To tell the time using the clock in the gallery.
Language focus telling the time
Technology Smart Gallery – Active Inspire Resource Browser

Before the class

Type the word *clock* in the search menu window and drag the clock you want onto the page.

Write down a number of times, in English, on a sheet of paper.

On another IWB page, drag the clock onto the page.

Procedure

1 With the class as a whole, review telling the time using the clocks on the IWB.

2 Divide the class into two teams and show the screen with the single clock.

3 Ask for a volunteer from team A. They come out to the front and read the time from one of the pieces of paper. One of their teammates has 30 seconds to move the hands of the clock on the IWB. If they are correct within the time limit, they score a point.

4 It is then the next team's turn.

Follow up

Repeat the exercise asking students to tell the times numerically, eg twelve forty-five, six fifteen etc.

Variation

Promethean provide a number of options with their clocks so spend a bit of time deciding how best to use the options available.

V7 Timed opposites

Level elementary
Interaction pairs
Aim To be the first to correctly identify opposites of words.
Language focus *In the example:* opposites
Alternatives: capital cities
Technology Smart LAT 2, all IWB software

Before the class

Open the *Question Flipper* tool and key in *high*, then click on back and key in *low*. Repeat this process for the following sets of words: *high, low; up, down; cheap, expensive; narrow, wide; tall, short; dry, wet; dark, light.*

Procedure

1 Show the page and elicit the opposite word of the first example. Tap on the tile to reveal the answer.

2 Tell students that they are going to work in pairs to write down the opposites of the other words shown. When they think they have all of them, one of them can come up to the front to check the answers. The piece of paper they are writing the answers on must stay on the desk so that the person who checks the answers must return to the desk to confirm whether or not the answers are correct.

3 Set students off and monitor to make sure nobody is cheating!

Variation

This game can be played with phrasal verbs and their single word equivalents.

V8 Noun sorter

Level pre-intermediate
Interaction teams, whole class
Aim To identify irregular nouns.
Language focus *In the example:* sorting regular and irregular nouns
Alternatives: any sorting activity
Technology Smart dual page display

Before the class

Write a list of regular and irregular nouns on the page, eg Irregulars: *foot, half, life, man, woman, that, roof, this, sheep, scissors.* Regulars: *boy, table, house, cat, car, onion, mile, saucer, guitar, bed, school, street.*

Activate the dual page display.

Procedure

1 Split the class into teams of four or five. Ask students to come to the board, one by one. Pick a noun and ask them if it is regular or irregular. If the latter, they must pull the noun over to the clean page. Ask them to type or write the plural underneath.

2 Checking the answers can be done as the exercise is carried out, or at the end of the activity. Colour code answers to clarify groups.

3 At the end of the exercise you will have a clean page of irregular nouns and their plurals, which you can print off and hand out. For presentation purposes, utilise handwriting recognition and correct any typos or errors.

Variation

Dual page display allows you to print off the answers to any sorting activity on a clean page with no surplus information attached.

V9 *They're* or *their*?

Level pre-intermediate
Interaction pairs
Aim To distinguish between *they're* and *their*.
Language focus *In the example: their* and *they're*
Alternatives: any other easily-confused pairs of words
Technology Smart table, cell shade

Before the class

Create the following table using your IWB software:

1 _____ exactly the kind of people we want here.	They're
2 We don't know if _____ coming or not.	they're
3 I called at _____ house earlier.	their
4 We took a ride in _____ new car.	their
5 _____ new around here, aren't they?	They're
6 _____ picking up _____ children from school.	They're, their
7 _____ not coming until later.	They're
8 It wasn't funny in _____ opinion.	their
9 _____ not the only ones to think like that!	They're
10 They put in _____ election manifesto and now _____ regretting it.	their, they're

Apply a cell shade to each of the cells in the right hand column.

Procedure

1 Display the first sentence and ask students if they can think of the missing word. Reveal the answer.

2 Put the students into pairs and ask them to complete the exercise.

3 When they have finished, ask students to come to the board and click on the cells to reveal the answers.

V10 Formal language sorting

Level pre-intermediate to intermediate
Interaction individual, whole class
Aim To distinguish between informal and formal language.
Language focus formal and informal language
Technology Smart LAT

Before the class

Open the *Vortex sort* tool – this is a tool which categorises words or images into two groups. Enter the following terms at random and then click on OK.

hi, cheers, ciao, bye, thanks, hey, yeah, gonna

Dear, Best regards, Goodbye, How do you do? Pleased to meet you, May I...

Procedure

1 Show the list of phrases to the class and draw attention to the first one. Ask students to decide if it is formal or informal and drag it into place.

2 Divide the class into pairs and ask them to discuss the other phrases.

3 Conduct feedback by inviting students up to the front to drag the words before confirming.

V11 Word building

Level pre-intermediate to intermediate
Interaction individual, teams
Aim To create compound words.
Language focus vocabulary building
Technology Promethean Resource Library (path: *Activities, Word Building, Compound words.ap 2 activity*)

Before the class

Open the Compound words activity. This is an activity which consists of two lists of words, one on the left, one on the right, which can be moved up and down in order to create compound words.

Procedure

1 Display the words you are going to use and show students how the words can be moved together to make new compound words.

2 Students come to the front of the class and attempt to create one new word by moving the left and right-hand columns into place.

3 Make a note of all compound words that are correct and write them up on the board to refer to at the end of the lesson.

Variation

Smart users can make a list of words that can be jumbled on the page. Remember to colour code the words for clarity.

V12 Keyword match

Level pre-intermediate to upper intermediate
Interaction pairs
Aim To identify words via simple clues.
Language focus reading, speaking
Technology Smart LAT 2. A simplified version without a checking device can be made using regular IWBs.

Before the class

Access *Keyword match* in the LAT2 Activities menu.

Press edit and enter your keywords and their descriptions in the spaces provided, eg *Car – you drive this. Bed – you sleep in this* etc. You can input eight clues and answers per page so compile as many as you will need to go around your class several times.

Press okay to reset the page.

For users of other boards, write the clues on the left-hand side of the board and enter the keywords, separately to the right, in a different colour and in a random order.

Procedure

1 Show the page to the class and draw attention to the first clue. Elicit the answer.

2 Divide the class into pairs and explain that they are going to use the crossword to play a game. The object is to be the last pair still in the game. Ask the first pair to choose a clue and to also choose another pair to answer the clue. One of the second pair then comes out and writes the answer on the board.

3 If the nominated pair is able to answer correctly they can then choose the next clue to be answered and the pair that they wish to answer. If they can't give the correct answer they are out and the original pair can choose again.

V13 Picture labelling

Level pre-intermediate to upper intermediate
Interaction whole class
Aim To describe a picture.
Language focus vocabulary
Technology Smart dual page view

Before the class

Insert your picture of choice onto a page. A good example for this kind of activity is to use a news image, contemporary or historical, eg a picture of East and West Germans standing on the Berlin Wall in 1989.

Procedure

1 Show the picture and brainstorm information about it. Write down the words on the image and use handwriting recognition to turn your writing into a fixed font. Here you are looking not just for adjectives describing physical details but background information, political, social, economic etc.

2 Add any words that you think are applicable. Click on the *dual page display* icon.

3 Drag the words over to the right-hand page.

4 Lead into a discussion about western values, democracy, capitalism etc. In the light of recent world economic events, are western systems of running economies the best? Were there any advantages to living in old Eastern Europe?

5 Ask students to compose a short written piece looking at two opposing sides of the argument, choosing which side they agree with. Ask them to include some of the vocabulary brainstormed from the activity.

Follow up

Show the image and repeat the activity as a quick starter activity a few lessons later. You can then bring in the words from the original activity to compare at the end of the activity.

V14 Spotlight record

Level pre-intermediate to upper intermediate
Interaction pairs
Aim To talk about an image and to discuss the topic.
Language focus discussion
Technology recorder, *spotlight* tool

Before the class

Insert an image on a page, eg a picture showing evidence of deforestation, and increase size to fill page. Access the recorder and then access the *spotlight* tool. By guiding the spotlight over the recorder, press *Record* and then start revealing parts of the image, as you would if you were using the *spotlight* tool in class. Gauge how long you need to spend on each part of the image.

Change the dimensions of the spotlight to reveal more, or less, of the image. When you have revealed the whole picture, write the topic, *Deforestation*, underneath, or on the image. Press *Stop* on the recorder.

Procedure

1 Tell the students they are going to see an image and that they need to guess what it shows.

2 Call up the film and press *Play*. You can pause the recording if you want the students to have time to discuss the image in more detail.

3 As the film plays, monitor and help as necessary.

V15 Adjective, verb or noun?

Level intermediate
Interaction individual and pairs
Aim To sort word types onto a Venn diagram.
Language focus word types
Technology all IWB technology

Before the class

Create a three-circle Venn diagram on your IWB.

Write the criteria outside each circle: *Adjective, Verb, Noun*. Write the words you want to use on the page, or on the labels if using the LAT (eg *set, fine, holy, red, guitar, help, create, live*) and number the words.

Procedure

1 Write the following sentences on the board and ask students to suggest one word which can fill both of the gaps.

> *The weather forecast said that it would be _____ all week.*
>
> *Maria was given a _____ by the police for driving too fast.*

2 Ask students to identify the word class of *fine* in each sentence.

3 Display the Venn diagram and ask students to draw it in their books or on a laminate board. Explain what the different areas represent and ask them where they would place *fine*.

4 Display the other words and ask students to write the numbers in the right places.

5 Feedback can be done on a word by word basis, with students writing the initials to show their answers on the back of their laminate boards, eg you call out 'red' they show their answers 'A, N'.

Follow up

Put students into pairs and ask them to write more gapped sentences for another pair to fill in.

Answers

set (VN), fine (VNA), holy (A), red (AN), guitar (N), help (NV), create (V), live (VA).

V16 Large numbers

Level intermediate
Interaction small groups
Aim To talk in detail about differences between countries. To identify and name large numbers.
Language focus numbers, country names
Technology Smart (for animation), all other IWBs for simpler reveal

Before the class

Go to the *Gallery* and from *Maps*, drag your continent of choice onto a new page. Look up population sizes of specific countries and place them within the country areas. Lock these numbers into place.

Next, write the names of the countries and group them with the relevant country lids. Go to *Properties*, and then click on *Object Animation*. Under *Type*, choose *Fade out*. Under *Occurs*, choose *When the object is clicked*.

Next, when all the labelled lids are in place, find the relevant country lids again and choose exactly the same *Object Animation* effects. Finally, drag them into the right places and snap into position.

Procedure

1 Divide the class into small groups. Take turns asking students from both groups to come to the board and name a country. Their teammates can help.

2 Ask the student to tap on the country. It will disappear to reveal the country name. They get a point if it's correct.

3 Next, ask the student what the population of the country is. Wild guesses are fine. The student can also confer with teammates.

4 The opposition team then decide if they want to go higher or lower. Tap on the country lid to reveal the answer.

5 Keep score and announce the winning team at the end.

V17 Loan words

Level intermediate
Interaction pairs, whole group
Aim To decide which countries a set of loan words come from.
Language focus vocabulary
Technology world map

Before the class

Prepare a flipchart. Insert the world map from the resource bank. Type the following 'loan words' on the flipchart:

angst, au fait, matador, glasnost, dome, karaoke, sauna, bungalow, kiwi, goulash

Procedure

1   As an introduction, ask students if there are any English words which are commonly used in their own language, because they don't have translations. Tell students that many words came into English from other languages. In this activity, they will focus on these loan words.

2   Display the flipchart and draw attention to the first word (*angst*). Ask students if they know where the word originally came from. After the students have guessed, drag the word and place it over Germany on the map.

3   Put students into pairs and ask them to do the same for the other words.

4   Ask students to come out to the whiteboard in turn and drag each word to its country of origin. Get whole class approval.

Follow up

See if students can add any more 'loan words' to the list, either from the same countries or others. If so, they can come out and write them on the world map. Check any examples you are not sure about using the Internet or the etymology section of a CD-ROM dictionary. Students could also research five more loan words on the Internet for the next lesson. They should copy down any new words into their vocabulary notebook.

Answers

angst – German / *au fait* – French / *matador* – Spanish / *glasnost* – Russian / *dome* – Italian / *karaoke* – Japanese / *sauna* – Finnish / *bungalow* – Hindi / *kiwi* – New Zealand / *goulash* – Hungarian

V18 Phrasal verb files

Level intermediate
Interaction individual, pairs
Aim To identify pairs of adjective opposites.
Language focus phrasal verbs
Technology Smart LAT 2, shapes tool on other IWB software

Before the class

Create a 4 × 4 grid of tiles with phrasal verbs on one side and their meanings on the other. For example:

Turn out – take part; Pass out - faint; Leave out – omit; Take after – resemble; Chip in – volunteer / suggest; Kick out – expel; Take away – remove / take with; Let down – disappoint; Let go – release; Blow up – explode / inflate; Come into – inherit; Look after – take care of; Look for – search; Make off – leave in a hurry; Go for – choose; Eat out – have a meal in a restaurant.

Set the tiles so that the sides with the phrasal verbs are showing and so that they will flip to reveal the meanings when they are tapped.

Procedure

1   Ask the students to look at the phrasal verbs in pairs and to discuss the meanings and to come up with an example sentence.

2   When they have finished, choose an example and elicit the meaning.

3   Click on the tile to reveal the answer. There isn't enough space to provide multiple meanings so, where applicable, ask other groups for alternative definitions.

Variation

Add a competitive element by using the grid from a Tic Tac Toe game.

V19   Prefix/suffix word builder

Level intermediate to upper intermediate
Interaction individual, pairs, whole class
Aim To create words using prefix, suffix and root word cues.
Language focus suffixes and prefixes
Technology Smart Gallery, all IWBs

Before the class

Go to *Gallery Essentials* and click to access the drop down menu. Choose *Grammar* and then *Prefixes*. Drag all of the prefixes onto the left-hand side of the page. Next go to *Suffixes* and drag them onto the right-hand side of the page.

Now, create a new page. Draw your cursor around all of the words on the original page and then paste them on to the new, blank page.

Then go to *Root words* and arrange them in a column down the middle of the page. You won't be able to fit all of the root words on one page so arrange 14 on one page and 13 on another.

Procedure

1   Activate the *dual page display* function to display the material and divide the class into pairs.

2   Choose a root word and relay a sentence leaving a vocal space to create a 'blank', or describe the word. Ask students to identify the word and then drag the word end or beginning into place to complete it.

3 Ask students to do the same, in pairs – nominating root words, coming up with a suggested sentence or describing the words, and getting their partners to identify them. When they have gone through all of the examples, ask students to come to the board to move the media into place to create the words and give example sentences.

4 Get them to go through all of the root words, making a list of as many words as they can. Count up at the end to see who has most, checking for context.

V20 Word biz quiz

Level intermediate to upper intermediate
Interaction teams
Aim To read questions and respond by typing in answers from random letters in a grid.
Language focus spelling
Technology Smart LAT 2

Before the class

Open the *Word biz* activity from the *Lesson Activity Toolkit 2.0*.

Key in the following clues and answers:

Place where you post letters – Post box. The Capital of Scotland – Edinburgh. Place where you buy medicine – Chemist. Person you see when you are ill – Doctor. British national dish – Fish and chips. You catch a bus here – Bus stop. Famous Indian food – Curry. After Winter comes. . . – Spring. Capital of Wales – Cardiff. Britain's national sport – Football. The Queen's first name – Elizabeth. Who lives at No 10 Downing Street? – Prime Minister. BBC stands for British Broadcasting. . . – Corporation. Location of Nelson's Column – Trafalgar Square. Game played at Twickenham – Rugby.

Capitalising answers gives students the chance to choose the first letter correctly but to make it more difficult, key in the answers in lower case.

Procedure

1 Divide the students into groups of four or five and explain that they are going to take part in a quiz. All they have to do is choose the right letters to spell out the answers from a selection on the board.

2 Show the first clue to the class and elicit the answer. Demonstrate the procedure by dragging out the correct letters yourself.

3 Ask one group to come to the front of the class and give them three questions to complete. They must press each letter only once. Then the next group takes a turn.

4 Record scores and announce the winning group at the end.

Follow up

You can use the quiz again at a later date to help students reinforce the information.
Students could also generate their own questions instead of these.

V21 Confusing words

Level intermediate and above
Interaction whole class, individual
Aim To help students identify the differences between confusing words.

Language focus reading, comprehension
Technology Smart LAT 2

Before the class

Open the *checker* tool from the tool section and type in the following sentences:

1 *I am very interested | interesting in applying for the job.*

2 *I must say, the job does look interested | interesting.*

3 *Last year our company expended | expanded by 10%.*

4 *When running long distances you must be careful not to expend | expand too much energy in the early stages.*

5 *The film was amazing and the special affects | effects were just incredible.*

6 *He joined the team but was unable to affect | effect any change.*

7 *Call me later, maybe | may be I can help you.*

8 *Call me later; there maybe | may be a way I can help you.*

9 *I've brought | bought some biscuits with me in case we get hungry.*

10 *I went to the shop and brought | bought these biscuits in case we get hungry.*

In another window type the words, *interested* and *interesting*, remembering to click into a new space so that the words are not joined together. Put these words well clear of the end of the sentence, above the *checker* tool.

Next click on the arrow heads at the top left of the *checker* tool and input the correct answer. You can make the answer case sensitive if you wish.

Procedure

1 Show the first sentence and ask your students for the correct answer. Drag the answer into the *checker*. If it is the wrong word, you will be told. If correct the answer is ticked.

2 Ask the students to work in pairs and to do the same for the other sentences.

3 Ask students to come to the board to volunteer their answers and drag the right words into the *checker*.

Answers

1 interested 2 interesting 3 expanded 4 expend 5 effects 6 affect 7 maybe 8 may be
9 brought 10 bought

V22 Stereotypical traits

Level upper intermediate to advanced
Interaction pairs
Aim To identify and recognise adjectives, in this case to discuss perceived male / female stereotypical traits.
Language focus adjectives to describe character
Technology Smart screen shade or Promethean Revealer

Before the class

In separate boxes, at the top of a blank page, write the words *Male* and *Female* and underneath type the following adjectives:

bossy, jealous, nurturing, sensitive, aggressive, competitive, talkative, caring, gentle, passive, ambitious, loud, physical, extrovert, cautious.

On the next page, insert pictures of famous men and women who both reinforce and contradict the stereotypes. Put them into pairs, descending down and across the page and activate the screen shade.

Procedure

1 Introduce the topic of stereotypes, eliciting character adjectives from students.

2 Put students into pairs and reveal the character traits. Ask students to discuss where they think each word should go.

3 Conduct feedback. Invite students to drag the words under the suggested headings.

4 Go to the next page and use the screen shade to reveal each face or pair of faces. Ask the pairs to decide if the stereotypes apply.

Follow up

More complex discussion can take place around changing roles in societies, equality of rights, pay etc.

LISTENING

L1 The director's cut

Level pre-intermediate
Interaction whole class, individual
Aim To listen to a picture description and identify differences.
Language focus features of a town
Technology recorder

Before the class

Insert an image onto the page which includes the vocabulary you want to focus on, eg a street scene in the morning: children walking to school, a lollipop man, cars and traffic, a queue at the bus stop etc.

Activate the recorder and check that your internal microphone is working. Talk about the picture / pictures, using your mouse to pinpoint exactly what you are talking about at any one time. Include some errors that you want students to identify.

Procedure

1 Display the picture and brainstorm related vocabulary. Explain to students that you are going to show them a film and that you want them to make a note of any descriptive errors.

2 Play the film and ask students to make a note of the mistakes.

3 Ask students to come up to the board to annotate the picture or to highlight differences.

Follow up

Students can make their own films as extra project work or homework using the school computer.

READING

R1 Dual page reading comprehension

Level pre-intermediate to upper intermediate
Interaction pairs
Aim To read a text and to answer questions about it.
Language focus reading skills
Technology Smart dual page display

Before the class

Insert or write a text of around 400–500 words that will be of interest to your students. It could be a short life story of a famous actor, pop star or politician, or it could be a piece about the natural world or history.

On the following page, write down questions with multiple-choice answers, eg *Where was Barack Obama born? A) Honolulu B) Miami C) New York D) Alaska*

Procedure

1 Ask students to brainstorm in pairs what they know about the main subject of the piece. Collect answers on the board.

2 Display the questions and ask the students to discuss what they think the answers might be.

3 Activate the dual page display and then go to *View, zoom* and then *Pin page*. This will enable you to pin the page with the questions into place, whilst also showing the text. Give students a fixed time to answer the questions.

4 After they've completed the questions, you can check the answers using laminate boards or by asking students to volunteer answers.

R2 Document camera reading

Level upper intermediate to advanced
Interaction whole class
Aim To read an article and describe its main ideas.
Language focus reading comprehension
Technology document camera

Before the class

A week before the lesson, ask students to find a passage of written English from a newspaper or magazine. It should be something that they would not normally read. Ask them to read the piece for comprehension and then to bring the piece into the class.

Ensure that the document camera is attached and functioning or be prepared to display the texts using the IWB.

Procedure

1 Divide the class into pairs and ask them to describe the text that they read for their partner.

2 Ask one of the students which newspaper or magazine they brought, or which Internet site they accessed. Ask them to describe the article and to discuss its main points.

3 Place the article on the document camera pane so that all of the students can see it. Ask the student to point to the words they found difficult using a pen. Also, ask them to identify any key phrases that they were not sure of. Did they take a guess at anything?

4 Repeat the process with other students' pieces.

Follow up

Keep the written pieces and show them at a later date to show how far the students have progressed.

SPEAKING

S1 Shape recognition guessing game

Level elementary
Interaction pairs
Aim To guess objects hidden by the shape recognition pen.
Language focus *In the example:* furniture vocabulary
Alternatives: any lexical items
Technology Shape recognition pen in Smart 10 Toolbar

Before the class

Insert a photograph of a sitting room and draw around the perimeter lines of various items in the picture, eg chair, television, to create closed shapes. Fill the shapes with colours and label each with a number.

Copy the page so you have two copies.

Procedure

1 Arrange the class into pairs and ask them to discuss what they think lies behind the shapes, first eliciting and exemplifying the speculative language needed.

2 When they have discussed their ideas, go through all of the shapes, asking for students' suggestions before revealing and naming the objects. Go through all the pages you have prepared until the end of the first set.

3 Show the duplicate of the page, with the items numbered, and ask the students to write down what they remember being behind each number. Check their answers using the pages in the first set.

Follow up

Returning to the activity in a couple of lessons' time, this time simply as a quick run through, will give students a much better chance of lodging the vocabulary in their long-term memory.

S2 Colleague connector

Level pre-intermediate and above
Interaction pairs
Aim To discuss and support points of view.
Language focus supporting arguments, making a case
Technology Promethean Active Inspire, digital camera

Before the class

Take photos of seven willing colleagues and insert them on the page, line them up at the bottom of the page. Also insert a surprising piece of information. You can do this either by entering text or by inserting images along the top of the page. Try and keep it interesting and unpredictable (ironically, this can be achieved by making one or two examples very predictable).

Procedure

1 Divide the class into pairs and ask the students to discuss the images and the information and to draw up a list of which face they think is connected to which piece of information. They can ask you *yes / no* questions about the pictures to get an idea as to their relevance.

2 The whole class discuss their decisions (in their pairs), justifying their opinions.

3 Ask the pairs to swap their lists for marking and ask students to come out, one by one. Ask them where they think the face should go.

4 Collect the scores at the end of the activity and see who got most right. Discuss the results: were there any real surprises?

Variation

This is a good activity when students become familiar with staff. You can also use famous faces but in this case, you should find out an interesting and, if possible, little known fact about them. Or, you could ask students to tell you something about themselves, privately, and play the game individually. You could write their names on the board instead of inserting photographs.

S3 Object taboo

Level intermediate
Interaction pairs
Aim To describe an object without using certain words.
Language focus verbs, nouns, adjectives
Technology Smart document recorder

Before the class

Find a range of pictures or objects that you would like to use in the class and then write down five words that you want to ban, eg *car* (*wheels, transport, travel, go, engine*).

Procedure

1 Divide the class into pairs. Arrange them so that one student has their back to the board and the other can see it.

2 Call up the document camera and place the first object or picture on the screen.

3 Access the dual page display so that on the second page, the taboo words are showing. The student has to describe the object without using any of the taboo words on the board. Repeat with different objects so that all students take a turn.

Follow up

Show the words – minus the images – at the end of the class to see if students remember the objects. If you don't have access to a document recorder you could run this activity using images of the items from an Internet search engine.

Variation

This activity can be used by lower level groups but in this case, insist that the listed words are used!

S4 Delegates

Level intermediate to upper-intermediate
Interaction pairs
Aim To discuss how suitable celebrities are to represent their country.
Language focus discussion
Technology Smart LAT 2, all IWB software

Before the class

Find pictures of 12 celebrities from different countries and place squares over each of them. Set the squares so that they disappear when they are tapped and insert the names of the countries the celebrities are from on each of the shapes. This will give 12 boxes that, when clicked, reveal a famous face from that country.

Procedure

1 Display the country names and elicit the names of famous people from those countries.

2 Reveal the pictures and then choose one of the names. Elicit reasons from the students why this person would or wouldn't be a good representative for their country. Can they suggest other suitable people?

3 Allocate each pair a celebrity and ask them to draw up a list of reasons why that person would be a good ambassador to represent their country.

4 When students are finished ask them to come up to the IWB to outline their reasons for the rest of the class, who are free to challenge and question.

5 Move on to a discussion about celebrity and gauge how opinion differs through nationalities, age-groups etc.

Follow up

Students can prepare a short piece to read out in which they nominate a person whom they think represents their country or region positively. The rest of the class will ask questions surrounding worthiness, suitability etc.

S5 Changing the subject

Level intermediate to advanced
Interaction small groups
Aim To practise changing subject while making small talk.
Language focus small talk topics
Technology Smart Notebook

Before the class

Go to the *Gallery* and search for *timer*. Open the *Interactive and multimedia* section of the results and drag one of the timers onto a page.

Procedure

1 Divide the students into small groups and ask them to brainstorm as many topics as they can think of that are suitable for small talk.

2 Write a selection of topics on the board under the timer. Give each topic a number.

3 Allocate a number to each group and explain they are going to make small talk about that topic for a set period of time. When that period finishes they have to move onto the next topic on the list.

4 Set the timer. The period depends on the level of your students, eg five minutes for higher levels but less for lower. Start the timer and tell the groups to start their conversations. Monitor and provide support. When the timer goes off, reset it for a further period and start it running immediately.

Follow up

Ask the students which topics they found most difficult to talk about and plan future lessons to cover vocabulary useful for those topics.

Repeat the activity but ask students to incorporate new vocabulary or specific phrases for changing topics, eg *That reminds me of the time I. . . .*

Variation

This can be used as a 'getting to know you' style activity for new classes. In this case divide the students into pairs and have a list of topics designed to elicit information about themselves suitable for a first conversation.

S6 Interrupting

Level intermediate to advanced
Interaction pairs
Aim To practise interrupting while making small talk.
Language focus small talk topics
Technology Smart Notebook

Before the class

Go to the *Gallery* and search for *timer*. Open the *Interactive and multimedia* section of the results and drag one of the timers onto a page.

Procedure

1 Divide the students into small groups and ask them to brainstorm as many topics as they can think of that are suitable for small talk.

2 Write the topics on the board under the timer. Give each topic a number.

3 Divide the students into pairs and allocate a number to each pair. Explain that one of them is going to talk about that topic for one minute. When that finishes the other member of the pair has to politely interrupt with a question or to talk about the topic themselves.

4 Set the timer. The periods can be completely random, from a few seconds to two minutes. Start the timer and tell the first person to start talking about their topic. Monitor and provide support. When the timer goes off, reset it for a further period and start it running immediately. Discourage the students from watching the timer. They should listen out for the sound it makes when it reaches zero.

5 After three or four interruptions, tell the pairs to move to the next topic on the list and repeat step 4.

Follow up

Ask the student which topics they found most difficult to talk about and plan future lessons to cover vocabulary useful for those topics.

S7 Tickertape test

Level upper intermediate to advanced
Interaction pairs
Aim To read and respond to written questions.
Language focus discussion skills
Technology Smart LAT, Promethean Active Studio / Inspire

Before the class

Locate the *Scrolling text banner* or *Tickertape* tool in your IWB software. Input five or six vocabulary items for four different lexical sets (ie furniture, food, colours, jobs).

Procedure

1 Divide the class into pairs and explain that they are going to play a vocabulary sorting game. They will see 20 words for one minute and, without writing anything down, will then have to remember as many as they can.

2 Activate the *Scrolling text banner* or *Tickertape* tool and let the text scroll for one minute.

3 When the time is up, ask the pairs to write down as many words as they can remember and to sort them into four vocabulary groups.

4 Follow up by eliciting any other items for each of the groups.

S8 Picture descriptions

Level all
Interaction pairs
Aim To label a picture and discuss activities taking place within it.
Language focus vocabulary building and discussion skills
Technology Smart / Promethean

Before the class

Download or scan a picture with a lot of detail or activity taking place such as a factory production line or a street scene with people involved in a number of situations.

Number the objects that you wish the students to identify.

Underneath the image, write the names of all the things that have been numbered, in columns, with a space at the side in which to write the numbers.

Procedure

1 Display the picture and put the students into pairs. Ask the students to study the picture and write the numbers next to the words under the picture.

2 When they have finished, use the *Spotlight* tool to focus on images, one by one, and ask students to identify what they are.

Follow up

Pictures with more complex detail / ambiguities can be used to inspire discussion among more advanced groups.

WRITING

W1 Apostrophes activity

Level beginner
Interaction individual, whole class
Aim To add apostrophes to incomplete sentences.
Language focus *In the example:* possessive apostrophes
Alternatives: contractions, *it's* vs. *its*
Technology cell shades

Before the class

Insert the following text into a 2 × 16 table:

1 *Sues cat was on her mothers table.*

Sue's cat was on her mother's table.

2 *That is Bobs pen.*

That is Bob's pen.

3 *Did you put Rozs sandwiches in her bag?*

Did you put Roz's sandwiches in her bag?

4   *These are the childrens sweets.*

    These are the <u>children's</u> sweets.

5   *I put that boys bike in the shed.*

    I put that <u>boy's</u> bike in the shed.

6   *I put those boys bikes in the shed.*

    I put those <u>boys'</u> bikes in the shed.

7   *Who thinks that Real Madrids fans are better than Manchester Uniteds?*

    Who thinks that <u>Real Madrid's</u> fans are better than <u>Manchester United's</u>?

8   *The President of Gambias plane touched down an hour ago.*

    The President of <u>Gambia's</u> plane touched down an hour ago.

Put one sentence into each cell and add cell shades to all cells containing the answers.

Procedure

1   Show the first sentence to the class and ask students what's wrong with it.

2   Uncover the answer by removing the cell shade.

3   Ask students to work in pairs to look at the other sentences.

4   Reveal the answers when the students are finished by clicking on the cells.

W2   Spelling the days of the week

Level beginner
Interaction pairs, individual
Aim To answer questions about the days of the week.
Language focus spelling – days of the week
Technology Promethean Active Inspire

Before the class

Follow the path, *Shared Resources, Shared Assessments, Primary English, word level.* Drag the thumbnail onto the screen and double left-click on it to import the file and fill the screen.

The task consists of seven questions that ask students to identify days of the week, eg *Which day comes after Monday?*

a) Tuesday b) Thursday c) Teusday d) Tewsday

There is no checking device. After the first question, navigate through the pages to run through the activity.

Procedure

1   Access the first question and ask for a volunteer to answer it. Go through the reasons why the other answers are wrong, eg are they the wrong days or the wrong spellings?

2   Students remain in their seats to answer questions in their pairs. Rotate the questions so that all pairs have a chance to answer.

3   When you have finished the quiz, go through it again so that pairs answer different questions. If this is a challenge for them, repeat the quiz several times.

Follow up

This is an elementary quiz for beginners. A nice way to remind students of the progress
they've made is to replay this kind of quiz some weeks / months on.

W3 Anagrams

Level intermediate to upper intermediate
Interaction individual, teams
Aim To arrange letters into the correct order to form words.
Language focus spelling
Technology Smart LAT, Promethean Alphabet Activities

Before the class

For Smart users: from the *Activities* menu in the LAT access *Anagrams* and type in
the words you wish to use, eg *achieve, ceiling, accommodation, millennium, leisure,
acceptance, marriage, carriage, separate, conscious, necessary, necessarily, approximately,
faithfully.*

For Promethean users: access the *Alphabet activities* from the Resource Browser.
With this activity the anagram is constructed using the alphabet cubes or magnetic
letters. There is no device for checking the answers so this is always a wholly
teacher-led activity. Timing each turn can be done by using the clock from the
browser.

Procedure

1   Explain to students that they are going to look at some anagrams, and divide the class
into two teams.

2   Access the activity and ask students, one by one, to come to the board to arrange the
letters to make one word each. Other team members can call out what the word is but
the student at the board has to spell it correctly.

If using Smart, play the activity on *slow* the first time you use it as a speeding time bar
will distract and possibly panic some students. You can speed up the activity when you
have used it a couple of times.

W4 Business letter video demo

Level intermediate to upper intermediate
Interaction whole class, individual
Aim To write a business letter.
Language focus *In the example:* Business English, letter writing
Alternatives: describing processes like using a computer, how to surf the Internet, how
to use an online dictionary
Technology Recorder

Before the class

Access the recorder. Press *Record,* type a business letter and talk through the instructions
as you go. After inputting the addresses and date, dictate the letter as you type.

Procedure

1 On an IWB page, brainstorm the features needed for a business letter.

2 Play the video and stop it after 30 seconds. Put students into pairs to predict what is coming next.

3 Play the rest of the video and ask the students to check their predictions.

4 Ask your students to write a business letter after providing them with cues.

Follow up

Students can access any video if you put it on the school system or they can save it to a memory stick.

W5 Possessives and contractions

Level intermediate to upper intermediate
Interaction whole class
Aim To identify the differences between contractions and possessive apostrophes.
Language focus apostrophes
Technology Smart screen shade or Promethean revealer

Before the class

Type the following sentences on the board (Note: the apostrophes are all missing):

1 *That is Bobs pen.*

2 *The President of Gambias plane touched down an hour ago.*

3 *Wheres Roz going today?*

4 *These? These are the childrens sweets.*

5 *I have taken that boys sweets away and hes really angry.*

6 *The government may have injected tax payers money into the banks but is it really looking after the peoples interests?*

7 *I put those boys bikes in the shed.*

8 *Dont you want to come to the football match?*

Copy and paste the sentences onto another page. Next, copy each individual sentence, paste a copy underneath the original and add the apostrophes. Insert a red apostrophe for a contraction and a blue apostrophe for a possessive. Activate the screen shade on this page (or use two pages if you want to make it easier to read).

Hand out red / alternative coloured pens to students or use four-coloured pens.

Procedure

1 Return to the first page. Display one of the sentences and ask students what is wrong with it. Then add the missing information.

2 Reveal all the sentences on the first page. On a piece of paper, ask students to write the sentences, inserting the colour-coded apostrophes in the right places.

3   When they have finished, show the second screen, with the screen shade revealing the second sentence. Ask individual students to come to the board and insert the colour-coded answers into the right places. Ask students if they agree or disagree with the answer provided.

4   Use the screen shade to reveal the answers as each sentence is corrected.

Answers

1 That is <u>Bob's</u> pen.   2 The President of <u>Gambia's</u> plane touched down an hour ago.   3 <u>Where's</u> Roz going today?   4 These? These are the <u>children's</u> sweets.   5 I have taken that <u>boy's</u> sweets away and <u>he's</u> really angry.   6 The government may have injected <u>tax payers'</u> money into the banks but is it really looking after the <u>people's</u> interests? 7 I put those <u>boys'</u> bikes in the shed.   8 <u>Don't</u> you want to come to the football match?

W6   Spelling difficult words

Level upper intermediate to advanced
Interaction pairs, teams
Aim To identify correct spellings for difficult words.
Language focus spelling
Technology Smart LAT 2

Before the class

Follow the path, *LAT 2, Activities, Multiple Choice*. Double left-click the thumbnail or drag it onto the page and click on *Edit*. In the spaces provided insert the multiple choice answers in the boxes labelled A, B, C, and D. Click the box next to *Number of questions* and input the number 10. You don't need to write any questions because you're going to tell your students all they need to know at the beginning of the exercise.

Now, in the spaces, type in the following words. The correct spellings are in bold.

1 ***Occasional*** – *Occassional* – *Ocassional* – *Ocasional*

2 *Gullable* – *Gulible* – ***Gullible*** – *Gullibul*

3 *Miscellenious* – *Misselaneous* – ***Miscellaneous*** – *Misellaynious*

4 ***Benevolent*** – *Bennevolent* – *Bennevollent* – *Benevolant*

5 *Suxinct* – ***Succinct*** – *Succinkt* – *Suksint*

6 *Ressussitate* – *Resusitate* – *Ressuscitate* – ***Resuscitate***

7 ***Wherewithal*** – *Werewithall* – *Werewithal* – *Wherewithall*

8 ***Entrepreneur*** – *Entrepreneure* – *Entrepaneur* – *Entrepraneure*

9 *Mischievouse* – *Mischeivous* – *Mischevious* – ***Mischievous***

10 *Sacrilegiouse* – ***Sacrilegious*** – *Sacraligious* – *Sacrilligious*

Procedure

1   Ask students if there are any words that they continually misspell. Write any suggestions on the board.

2   Tell students that you are going to show them a list of words and that they need to work in pairs to identify the correct spelling.

3   Use the quiz to reveal the right answers. At the end, go through the quiz again so that students can correct any errors.

Follow up

Go through the word meanings. This is a good way to build vocabulary.

PRONUNCIATION

Pron 1   Alphabet challenge

Level beginner
Interaction individual, pairs
Aim To identify consonants and vowels which appear randomly on the board.
Language focus pronunciation of the alphabet
Technology Smart *Gallery*

Before the class

Type *Dice* into the *Gallery* search window. In the window below, click on *Related Folders* and then double-click on *Consonants or Vowels*. From the new window, drag or double-click *Dice consonants or Dice vowels*. The virtual dice will appear on the screen.

Procedure

1   Tell students that they will see ten vowels or consonants displayed at random on the board and that their task is to copy them down.

2   Set the dice in motion and ask students to copy down the letters.

3   When this stage is finished, ask students to work in pairs to pronounce the letters that they have written down.

4   Conduct feedback, using the speaker icon to confirm the correct pronunciation.

Variation

From the same window you can also drag all the letters of the alphabet onto the page.
Students can then click on the speaker icon to see if their answer is correct.

Pron 2   Letter pronunciation

Level beginner
Interaction individual
Aim To pick a letter on the board and check pronunciation against that stored in the software.
Language focus pronunciation of alphabet letters
Technology Smart

Before the class

Go to *Gallery Essentials* and from the drop down menu click on *English and Language Arts*. Next click on *Alphabet* and then drag each letter out onto the page, lining them up in order at the top of the page.

Procedure

1 Ask a student to come to the front of the class and drag a letter down into the middle of the screen. Ask them to pronounce the letter and then get them to click on the speaker symbol at the bottom left of the image. If their pronunciation was not correct, get them to try again after they have heard the sound file.

2 Repeat until all of the letters have been used.

Pron 3   Minimal pairs dice

Level elementary to intermediate
Interaction whole class
Aim To practise the pronunciation of words with similar sounds
Language focus minimal pairs: /ɪ/ and /iː/, /ʃ/ and /tʃ/
Technology virtual dice

Before the class

Open the virtual dice and place one of the following words on each face of the dice:

ship, sheep, chip, cheap, shoes, choose.

Create a separate page with these words.

Procedure

1 Display the page with the words. Model the pronunciation of each one and ask the students to repeat them after you. If necessary, explain and drill the difference between the short and long vowel sounds: /ɪ/ and /iː/, and between the consonants: /ʃ/ and /tʃ/.

2 Now display the page with the dice. Click on the dice and ask the students to say the word that is displayed. Do this 10 or 12 times so that all the words come up at least once.

3 If you have a small group ask for volunteers to do this individually. Give feedback on those words or sounds they find more difficult.

Follow up

Return to this activity as a warmer in subsequent lessons until the students are making the sounds correctly most of the time.

Pron 4   Minimal pairs pelmanism

Level elementary to intermediate
Interaction whole class then teams
Aim To identify words with similar vowel sounds.
Language focus vowel sounds minimal pairs
Technology SMART Notebook LAT 2

Before the class

In LAT 2, click on the folder called *Examples,* then the folder called *Activities* and drag the *Pairs* onto a page. Click on the *Edit* button, set the number of pairs to 8 and type the following words, one per tile:

big, build; ten, dead; bad, hand; cup, young; light, white; both, phone; they, gave; beach, ski.

Click on *OK* to finish.

Create a separate page with these words, each as a separate item.

Procedure

1 Display the page with the pairs exercise. Explain that each tile hides a short, simple word and that the aim of the game is to match the words with the same vowel sound. Write *sleep* and *leave* on an empty page. Invite a student to say the two words. Draw the students' attention to the fact that, despite the different spelling, both words have the same vowel sound, ie /iː/.

2 Now display the page with the pairs again. Invite a student to the board to click on a tile. Ask the student to say the word on the tile and the vowel sound, eg *beach* and /iː/. The student then clicks on another tile in search of the other word with the /iː/ sound.

3 Repeat step 2 with different students. Whenever someone finds a match, the two tiles disappear. Continue until all the tiles are gone.

4 Divide the students into two teams and play again, alternating between members of the teams. Award points for every pair a team finds.

5 Display the page with the words listed and ask for volunteers to say the words.

Follow up

The words as listed in the second page can be jumbled up and step 5 repeated. You can also ask the students to use a pronunciation chart to identify the different vowel sounds used in the exercise. Students can also be asked to work in pairs and create sentences using the words in context.

Pron 5 Homophone quiz

Level intermediate
Interaction pairs
Aim To choose the right meanings from pairs of homophones and multiple choice questions.
Language focus homophones
Technology Promethean Active Inspire

Before the class

Follow the path *Shared Resources, Shared Assessments, Secondary English, sentence level.* Drag the thumbnail onto the screen and double left-click on it to import the file and fill the screen. The quiz consists of six questions that ask you to pick the correct word, and six questions that ask you to choose the correct meaning, eg

Cornflakes are Betty's favourite serial / cereal.

Which is the correct meaning of 'feint'?

A) like being asleep or feeling weak B) a pretend attack

Procedure

1 Open the activity and show the first question to the students. Elicit what they think is the correct answer.

2 Display the rest of the activity and put the students into pairs to discuss their answers.

3 When the students have finished, run through the activity, eliciting answers.

Follow up

Ask students for definitions of the other examples that appeared in the exercise but which were not discussed.

Variation

Write other examples that were not discussed on a clean page and ask students to write sentences containing the words.

Pron 6 Sound maze

Level intermediate
Interaction individual, whole class
Aim To focus on a particular vowel phoneme independent of spelling.
Language focus *In the example:* words containing the sound /ɔː/
Alternatives: words with any particular sound in common
Technology IWB software

Before the class

Prepare the following grid. **Bold** is used in the grid below to identify the correct words, but should not be used in the grid you prepare for the class.

Sound maze /ɔː/
START

bought	boat	become	catch	mouse	watch	long	sit	chair	food
talk	**saw**	**boring**	wake	house	ten	**thought**	**store**	**floor**	boot
world	shoe	**walk**	work	**brought**	**for**	**poor**	rich	**taught**	ago
buy	show	**four**	**law**	**before**	know	woke	meet	**daughter**	**short**
she	rich	book	suitcase	bring	put	think	meat	paid	**caught**

FINISH

Figure 2.1 Sound maze

Procedure

1 Display the grid on the whiteboard. Explain that the challenge is to connect the top left corner to the bottom right but only going through words with the /ɔː/ vowel sound.

2 Ask a student to say the first word *bought*. Conduct a drill so that all the class are pronouncing it correctly.

3 Ask the class to identify the next word that contains the sound. If all the students agree, the student uses the pen to link this word to the first.

4 Continue through the grid to the end. Make sure every student has an opportunity to choose, say and link a word.

Follow up

Students compose a short presentation / dialogue using as many of the words as possible.

Pron 7 Pronunciation sorting

Level intermediate to upper intermediate
Interaction individual
Aim To identify pronunciations and sort them into categories.
Language focus *-ed* endings
Technology LAT (Smart), Smart Notebook, Promethean Active Studio / Inspire

Before the class

In the LAT menu, select *Activities* and *Category sort – text*.

Having accessed *Edit*, enter the words in the right columns. In one column write the unvoiced words: *looked, booked, smacked, laughed, hoped, watched*.

In the other column write the voiced words: *lived, loved, moved, shoved, allowed, played*.

Press *OK* to scramble the words.

For users of other boards, write the words on the screen and construct the categories by drawing a straight line down the middle of the screen, or by creating two large boxes.

Write the criteria at the top of the page: *Voiced* and *Unvoiced*.

Procedure

1 Elicit from students the different ways in which *-ed* endings can be pronounced. Drill.

2 Display the words and ask students to sort them into the correct columns. Students can use their books, paper or a laminate board.

3 Check answers individually, eg on laminate boards or on a piece of paper. Ask them to write *U* (unvoiced) on one side and *V* (voiced) on the other side. As you refer to each word on the board, ask them to show the letter which represents the answer.

4 To reveal the answers, ask students to come to the board, one at a time, to drag words into the correct areas.

Pron 8 Vortex vowel sort

Level intermediate to upper intermediate
Interaction individual, whole class
Aim To distinguish between long and short vowel sounds.
Language focus long and short vowel sounds
Technology Smart LAT 2

Before the class

Type *Vortex sort* into the LAT search window or go to LAT 2, *Activities* and *Vortex sort – text*. Drag the thumbnail onto the page and click *Edit*. In the boxes at the top write *Long* and *Short* and then enter the following words:

cat, lit, hat, ask, copy, orange, next, pan, see, chair, bar, car, like, cake, game, smile.

Make sure you enter them randomly and not one type on the left and one type on the right (otherwise they will appear in groups when the activity is used, thus revealing the answers).

Clicking the arrow on the right-hand side of the box will enable you to sort your words. When you have finished, click *OK*.

Procedure

1   Go through the first few words with the class, dragging the words into place to show the answer.

2   Next, ask students to volunteer their answers individually, getting them to pronounce the words to exemplify their opinions. Remember to challenge or confirm their answers by pronouncing the words yourself.

Answers

Short: cat, lit, hat, ask, copy, orange, next, pan, see, chair
Long: bar, car, like, cake, game, smile

Pron 9 Word endings test

Level intermediate to upper intermediate
Interaction individual and whole class
Aim To identify and pronounce different past verb forms.
Language focus pronunciation
Technology Smart Version 10

Before the class

Refer to notes in G16 in this chapter for more details on how to create this activity. In this case the activity focuses on the pronunciation of words ending with the sounds /t/, /d/ and /ɪd/.

In the first box, write the infinitive of the verb *look*. The answer for this example is /t/.

want – ɪd, enjoy – d, visit – ɪd, work – t, play – d, marry – d, save – d, look – t, ask – t return – d, suggest – ɪd, negotiate – ɪd.

Insert a new page before the current page and write /d/, /t/ and /ɪd/ and space these equally at the top.

Procedure

1 Ask students to write down five verbs connected with their daily routines or their leisure pursuits. Elicit suggestions and write down, on your first page, a handful of regular verbs on the board. Ask students to call out example sentences using the verbs in the past simple form, eg *Yesterday I listened to some music on my mp3 player.*

2 Focus on the pronunciation of the past verb forms and elicit from students the endings to these verbs. Point to the references (*d*, *t* and *ɪd*) for guidance.

3 When you have covered a few examples, go to the next page and start using your prepared activity.

4 Go through each example, eliciting an answer from at least two students each time, and then drag the rectangle into the top box to reveal the answer.

Follow up

Ask students to write down two more words ending in *ed*. Go back to your first page and erase the previous work, leaving *t, d* and *id* at the top, and ask a student to come to the board and write their words. Then get another student to drag the words under the correct headings. Ask the original student if the second student has got it right and repeat the process until every student has both written and sorted two words.

Pron 10 Pronunciation generator

Level all
Interaction whole class, individual
Aim To pronounce difficult, confusing words.
Language focus reading, speaking
Technology Smart LAT 2

Before the class

Type *Tools* in the Smart *Gallery* and from the window below pick *Random word chooser*. Fill in the following words: *rough, cough, through, though, doubt, although, thorough, high, height, might, weight, wait, straight, late, great, bear, wear, ware, bare, barred, bath, care, could, would, wood, put, shut, nut, horse, worse, hoarse, new, know, knew, no, mind, wind* (*wind* has two pronunciations and meanings).

Procedure

1 Press *Select* and let the generator pick out words for students to pronounce. If you don't want repeats, click the box *No repeat*. This is a great starter or plenary activity that can be used time and time again to reinforce difficult and inconsistent pronunciations.

Variation

This is also a great way to randomly pick 'volunteers' for answers. Simply type in the names of the students and use the generator to pick the name for you. If, at the beginning of the year, you type in all student names, you will be able to use the generator throughout the year.

Games 1 Beginners' name game

Level beginner
Interaction individual, pairs, teams
Aim To link pictures and words through the medium of an interactive quiz.
Language focus vocabulary
Technology Promethean Active Inspire

Before the class

Follow the path *Shared Resources, Shared Activities, Primary, KS1 Literacy*. In the *Items* menu beneath, scroll down to the thumbnail *Pick a picture* and drag it into place.

Procedure

1 Divide the class into teams depending on class size and ability and tell them that they need to click the pictures that match the names that appear underneath. Do an example to show the students how the game works. Demonstrate that they must click on the object and not in the space around it for the game to work and explain that they are penalised for each incorrect answer. Students have 20 attempts per turn. If you want to increase the pressure, put the timer on and give each group 30 seconds to get as many as they can.

2 Ask a group or pair to come to the board and start the game.

3 Record their score and repeat the game so that every team or pair has taken a turn. Announce the winner.

Follow up

To keep this competitive you could ask stronger students to take their turn first, thus allowing weaker students to learn some answers they might not have otherwise known.

Games 2 Colour snap

Level beginner
Interaction individual, pairs
Aim To play a game of snap to identify colours.
Language focus *In the example:* colours
Alternatives: counting, numbers, shapes and animals
Technology Promethean Active Browser

Before the class

Follow the path *Active Browser, Shared Resources, Shared Activities, Gadgets and Widgets, Educational Games*. Scroll down to find *snap game colours words* and drag the thumbnail onto the page.

The activity consists of a large box containing two rectangles. When you click on the *Play* button, the left-hand box will display a coloured shape and the right-hand box will display the name of a colour. Your students' task is to click the *hand* symbol when the colour in the left-hand box matches the name of the colour in the right. Although the activity has a scoring device, students aren't penalised for mistakes so make a note of each incorrect answer, removing a point for each one.

Procedure

1 Ask two students to come to the board and hand them each a stylus. Explain the rules and click on *Play* to start the game.

2 Let each pair play until one of them has scored five points.

Variation

Try some of the other 'snap' games and pairs activities to round off a lesson and recap earlier work.

Games 3   Spin the wheel

Level beginner
Interaction individual, pairs, teams
Aim To identify words spelled out by a random generator.
Language focus vocabulary, especially short words
Technology Promethean Active Inspire

Before the class

Follow the path *Active Browser, Shared Resources, Shared Activities, Gadgets and Widgets, Educational Widgets*. Scroll down to *cvc slot machine*.

Procedure

1 Ask a student to come to the board and press the *play* button. The generator will spin its three wheels, each with a letter on it. When it stops spinning and rests it will either spell a word, or not. The student has to say whether or not the three letters make a word.

2 They then choose whether to hold one letter, or two, or spin the wheels again without holding any letters in place. They have ten turns, winning five points for every word and losing two for each failed attempt.

3 Add up the score and ask the next student to come to the board. Keep going until everyone has had a turn.

Games 4   Fridge magnets

Level elementary
Interaction groups
Aim To create and solve anagrams.
Language focus spelling
Technology Smart *Gallery*

Before the class

Type *Fridge magnets* into the *Gallery* search window. In the window below double-click on *spelling* and then double-click on, or drag out the *Fridge magnets* flash file onto the page.

Procedure

1 Split the class into small teams and ask each group to think of five words relating to a different topic, eg fruit, vegetables, the classroom, rail travel, holidays.

2   Demonstrate by telling the class you are going to give them a word connected to music. Drag the letters for *violin* onto the page but in a random order. The team which guesses correctly must present a volunteer to come to the board and arrange the letters in the right order.

3   That team now create an anagram of one of their words, first telling the rest of the class what the topic is. The team which identifies this word then takes a turn. The winning team is the first to present all five of its words to the class.

Games 5   Imperatives game

Level pre-intermediate to upper intermediate
Interaction pairs
Aim To use imperatives to tell a partner how to fill an image with shapes.
Language focus imperatives
Technology Promethean Active Inspire

Before the class

Follow the path *Active Browser, Shared Resources, Shared Activities, Gadgets and Widgets, Educational Widgets*. Scroll down to *tangrams activity*. Drag the thumbnail onto the page and increase its size.

Choose one of the templates from the *Templates* menu. The purpose of the exercise is to fill this image with shapes from the *Shapes* menu so that the image is filled completely with no overlaps or gaps. Note that when a shape is dragged from the menu into the main area it increases in size and cannot be resized. It can only be rotated and moved using the handles, which appear at the sides when the shape has been selected.

Divide the class into pairs.

Procedure

1   Review the form of imperatives.

2   Tell the students what they will be doing by showing them a template, bringing some shapes into view and inserting them into the template. Ask them what kind of words and phrases they'll need, eg *drag, rotate, put, at the top, to the right, to the left, underneath, above, triangle, square, parallelogram, red, yellow* etc.

3   Choose an image and ask two students to come to the front of the class. Their job is to tell you how to complete the puzzle. Put the timer on and follow their instructions. Give them a maximum of three minutes.

4   If the template has not been completed in the allotted time, count up how many shapes have been added accurately and keep all teams' scores.

Games 6   Multiple choice language and culture quiz

Level intermediate
Interaction teams
Aim To read and answer questions about language and Britain.
Language focus reading, grammar, spelling
Technology Smart LAT 2

Before the class

Follow the path *LAT 2, Activities, Multiple Choice*. Double left-click the thumbnail or drag it onto the page and click on *Edit*. In the spaces provided, write your question (at the top) and the multiple choices in the boxes labelled A, B, C, and D. Click the box next to *Number of questions* and input the number *8*.

Then input the following questions and answers, making sure you indicate the correct answer (shown below in **bold**) in the space provided:

1 *Spot the correct spelling.* **Occasion** | *Occassion* | *Ocasion* | *Ocassion*
2 *The number of curries eaten in restaurants in Britain each week. 1 million | 1.5 million | 2 million | 2.5* **million**
3 *Complete the sentence. If it rains . . . I'd take an umbrella* | **I'll take a taxi** | *they'd take an umbrella | they took an umbrella*
4 *An uncountable noun. Egg* | **Water** | *Shoe | Chair*
5 *You cannot get medicines here. Hospital | Chemist | Pharmacy* | **Delicatessen**
6 *Who are your siblings? Your mum and dad | Your children | Your aunt and uncle |* **Your brother and sister**
7 *The superlative of big.* **Biggest** | *The most big | The most biggest | Bigger*
8 *Where is Birmingham? Wales | The North of England |* **The Midlands** | *London*

Once you have made this quiz, make another with eight questions.

1 *The past participle of fall.* **Fallen** | *Fell | Felled | Falled*
2 *After winter comes . . . autumn |* **spring** | *summer | fall*
3 *From which of these places can you not withdraw money? Cash machine | Cashpoint |* **Cash and Carry** | *Cash dispenser*
4 *The plural of tooth. Tooths | Toothes | Teeths |* **Teeth**
5 *Find the incorrect sentence: We live in London | He lives in London | They live in London |* **He live in London**
6 *'I have been waiting for two hours.' Which tense? Present Perfect | Past Perfect | Present Continuous |* **Present Perfect Continuous**
7 *The plural of potato.* **Potatoes** | *Potatos | Potatose | Potata*
8 *You do this on a computer. Log to |* **Log on** | *Log down | Log up*

Bring the interactive clock onto the page from the *Gallery* and set it to 90 seconds.

Procedure

1 Divide the class into two teams. Ask for a volunteer to come to the front.
2 The volunteer will tap on what they think is the right answer as they go through the quiz. The idea is that the other members of their team will call out to help them. Make a note of each wrong answer, including multiple wrong answers within the same question (ie if someone presses three incorrect answers before hitting the correct one, mark down three errors). Start with a total of 40 marks and deduct one for each error made – you must be quick to spot the errors so just make a mark on a piece of paper. Start the clock countdown and let the game commence.

3   After the first team have taken their turn, call up a volunteer from the other side and follow the same procedure with the other quiz. To help comprehension you can read out the questions that appear, or get an able student to read them.

4   Add up the scores and announce the winner.

Games 7 Interactive Tic Tac Toe

Level all
Interaction teams
Aim To review any previously covered material.
Language focus any (grammar / vocabulary / spelling / speaking)
Technology IWB / Smart Notebook

Before the class

Use the Smart Notebook to create a 3 × 3 grid and number the squares from one to nine. Link each square to a separate slide and write a question there. (You need one slide with the grid and nine slides with one question each in total.) Use all sorts of questions like 'What's the difference between . . .', 'Give five examples of . . .', 'When would you use third conditional' etc, depending on what you have done recently with your class. Each slide should have a link back to the first page with the grid.

Procedure

1   Choose two students to come to the IWB to play a game of Tic Tac Toe or noughts and crosses. You can divide the rest of the class into two teams supporting the students.

2   Before the students mark a square with a X or O they touch the number which takes them instantly to the pre-prepared question. If the student answers the question correctly (with the help of their supporting team, maybe) they can go back to the slide with the grid and 'win' the square.

3   The students keep playing until one of them gets three marks in a row (the game very often ends up in a draw).

Follow up

As a whole class you can answer all the remaining questions that were not used in the game (if there are any left).

Variation

You can easily adapt the questions to make the task more or less challenging, depending on the level of your students. If you insert a timer into your Notebook slides, you can also give your students questions like 'Talk for a minute about. . .'.

Idea contributed by Agata Biernat

Case study: Which board should I buy? (1)

Martin owns a small language school on the outskirts of Madrid. He wants to install two IWBs but he also, quite reasonably, wants to keep his traditional whiteboard, which he uses regularly and with which he is comfortable. His classes are too small to have both so he opts to purchase a Mimio device, which he can clip to the side of his whiteboard to make it interactive, and which he can turn off when he wants to use the non-interactive board with a dry-wipe marker.

The problem, however, is cost, with a local company charging around £3,500 for two installations. This is a big risk as Martin is not sure exactly how much use he will get out of the boards, though he does feel that having them in his school will reflect well and help to keep business coming in.

After a consultation with a neutral third party, it is suggested that Martin purchase a Mimio device for around £460. Martin is lucky that his brother-in-law will install a £400 projector on the ceiling for free, though installation of this kind of apparatus should be fairly cheap anyway. If Martin wants to install this technology in his other classroom he simply doubles the cost, though he will be working without backup should anything go wrong with the products. He should, though, ensure that the products come with a guarantee so that he can send the equipment back if it breaks down in the first year. He may also miss out on an initial training session from the company but these don't tend to be more than brief introductions and Martin is lucky that he has a friend who can talk him through the set-up and the learning of the software.

One other piece of advice that Martin would do well to take heed of is that if he is thinking of buying more than one projector, they should be the same brand and model number. This means that he only needs to keep one spare bulb (projector lamp) in his store room so that when a bulb runs out, he's got an immediate replacement on hand for whichever projector needs it.

Case study: Which board should I buy? (2)

Mark Holt runs a language school where the manager has just given the OK for the purchase of three IWBs. He now has the task of choosing which brand to opt for and so makes a checklist of the factors to consider: cost, size, projector, training, support. As he has relatively little experience of IWBs he emails a couple of colleagues to see what they have chosen. Here are their replies:

Hi Mark

We decided to buy a SMARTboard. The teachers tell me they find it easy to move all the objects around with their fingers - actually, they use fingernails. They also like using the multiple functions like the Magic pen tool (which, among other things, enables you to enlarge images instantaneously), and the Lesson Activity Toolkit which has hundreds of lesson templates, easily adaptable to suit your needs.

Perhaps the best thing about the software is its intuitiveness. Once you've got the basics nailed, progress really rockets. Menus are easily accessed and the graphics are bold and nice to look at which makes it a joy to use and to create lesson activities with. You'll find a lot of teachers post ideas online showing how to perfect various techniques and ideas.

The only problem we've encountered is that the pens from the tray can go missing but even that's a minor inconvenience as it's the tray that is interactive, not the pens.

All in all, we're more than happy with it.

Jennifer

Hi Mark

We decided to buy the Promethean Activeboard. We've had a lot of fun with it and we wouldn't go back to being non-IWB board users if you paid us!

The software we use is Active Inspire, which is the latest software from Promethean. It's easy to use once you've got to grips with the functions and I hear it's a lot easier to use than the previous versions of Promethean, which also had some glitches here and there. The board is very robust and the stylus enables you to click on the fine details, though you do have to keep these safe as you cannot use the board interactively if you lose them. Replacing them takes time and money so it's a good idea to keep them locked up at night.

Linking files to objects is straightforward so accessing video, audio or any other type of file on your computer is easy – although I think this is the case for all boards.

We didn't look at any other board and I've only used this kind so can't speak about comparing it with other brands though I have to say we're delighted with the purchase.

Hope this helps

Terry

Although the messages are positive, Mark still feels that he wants to know more. After several calls to friends he manages to get a contact in the UK. Phil Evans is the business manager of a high school in the UK and Mark calls him with checklist in hand. After a lengthy discussion, here are his findings . . .

The most important thing Mark must do is to decide on *one* brand of board so that there is complete compatibility throughout the school. This means that teachers only have to learn one system and that all lessons and activities created are immediately usable on all the boards in the school.

Mark's decision may well have been made for him due to the size of classrooms in the school. Although two of the rooms are quite large, three are quite small. Mark wants boards for the larger rooms and for one of the smaller rooms. He doesn't want to dwarf the smaller room with a large board and he wants to keep his dry-wipe board so he may well opt to purchase a 'traveller board' for this room.

With regards to training IWB sellers often provide training with their installation but these can often take the form of one-hour sessions which show you little more than how to access the software once the computer is turned on, plus some various, simple techniques. Mark should ask just what the school are getting for their money and how long the session will take. He'll want to run through the tools on the toolbar and be shown how to access the *Gallery* / browser as well as be given information on how to link to other files on his computer. Any company that cannot provide this service cannot realistically claim to be offering training and if this is the case, then at least he should ask if they can reduce the cost of the installation.

Mark also needs to check on the level of technology support and the cost of installation from the various providers.

Phone call over, Mark sits back and smiles. He has a meeting with a Hitachi Starboard rep this afternoon, before he finally makes up his mind. He thought he was only buying a board, but he's fast realizing that there is a lot more to it than that . . .

3 USING PUBLISHED MATERIALS

INTRODUCTION

Do you use a coursebook with your students? If so, it may have accompanying 'whiteboardable' software. This is a version of the coursebook which has been created specifically for use with an interactive whiteboard. A growing number of coursebooks have IWB software, such as New Headway iTools (OUP), Cutting Edge Digital (Longman), face2face (CUP) and New Inside Out Digital (Macmillan).

There is a wide range of software packages. At one end of the spectrum, the software consists simply of the coursebook pages accessible for projection. These versions are designed to be used in class, so the teacher can click on an exercise to enlarge it. At the other end of the spectrum, the whiteboardable version includes an integrated set of tools (pen, highlighter), extra interactive learning materials and sophisticated features such as customisable language games. A special Teacher's Area within Macmillan's New Inside Out Digital provides a digital 'blank canvas' which can be accessed at any point in a lesson and allows teachers to author and build up a complete repository of teacher- and student-generated material to support each unit of the coursebook. This arguably gives teachers the best of both worlds – quality material from the publisher working seamlessly alongside a locally produced, personalised and re-usable materials bank.

Whiteboardable software is not intended to replace the coursebook. Rather, the teacher can use the IWB to go over or mark the students' work. On-screen symbols for audio and video mean that teachers can access and use these assets without leaving the program, so there is no need to switch to the CD-audio player or the DVD.

There are a huge number of benefits for classroom teachers using whiteboardable versions of coursebooks. You can:

- click on specific questions to focus on the answer
- access the tapescript of all the audio clips. Clicking a single sentence in the tapescript allows you to listen to it
- integrate the other tools of the IWB, such as the pen tools or highlighter and use these in conjunction with the course materials
- use the marquee zoom tool to blow up a specific section of a picture
- 'toggle' to other materials, such as the Internet, CD-ROM dictionaries or an interactive version of the phonemic chart, at any time during a lesson.

The activities in this section all exploit this whiteboardable software, as well as other publisher-produced software such as websites, DVD-ROMs or CD-ROMs, or other digital materials on learning platforms such as the Macmillan English Campus or English360 (CUP). Most of the activities in this section can be adapted to whichever course and coursebook you are using. All of them mean you can exploit these digital learning materials in new and exciting ways.

GRAMMAR

G1 Interactive review

Level elementary
Interaction pairs, whole class
Aim To classify adjectives according to their comparative form.
Language focus *In the example:* comparative adjectives
Alternatives: interactive exercises are available for a wide range of teaching points
Technology New Inside Out Digital (Elementary)

Before the class

Check you are familiar with the interactive exercises in the unit you are working on. In the example, the students are working on comparatives.

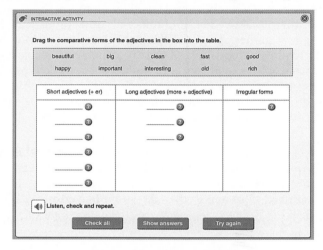

Figure 3.1 New Inside Out Digital (Elementary), Unit 12 Money

Procedure

1 Open the interactive exercise.

2 Invite students up to the whiteboard in turn to drag one of the words in the box to the correct part of the diagram.

3 Wait until the students have completed the activity and then click on *Check all*. On interactive exercises of this type, the answers are not displayed automatically, allowing for class discussion of language points. Alternatively, click on the audio symbol so that students can listen and check their answers.

G2 Picture matching

Level elementary
Interaction groups, whole class
Aim To review vocabulary previously taught through playing the memory game, *Picture Matching.*
Language focus vocabulary review; fluency practice
Technology New Inside Out Digital (Elementary) Picture Matching

Before the class

Decide how many teams you wish to play the game: two, three or four. Go into the Teachers' Area and click on *Picture Matching*. Click on *Add word* and add a word. Continue until you have all the vocabulary you wish to review.

Procedure

1 Open the activity by clicking on it.

2 Explain the rules to students. Include a short demonstration. They turn over one picture card with a pink star and one vocabulary card with a blue star.

3 Ask a student to come out to the front and click on a blue star card and a pink star card. Note: the cards will stay face up if they are pairs; the cards will turn back down if they are not pairs.

4 Continue with a student from the other team. Encourage the students to discuss which cards they want to turn over at each turn. Continue until the game is completed.

Comments

Teachers can customise the game with their own words and pictures.

G3 Using the screen shade / revealer tool

Level elementary
Interaction whole class
Aim To use the screen shade / revealer tool to focus attention on specific questions.
Language focus any
Technology screen shade / revealer tool

Before the class

Open the page in the digital coursebook. Click on the zoom tool in order to zoom in on the exercise you are working on. In this example, students are practising the modal verb *can*. Open the screen shade tool in order to uncover the questions. Close down the screen by clicking on the *Close screen* icon.

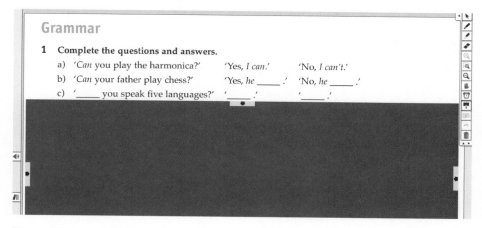

Figure 3.2 Screen shade

Procedure

1 Open the screen.

2 Reveal each question in turn and elicit the students' answers.

Follow up

Ask students to complete the exercise in their own coursebook.

Comment

Using the screen shade allows you to control the pace of the lesson. You can respond to students with problems by taking time to work on peer correction, peer support, or speed up and complete the exercise quickly.

G4 Freeze frame

Level elementary to pre-intermediate
Interaction pairs, whole class
Aim To use the 'freeze frame' technique and describe events that have just happened.
Language focus *In the example:* present perfect, restaurant vocabulary
Alternatives: this technique is possible with all video clips
Technology New Inside Out Digital (Elementary), or other courseware video

Before the class

Select the video clip you will be working on with your learners, eg *In the restaurant* on New Inside Out Digital (Elementary).

Procedure

1 Brainstorm topic vocabulary with the class (eg restaurant vocabulary). Collect ideas on the board as students call them out.

2 Tell students they will be watching a video clip and that you will pause it from time to time and ask questions. Click to play the video clip.

3 Pause the video occasionally and ask the students what just happened, eg *the waiter took them to their table, they asked for the menu* etc.

Follow up

Note any language mistakes and deal with these at the end of the activity or at the end of the lesson.

Comment

With some programs, it is possible to use the pen tool to annotate the still video picture. Students can label the picture, or draw speech bubbles next to characters to create a mini-dialogue.

G5 Word ordering

Level pre-intermediate
Interaction individual, whole class
Aim To put words in the correct order to make question forms.
Language focus question forms
Technology New Inside Out Digital (Elementary)

Before the class

Check you are familiar with the exercises in the unit you are working on.

Procedure

1 Open the exercise and explain that the students need to put the words into the correct order to make questions. Do the first one as an example.

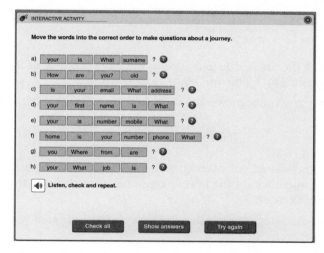

Figure 3.3 Ordering activity on New Inside Out Digital (Elementary)

2 Put students into pairs and set a time limit for them to do the other questions.

3 Invite students to come out in turn and drag the words to create the correct sentence. Encourage peer correction.

4 When the exercise is complete, click on the *Check answers* button.

Follow up

Do the exercise in the coursebook for consolidation.

G6 Jump review

Level intermediate
Interaction group
Aim To use the *Insert link* feature of New Inside Out Digital to provide a quick link to a review of an exercise.
Language focus tense review
Technology New Inside Out Digital (Intermediate) – Teacher's Area

Before the class

In this example, the teacher is going to do a lesson on reported speech (Unit 9) but wants to review tenses first: the present perfect and simple past distinction (from a previous unit), and the past perfect (from the last unit).

Open the Teacher's Area. Click on the *Insert link* icon in the menu.

Figure 3.4 *Insert link* box, Teacher's Area. New Inside Out Digital (Intermediate)

In the *Insert link* box, give the link a title and type in the page number of the exercise you wish to review (eg page 14). Click on *OK* to close the box.

Repeat the procedure for any other pages you wish to review (eg past perfect / page 73).

Procedure

1 Before proceeding with the lesson, tell students you are going to do a quick review. Open the Teacher's Area and click on the first link you have created. Do the review exercise (in this example, exercise 3).

2 Return to the Teacher's Area. Repeat the procedure for the second area you wish to review (in this example, exercise 2).

3 Using the menu, return to your original lesson and proceed with the target unit on reported speech.

Comment

The *link page* feature allows you to link to any coursebook page you wish to review.

G7 Grammar focus – right or wrong?

Level all
Interaction whole class
Aim To provide language practice on problematic areas of grammar.
Language focus common errors
Technology digital flipcharts

Before the class

Open a new flipchart and add a smiley face and a sad face icon. Right-click on each icon and click on *Infinite cloner* (Smart terminology). It is also possible to clone objects in Promethean software.

On the same flipchart page, type in a number of language mistakes which students made during a fluency activity. Include correct examples of the target structure, eg

He likes listening music.   *She likes to speak English.*

He likes watching cinema.   *She is feel relaxed.*

She's not speaking Chinese.   *He live in New York.*

I am not agree.   *She lives in Rome.*

She stays at the Chelsea hotel.   *She's staying in Florence.*

Procedure

1   Open the flipchart. Ask the students to read the sentences and decide if they are correct or incorrect.

2   Ask a student to come out to the whiteboard and tell them to drag the smiley face or the sad face to the first sentence, depending on whether they think it is correct or incorrect. Ask for whole-class agreement.

3   If anyone disagrees with the answer, they should come out and change the answer by dragging the other symbol next to the sentence. They should explain why they disagree. Encourage the class to comment. Provide the correct answer where necessary. On a traditional CD-ROM, the examples for grammar practice are usually written with a clear *yes / no* answer in mind. Grey areas of language are usually avoided. Here, the teachers can provide clarification where necessary.

4   After students have completed the exercise, you can print out the exercise with answers as a handout.

Variation

1   Increase the level of difficulty of the activity by providing examples which are unlikely, or only correct in limited contexts.

2   Cut and paste the language feedback from a previous lesson to provide the examples.

3   Ask students out to the whiteboard to use the pen tool in order to annotate examples by adding time-markers such as *usually / at the moment*.

G8   Grammar quiz

Level any, various levels available
Interaction whole class
Aim To review grammar at the end of a unit.
Language focus grammar
Technology ready-made quiz in New Headway iTools

Before the class

Check that you are familiar with the Grammar Quiz on the courseware. This is a multiple choice quiz to review grammar specific to units in the accompanying student's book. Students score ten points if they guess the answer at the first attempt, and five if they guess on the second attempt.

Procedure

1 Divide the class into two teams – Team A and Team B. Ask them to choose someone to go to the IWB and click on their team's answer.

2 Open the screen. Click on the *Start* button to begin the quiz. Students discuss their answer, decide and tell their team member to click on their choice. If the answer is wrong, the team has a second chance.

3 Continue with Team B.

4 When the game is over, the computer will show the final score.

Follow up

If students have made a lot of mistakes in the quiz, you will want to do further review.

Variation

Use the timer to set a time limit for answering each question.

VOCABULARY

V1 Labelling a picture

Level elementary
Interaction individual, whole class
Aim To use furniture vocabulary to label a picture of a house.
Language focus *In the example:* furniture vocabulary
Alternatives: any suitable picture in the courseware can be labelled
Technology New Inside Out Digital (Elementary); marquee zoom, pen tool

Procedure

1 Open the courseware at the picture of a house in Unit 9. Click on the *Marquee zoom* icon and mouse over the selected part of the picture so it enlarges. In the example, objects are numbered. Otherwise, circle any objects you wish your students to label.

Figure 3.5 Visual from New Inside Out Digital (Elementary), Unit 9 In a house

2   Ask students to come out and label the diagram by writing the names of the objects using the pen tool. Monitor the activity and input as necessary.

3   Students can copy any new words into their Lexical Notebooks.

Variation

Use a diagram which is already labelled. Cover the words with black highlighter pen and ask students to guess the words. Reveal the words using the eraser tool.

V2   The memory game

Level elementary
Interaction group
Aim To try and write down as many items from a list as possible.
Language focus vocabulary related to holiday items
Technology courseware; screen shade/revealer tool

Before the class

Open the page from the digital coursebook. Zoom over the picture and cover it with the *Screen shade* or *Revealer* tool.

Procedure

1   Tell students you will show them a picture for exactly ten seconds and then ask them some questions.

2   Reveal the picture for ten seconds and then cover it.

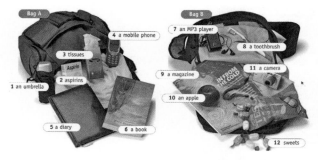

Figure 3.6 New Inside Out Digital (Elementary)

3 When the time is up ask students to write down everything they remember.

4 Ask students to compare their lists in pairs and see if together they can construct a list of all the items in the picture.

5 Elicit feedback and write up the students' list on the whiteboard.

6 Reveal the original picture again in order to check the group's answer.

V3 Note-able words

Level elementary
Interaction individual, whole class
Aim To record useful food-related vocabulary.
Language focus food vocabulary
Technology New Inside Out Digital note tool

Before the class

Check you are familiar with the *Add notes* function.

Procedure

1 Open the picture of the menu in Unit 15 of the courseware and ask students what kind of starters they like. Open the *Add notes* tool and type in the students' suggestions.

2 Continue as above with the other parts of the menu.

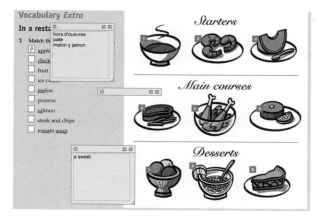

Figure 3.7 New Inside Out Digital (Elementary), Unit 15

3   At the end of the lesson, go back through your flipcharts and open the notes. Ask students to copy any new words they wish to remember into their vocabulary notebooks.

Variation

1   You can add a note at any time during a lesson. Use the notes to keep a list of all the words which come up during the class. At the end of the lesson, review all the notes.

2   Use notes to capture translations of words which your class find useful.

V4   Personalised family trees

Level elementary
Interaction group, individual
Aim To practise the language of families.
Language focus family vocabulary
Technology New Inside Out Digital (Elementary); digital coursebook and Teacher's
   Area

Before the class

Create a flipchart in the Teacher's Area with photographs of members of your own family. Click on the *Import picture* icon in the toolbar and select photographs from *Your Pictures*. Set these out to make a family tree (see figure 3.8).

Procedure

1   Students complete the exercise in their coursebooks, practising the language of the family.

2   Open the exercise in the digital coursebook. Check the exercise as a heads-up activity.

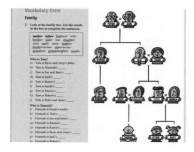

Figure 3.8 New Inside Out Digital (Elementary)

3   Tell students you would like to introduce your own family. Toggle to the Teacher's Area and show your family tree.

Figure 3.9 Teacher's Area New Inside Out Digital (Elementary)

4   Invite students to ask you questions about your family, eg *What does your wife do? Where does your daughter live?*

Follow up

For homework, ask students to create their family trees using presentation software and bring them to class on their memory sticks. In the next lesson, they can present their own families.

V5   Popular pets

Level elementary (young learners)
Interaction whole class
Aim To play a game and talk about pets.
Language focus language for describing animals and preferences
Technology Animal Explorers (available as part of Macmillan English Campus)

Before the class

Open up the Animal Explorers zone *Caring for pets.* The first activity is *Popular pets 1.* Using your IWB tools cover over the mixed up letters under each picture with a square shape. Then cover over each picture with a series of shapes.

See figures 3.10 and 3.11 below.

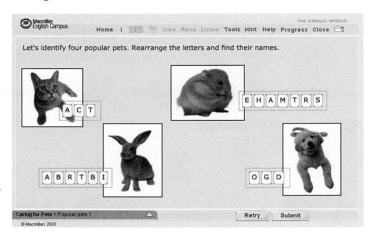

Figure 3.10 *Popular pets* screen

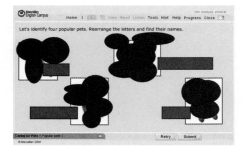

Figure 3.11 *Popular pets* screen with shapes

Procedure

1 Ask students to say a letter of the alphabet. If the letter is in the name of one of the pets you have covered, you can reveal one part of the picture. When the students have guessed the animal, you uncover the letters and ask a student to come up to the IWB and drag the letters in the right order. This goes on until the students guess each covered animal. You can also continue using *Popular pets 2*.

2 On the IWB draw an animal and tell the class why you like the animal. Write three sentences on the board. Ask your students to do the same and read them out to the person next to them.

3 To finish off divide students into two teams. One person draws an animal on the board and the teams have to shout out what it is in English.

Follow up

Ask students to find out as much as they can about their own pet or favourite animal.

Idea contributed by Sarah Milligan.

V6 Scrambled words

Level pre-intermediate
Interaction individual, whole class
Aim To rearrange letters into the correct order to form recently-studied words.
Language focus *In the example:* jobs
Technology New Headway iTools Anagram Activity

Before the class

No preparation necessary.

Procedure

1 In Headway iTools, click on *Anagram Activity*. This will display a list of words which have been scrambled to make anagrams.

2 Divide the class into two teams and set a time limit for the teams to work out what the words are.

3 When the time limit is up, one student from each group comes out in turn and drags the letters back into their correct place. At any point, click on *Check answer*.

4 Continue until the exercise is complete.

V7 Using the audio glossary for vocabulary review

Level pre-intermediate
Interaction pairs
Aim To review the vocabulary from a coursebook unit.
Language focus vocabulary from the unit
Technology New Headway iTools, (pre-intermediate) vocabulary glossary

Before the class

No preparation necessary.

Procedure

1 After you have finished a unit from the coursebook, tell students you are going to review the new words which came up. Access the *Glossary* for the unit. Words are displayed alphabetically.

2 Put students into pairs and ask them to look at the *Glossary* and to review the words.

3 Call out student's names at random and have that student remind the class of the word. They could put it in a sentence or provide a definition. Click on any words you want your students to hear again.

Follow up

Students can check they have written the new words in their lexical notebooks.

V8 Animation

Level upper intermediate
Interaction pairs, whole class
Aim To order the parts of the ear used when hearing sounds.
Language focus *In the example:* sound and hearing
Alternatives: on this CD, there are a wide range of topics from the science syllabus including electricity and magnetism, forces and motion, the respiratory system and the solar system.
Technology Macmillan Vocabulary Practice Series, Science CD-ROM (Topic 26: *Sound and hearing*)

Before the class

Prepare a flipchart with six terms, in jumbled order: *ear canal | ear drum | middle ear | inner ear | receptors | brain.*

Procedure

1 Tell students they will be watching the stages of an animation about how we hear sounds. As an introduction, open the animation graphic, click to enlarge it and see how many parts of the ear the students know. Then, open the flipchart to reveal the terms. Tell them to predict the order they expect the terms to be used in the animation.

2 Ask a student to come up and pull the terms into the expected order of 'how we hear'.

3 Open the animation *How the ear works*. Cover the script with the screen shade/revealer tool. Play the five parts of the animation and let students check their answer.

Follow up

Tell students to work in pairs to write the script from memory. Replay the complete animation so they can compare their efforts. Students transfer any new words to their lexical notebooks.

Variation

Ask the students to label the still picture of the animation instead of step 1.

Answers

1 ear canal   2 ear drum   3 middle ear   4 inner ear   5 receptors   6 brain

LISTENING

L1 Audio dictation

Level elementary to intermediate
Interaction individual, group
Aim To listen intensively to an audio clip and reconstruct it.
Language focus intensive listening
Technology audio clip and audio script from courseware

Before the class

Select the audio clip you wish to work with and number the sentences to correspond to the number of students in the group (ie if there are nine students, use the numbers one to nine). With a longer text you may need to use the same numbers for more than one sentence. Make sure the students cannot see the audio script on the screen while they are listening.

Procedure

1   Open the audio script of the recording. Give each student a number which corresponds to the number of one of the sentences in the script you wish to use. Tell students you will call out a number (1, 2, 3 etc) before each sentence, and the student with this number should write down the sentence. With lower level groups, you may wish to play each sentence twice.

2   Play each sentence in turn. Announce each sentence by number, eg *number one, number two*. Use the pause button to stop the recording after each sentence.

3   Ask students to work as a group to reconstruct the complete audio script. If they didn't catch something, encourage them to guess the missing words from context, or see if a classmate can provide the answer from memory. They should peer check their spelling.

4   Play the complete audio with the audio script visible so that students can check their attempt.

L2 Listen and read

Level all
Interaction individual, group
Aim To demonstrate the activity of listening and reading at the same time.
Language focus linking speech to text
Technology audio clip and audio script from courseware

Before the class

Select the listening comprehension you will be working on with your learners.

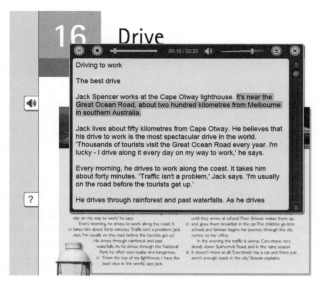

Figure 3.12 New Inside Out Digital (Elementary) audio script

Procedure

1   Before playing the audio, write a set of questions which demand that students catch some of the nouns or place names, eg *Where does Jack work? What does he drive past each day?*.

2   Play the audio. Put students in pairs to compare their answers. Elicit feedback: were students' answers the same? If not, what were the differences?

3   Tell students they will now listen to the audio again and this time they can read the audio script. Click the icon to reveal the audio script. Click *Play*. Tell students to follow the automatic highlighter guides which will guide them through the listening.

4   Elicit the correct answers to the questions.

Follow up

Debrief the activity. Was it helpful to be able to see the audio script? What do they think about listening and reading at the same time? Many students find this a useful activity which they can do in their eWorkbook in their own time. Remind students that if they always listen AND read, their listening may not improve. However, as a follow-up to a listening activity, it can be highly beneficial.

L3 Predicting visuals

Level all
Interaction pairs, group
Aim To predict the visual content of a video clip.
Language focus listening
Technology video clip from courseware

Before the class

Select the video you will be working on with your learners. Check you know how to hide the video. In some programs, you can blank out the whole IWB screen by clicking on a symbol in the software or you could turn off the projector itself with the remote control.

Procedure

1 Tell students they will hear a video clip although they will not be watching the picture. Dictate the following questions:

How many people do you hear?

What do you think they look like?

Where do you think they are?

2 Play the video clip with sound only. Short clips are effective in this activity.

3 Put students into pairs to compare their answers.

4 Elicit feedback from the students. Write up the answers and suggestions.

5 Play the video again, this time with the picture in order to check their predictions.

Follow up

Continue with an intensive listening activity to practise the target language.

Variation

This activity is very good for the language of possibility: *they might be / must be / could be.*

L4 Sentences out of sequence

Level all
Interaction individual, group
Aim To predict the content of an audio clip based on selected sentences.
Language focus listening
Technology audio clip and audio script from courseware

Before the class

Check you know how to turn off the projector display. This can usually be done using the remote control. Look at the audio script and select a few sentences you would like the students to hear beforehand, in order to create interest in the listening.

In this example, the teacher is playing a dialogue set in a lost property office. The selected sentences are:

What colour is it and what's it made of?
Yes, Hissy the snake.
It's black and it's made of leather.

Procedure

1 Turn off the projector so that students cannot see the screen. Open the audio script of the recording you are going to play. Click on a small number of sentences selected from the script. These can be played out of sequence.

2 Ask students to work together to predict what the content of the listening will be about.

3 Elicit some of the students' predictions. Open a flipchart and write some of these on the whiteboard.

4 Play the complete extract in order for students to check their predictions.

L5 Sound down

Level all
Interaction individual, group
Aim To predict the audio content of a video clip.
Language focus dialogue
Technology video clip from courseware

Before the class

Select the listening comprehension you will be working on with your learners. This example involves two people in a hotel. One calls the receptionist and makes a complaint.

Figure 3.13 New Inside Out Digital (Elementary), video

Procedure

1 As an introduction to the topic area, ask students if they have ever had to complain in a hotel. What was the problem? Was there a solution?

2 Tell students that you will play the video without any sound. Tell them they will be writing the script afterwards. Tell the students to take notes on anything they see which will help them.

3 Students work in pairs or small groups to construct the possible dialogue. Encourage the students to be imaginative. Monitor and help as necessary.

4 Ask one or two of the groups to read out their dialogues to the class.

5 Give language feedback as required.

6 Play the video with sound to allow students to compare their efforts with the original.

R1 Colour-coding text

Level elementary
Interaction individual, whole class
Aim To encourage learners to notice past simple verb forms.
Language focus *In the example:* past simple regular and irregular verbs
Alternatives: any other aspect of language
Technology New Inside Out Digital (or other courseware), zoom tool, highlighter pens

Before the class

Open a reading text from the student coursebook (in this case a text focusing on the past simple). Use the zoom tool to display the text or section of the text you wish to annotate.

Procedure

1 Tell students to read the target text in their coursebook and underline instances of the past simple tense.

2 Bring up the text on-screen.

3 Ask a student to come out and highlight any instances of past simple regular verb forms. Ask for whole class approval, additions or corrections. Ask another student to come out and highlight the irregular verbs, using a different colour. Monitor and correct as necessary.

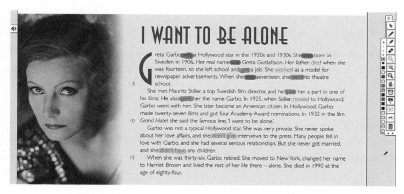

Figure 3.14 New Inside Out Digital (Elementary), reading text

4 Do any on-the-spot grammar practice arising from student performance. This might be focusing on the verb *to be*; practising the pronunciation of regular and irregular endings.

Follow up

For homework, students research and produce a short biography of someone famous.

Variation

1 Ask students to colour code words and phrases depending on their grammar, eg nouns, adjectives, adverbs, verbs.

2 Ask students to highlight the examples of past simple in one colour and present perfect in another. They can then explain the difference in the way the tenses are used.

Comment

Use this exercise when you wish students to focus on an aspect of language. The use of colour can be effective when annotating a text.

R2 Gapping text

Level all
Interaction whole class, pairs
Aim To identify key words from context; to develop reading skills.
Language focus reading; guessing and identifying words from context
Technology highlighter tool

Before the class

Use the zoom tool to select and enlarge the text from the coursebook which you wish to use. Select the pen tool and choose a thick line width. Blank out a number of words. These could be all the prepositions; five key words in the text which form a lexical set; all the examples of the past tense; the second word in a number of key collocations.

Procedure

1 As an introduction to the text, lead into the topic area as usual. For example, use the screen shade/revealer to reveal a picture or the title itself, and ask students to predict the content of the text.

2 Bring up the selected text from the coursebook. Ask students to work in pairs to guess which words could be used in the gaps.

3 Ask students to shout out what they think the first word is. Use the eraser to reveal the word so students can confirm their guesses. Continue until you have completed all the gaps.

Variation

1 Gap other text types, using the pen tool, eg the grammar reference summaries in the courseware; the script of an audio activity, which you can then play for students to check their guesses.

2 You can use this activity to revise the key words from a text that learners have read previously.

R3 Scanning

Level all, depending on the level of the courseware
Interaction whole class
Aim To practise scanning for numbers.
Language focus scanning
Technology zoom tool, pen tool, screen reveal

Before the class

Open the reading text you intend to use and use the black highlighter to blank out the numbers in the text. Use the zoom tool to enlarge the text and cover it with the screen shade/revealer tool.

Procedure

1 Reveal the text and ask students to skim it. What is it about?

2 Ask students to read the text more carefully and study the blanks. Tell students to work in pairs, and guess the figures, eg *At Primark, T-shirts cost £ . . ., pyjamas cost £ . . ., and women's tops cost less than £ . . . .*

3 Invite students to come out and write their guesses on the IWB around the side of the text.

4 Ask students to open their books and scan the text for the figures in order to confirm their predictions.

Follow up

Continue the lesson with an intensive reading activity.

R4 Speed reading

Level all
Interaction whole class
Aim To practise skimming a text.
Language focus skimming
Technology screen shade/revealer tool

Before the class

Open the flipchart and zoom on the text you intend to use. Cover the text with the screen shade/revealer tool.

Procedure

1 Set the pre-reading question. Reveal the text and ask students to skim it. You can use the stopwatch to set a time limit for this.

2 Cover the text. Elicit students' answers.

Follow up

Students read the text in their own books in order to do further work on the text.

Comment

In this heads-up activity, the teacher can control the exact time of the activity. When done with their coursebooks, students often haven't reached the end of the text by the end of the time limit.

R5 Textploitation

Level all
Interaction individual, whole class
Aim To identify specific language in a text.
Language focus scanning for synonyms
Technology New Inside Out Digital (or other courseware), zoom tool, highlighter

Before the class

Choose six challenging words in the text (eg *glancing at, trading*). Write synonyms on a flipchart (eg *looking quickly at, exchanging*).

Procedure

1 Show students the synonyms. Give them two minutes to scan the text in their coursebooks to find the original words.

2 Open the text on the whiteboard and enlarge the text by mousing over it with the zoom tool. Ask students in turn to come out and highlight the words they have identified.

Variation

Whenever you do feedback on pre-set questions, bring up the text on-screen and ask students to come out and show you and the group exactly where they found the answer.

R6 The gapping game

Level all, depending on the level of the courseware
Interaction individual, whole class
Aim To reconstruct a text in order to review topic language.
Language focus guessing words from context
Technology Automatic Text-Gapper from New Headway iTools

Before the class

Check you know how to use the Automatic Text-Gapper, this is a tool which automatically places gaps in texts. The default position is 50%. By clicking on a tab, this can be increased to 100% or reduced to 25%.

Procedure

1 When the students have finished reading a text in their coursebook, ask them to close their books.

2 Open the gapped text activity on-screen and set the tab at the figure you require.

3 Ask students to work together in pairs to work out the missing words in order from memory.

4 Students in turn shout out the missing words. Click on the word to reveal it.

5 Depending on how difficult it was for students to do the text, continue with the lesson or spend some time on problem areas.

Follow up

Repeat the same activity in another lesson, using the same text. For example, you could start by gapping 25% of the text, then move to 50% and finally 100%.

Variation

Clicking on the *Reveal answers* buttons will show the text for just a few seconds. This feature can help students if they are struggling.

R7 Using headings

Level all
Interaction pairs, whole class
Aim To predict the content of an article from the heading.
Language focus reading
Technology screen shade/revealer tool, reading text from any digital courseware

Before the class

Use the zoom tool to focus on the text you intend to use. With the screen shade/revealer tool, cover the text itself and just show the heading. Minimise the screen.

Procedure

1 Show students the heading and ask them to work in pairs and write down five words they think will come up in the text.

2 Open a new flipchart in the Teacher's Area and write up the students' ideas on the whiteboard.

3 Ask students to skim the text in their coursebooks in order to confirm their predictions.

Follow up

Continue with further reading activities you have planned.

R8 Vocabulary checker

Level all
Interaction individual, pairs, whole class
Aim To encourage students to work out meaning from context.
Language focus key vocabulary in a text
Technology zoom tool, screen reveal tool

Before the class

Select the text you are using in the coursebook and use the zoom tool to enlarge it and display it.

Hide the text with the screen shade/revealer tool.

Procedure

1 As an introduction to the text, ask students to predict the content from the title, or from a picture. Students read the text in the coursebook. When students have finished reading, ask them to look at the IWB. Reveal the same text.

2 Invite the students to come out to the whiteboard in turn and to highlight one word or expression which is new for them, or which they are unsure about and wish to check.

3 Students in pairs discuss the words. They should try and work out the meaning from context, and also use a dictionary if necessary.

4   Go through each word or expression with the whole class, eliciting meanings from the group. Only provide the meaning if no one in the class can supply one.

5   Let students read the text again. The text should now be easier, having spent some time focusing on meaning.

Follow up

Add any new words into the group vocabulary notebook (see note on eWorkbook in the Case study in Chapter 1).

SPEAKING

S1 Toggling

Level elementary
Interaction whole class
Aim To provide additional language practice and personalise the coursebook.
Language focus *In the example:* expressing likes and dislikes
Technology New Inside Out Digital (Elementary), Unit 4 Teachers' Area

Before the class

Open a digital flipchart in the Teacher's Area. Insert a set of photographs of locally famous people (a singer, an actor, a group, a footballer) selected from the Internet.

Procedure

1   Students do the activities in the coursebook, ie listen to the dialogues about Beyonce, Jude Law, The Rolling Stones and Wayne Rooney.

2   Toggle to the prepared flipchart in the Teacher's Area to reveal the photographs. Ask students to work together in pairs to ask questions from the dialogue, eg 'What do you think of . . .' and respond as appropriate: 'He / she / they're great / awful.'.

Follow up

Move on to the next stage in the unit, ie students write their own list of singers, actors, bands and writers.

Variation

Show the flipchart first with the screen shade tool as a lead-in to the coursebook exercise.

Comments

You can use the IWB to create a complete, parallel course to the coursebook, adding 'local' material. Within a given lesson, you can 'toggle' between the coursebook material and the personalised supplementary material which can be re-used and added to in successive classes and courses.

If you are not using New Inside Out Digital, you can use the flipcharts in your Smart or Promethean whiteboards to create your own materials.

S2 Video voice-over

Level intermediate
Interaction whole class and groups of three
Aim To watch a video, write a script about it and complete a sentence order activity.
Language focus writing skills, language used for social interaction
Technology Macmillan English Campus, or steps 1 and 2 can be done with any kind of video

Before the class

Open up the resource *It's your round!* from Macmillan English Campus and open the video so that it has had time to stream completely before the lesson.

Figure 3.15 *It's your round!* activity

Procedure

1   Play *It's your round!* with the sound off. Then ask your students the following questions: 'What do you think the people in the video are doing?' 'What do you think they are talking about?' 'What vocabulary might they be using?'.

2   Next ask your students to write their own script in groups of three and perform it to the rest of the class (if they're willing!). You then play the video with sound and compare their scripts to the real thing.

3   To finish off, get students to complete the matching and drag and drop exercises, first by writing their answers down, and then by coming up to the board and selecting the right answers until the whole class gets 100%.

Variation

Play the sound of the video but don't show the screen. Students have to guess the situation from the conversation and sounds.

Activity contributed by Sarah Milligan.

S3 Discussion scales

Level intermediate and above
Interaction individual, whole class
Aim To lead in to a discussion as a pre-reading activity.
Language focus speaking
Technology courseware; digital flipchart

Before the class

Prepare a digital flipchart. Draw a line from left to right. At one end, write: *agree strongly*. At the other end, write: *disagree strongly*. Write down a controversial statement relevant to the reading text you wish to use above the line, eg *People should become vegetarians*. The students will then read the text, eg *Is it time to give up meat?* (New Inside Out Digital Upper Intermediate).

Procedure

1 Tell the class the topic of the text. Show the flipchart. Ask students to think about their answer to the question. Ask them to think where they would put a cross on the line, depending on how much they agree or disagree with the statement.

2 Ask students to come out and using a pen, put a cross on the line which shows their own opinion.

3 When students have finished, you will have a map of opinions on the board. Ask someone who 'agrees strongly' to justify their answer. Then, ask someone who disagrees to do the same.

4 Close the flipchart and continue the class with the text. The brief introductory discussion will have predicted some of the vocabulary and issues in the text, making it more accessible to the students.

Follow up

After you have completed the text, go back to the original flipchart and ask if anyone would now like to change the position of their cross.

S4 Task repetition

Level all
Interaction small groups
Aim To build up confidence and fluency through telling the same anecdote a number of times.
Language focus speaking
Technology New Inside Out Digital (or other courseware), stopwatch

Procedure

1 Use the zoom tool to enlarge the coursebook activity, eg planning and then telling a short, personal story to another student in the class. Give students time to prepare.

2 Tell students that they will be telling their anecdote to three or four different people in the class. When the bell rings, they should change partners. Open the stopwatch. Set

the stopwatch to count down by clicking on the arrow buttons, and set a suitable time. Click on the *play* symbol to start the timer.

3 Students speak for the designated time. Re-set the stopwatch for a shorter time.

4 Continue for a further couple of times. Each time, ensure that you set the timer for a slightly shorter time.

Follow up

Provide language feedback on the students' fluency as usual. Debrief the activity by asking students if they found it easier to speak to the last person than the first, as task repetition is often highly beneficial and useful for confidence-building.

Thanks to the New Inside Out Digital Teacher's Guide for this idea.

S5 Timed speaking activity

Level all
Interaction individual, whole class
Aim To encourage speaking through a fluency activity.
Language focus speaking
Technology New Inside Out Digital (pre-intermediate), stopwatch

Before the class

Choose a suitable speaking activity from your courseware.

Procedure

1 Use the zoom tool to enlarge one of the activities. Tell the students that they are going to speak for a fixed time on a given topic, eg their favourite subject at school. Give them time to prepare.

2 Open the stopwatch. Give students a time limit for the activity; in this example, one minute. Set the stopwatch to count down by clicking on the arrow buttons, and then click on the *Play* symbol.

3 Students work in pairs and take turns to speak for a minute on the topic, while the stopwatch is running.

Comment

You can access and start the stopwatch running at any point in a lesson. The stopwatch is useful to get students in pairs to finish a speaking activity at the same time.

S6 Using the answer key

Level all
Interaction individual, pairs, whole class
Aim To use the key to check students' answers.
Language focus speaking
Technology New Inside Out Digital (or other courseware)

Procedure

1 When students have finished a coursebook exercise, ask them to check their answers in pairs.

2 In the courseware, open the *answer box* for the exercise, see figure 3.16.

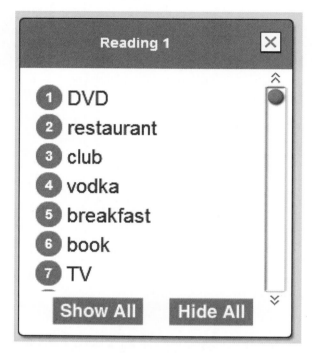

Figure 3.16 New Inside Out Digital (Elementary) Answer box

3 Ask each pair to tell you which answers they disagreed on and any which they felt unsure about and therefore want to check. Click on the numbers of only those questions in order to reveal the answers. Limiting the feedback through only revealing certain answers is a popular feature with teachers and students alike. It saves time and allows discussion of alternatives and so feels very different from mechanically checking every answer.

S7 Zoom tool guessing game

Level all
Interaction whole class
Aim To speculate about a picture as a lead-in to a lesson.
Language focus speaking / speculating about a picture
Technology zoom tool and screen shade/revealer tool

Before the class

Mouse over a photograph you wish to use as a lead-in to the lesson in order to enlarge it. Cover it with the screen shade/revealer tool.

Procedure

1 Reveal the photograph bit by bit and ask students to guess who or what is in the photograph.

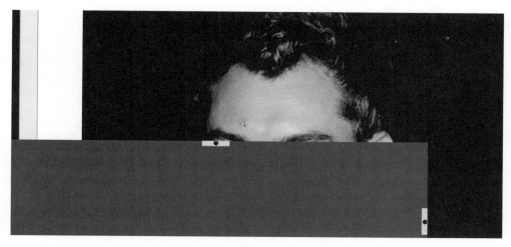

Figure 3.17 New Inside Out Digital (Elementary) and screen shade tool

2   When students guess successfully, reveal the complete photograph or drawing.

WRITING

W1 Compiling a glossary

Level intermediate and above, depending on the level of the courseware
Interaction whole class
Aim To focus on new vocabulary in a text.
Language focus guessing words from context; dictionary work; writing definitions
Technology New Inside Out Digital, zoom tool, highlighter

Before the class

Display the reading text you intend to study on the screen. The example looks at the text *Where to go to see a masterpiece?* from New Inside Out Digital, Upper Intermediate Unit 9.

Procedure

1   Check students know the term *glossary*. Zoom in on the selected text. Ask students to skim it.

2   Ask students to read the text again and to come out to mark difficult words with the highlighter. Assign a word to each pair of students. They should write a glossary entry for their word. They should see if they can guess the word in context, then use a dictionary for any words they cannot guess.

3   Open a new flipchart in the Teacher's Area. Invite students in turn up to the whiteboard in order to write out their glossary entries.

4   When students have finished, print out the whole glossary. Ask students to read the text in their coursebooks with the glossary. The example text has its own glossary in the coursebook material. Students can compare their own efforts with the coursebook entries.

Follow up

Debrief the exercise: were all the words / phrases in the dictionary? Which words will you need to use and which words are just for recognition? If there are any words students wish to remember, get them to write them in their lexical notebooks.

W2 Spelling

Level all
Interaction pairs
Aim To locate and correct spelling errors in a short text.
Language focus spelling
Technology highlighter tool and pen tool, coursebook

Before the class

Select a short text. Rewrite it with ten spelling mistakes and paste it into a flipchart. Print out a copy for each pair.

Procedure

1   Show the class the text and distribute copies. Ask them to work in pairs to find and correct the ten spelling mistakes.

2   Ask students to come up to the IWB in turn to highlight the misspelt words using the highlighter tool. Elicit whole-class agreement. Monitor and help as necessary.

3   Have students look at the original text to confirm their answers.

Follow up

Continue with the coursebook exercise.

Variation

You can make the activity more challenging by varying the number of mistakes in the text or by not telling students how many spelling mistakes there are.

Thanks to the author team of the *Straightforward Guide to Writing Skills* (Macmillan).

W3 Pretext for pre-text

Level all
Interaction individual and whole class
Aim To pre-teach vocabulary before a reading activity.
Language focus key vocabulary, writing definitions and examples, scanning
Technology courseware

Before the class

Select the text you will be dealing with in this lesson. Choose five key words which you wish to pre-teach and which you believe your students will not know. Draw an oval on a flipchart on the whiteboard and draw a few short lines coming out of the oval, creating a mind-map. Copy the flipchart four times. Write one of the five words in each circle. Also, write the words on individual pieces of paper.

Procedure

1   Divide the students into five groups. Give each group a piece of paper with one of the selected words on it. Ask students to create a simple mind-map. Tell students they should research key information on their word using a dictionary. Include meaning(s), stress pattern, any important collocations and any other useful information (such as opposite, different forms).

2   As each group finishes, invite them to the IWB in order to write down the key information for each word.

3   Have one or two students from each group come out to the front to present their word.

4   Ask students to open their coursebook and scan the text in order to find examples of the key words in context.

5   Continue to exploit the text as planned.

Follow up

Save the flipcharts and use them for revision. Ask students to write the new words in their lexical notebooks.

Comment

For an example of a mind-map, see Chapter 1, V10.

PRONUNCIATION

Pron 1   Silent consonants

Level elementary
Interaction pairs, whole class
Aim To practise pronunciation of words with silent consonants.
Language focus words with silent consonants
Technology New Inside Out Digital (Elementary); audio script

Procedure

1   Make sure the screen is switched off or hidden so students cannot see the words. Use the zoom tool to focus on the coursebook exercise. Click on the audio symbol and then click on the words to play the recording and ask students to write them down.

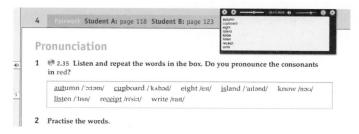

Figure 3.18 New Inside Out Digital (Elementary)

2 When all the words have been written down, students open their coursebooks and compare the spelling with their own attempts. Find out if students have included the silent consonants in red.

Pron 2 Phonetic spelling

Level pre-intermediate to upper intermediate
Interaction whole class
Aim To raise awareness of the symbols on the phonemic chart; to allow students to practise spelling words phonetically.
Language focus phonetic symbols
Technology New Headway iTools, phonemic chart

Before the class

Familiarise yourself with the pronunciation practice activities in Headway iTools.

Procedure

1 Select the first word you wish your students to practise from the word list on the left. You do this by clicking on it.
2 Click on the audio symbol next to the word to allow your students to hear it.
3 Invite a student out to drag the symbols they think are correct to the spaces under the word. Continue until they have completed the word.
4 Click on *Check answer.* If the answer is correct, congratulate the students and move to the next word. If there are any mistakes, click on *Try again.*
5 Continue until you have completed the list of words you wish to practise.

Variation

Don't click on the audio symbol (step 2) but let the students do the activity without hearing the word.

Pron 3 Annotating an audio script: phonology

Level in the example, intermediate
Interaction whole class
Aim To raise awareness of aspects of phonology.
Language focus *In the example:* intonation
Alternatives: weak forms, word stress
Technology IWB software and pens

Before the class

Select the audio script you wish the students to study.

Procedure

1   Open the audio script. Ask students to come out in turn and annotate the script for intonation pattern, ie draw an arrow up or down to show how they predict the first speaker will deliver the first phrase, eg

'Excuse me, are you one of the conference organisers?'

'Yes I am. Is there anything you need?'

Check the whole class agrees. If there is disagreement, add a question mark as something they need to check in the listening.

2   Annotate the rest of the script in the same way.

3   Play the audio. Use the pause button in order to give students time to check which answer was correct. Remember that you can click on individual sentences in the audio to check specific points, rather than play the complete audio.

Variation

1   Play the audio first. Then, have students annotate the script. Replay the audio to check students' annotations.

2   Focus on other aspects of pronunciation, such as strong / weak forms (eg ask students to circle *of* and write *weak* or *strong* depending on whether they expect the speaker to say /əv/ or /ɒv/) or word stress (ask students to highlight the stressed syllable).

Pron 4   Intonation check

Level all
Interaction whole class
Aim To identify likely intonation patterns.
Language focus intonation
Technology zoom tool and courseware audio script

Before the class

Select the sentences which you wish students to practise from the audio script of a listening exercise. This exercise works well with single sentence practice of high-frequency and useful functional exponents, such as *I'd like to buy a . . .*, and is beneficial for lower level learners.

Use the zoom tool to display the sentences.

Procedure

1   Ask students to come up in turn and use the IWB pen to mark the intonation pattern over the text. Demonstrate the use of up and down arrows, and curvy lines.

2   Play the audio to allow students to check their answers.

3   If appropriate, ask students to read out the sentences to practise their own intonation.

Pron 5 Just-in-time pronunciation

Level all
Interaction whole class
Aim To work on the pronunciation of individual sounds; to raise awareness of the phonemic chart.
Language focus individual phonemes
Technology phonemic chart from the courseware

Procedure

1 During the lesson, keep a list of any individual sounds which cause phonology problems in the class.

2 At the end of the class, open the phonemic chart. Read the words that the students have had problems with or dictate the sounds. Invite students to come out and click on the sound in the chart.

Follow up

Tell students to download the phonemic chart from the Macmillan English website onto their home computers in order to do extra practice with confusing sounds. See Macmillan English website, Methodology Resources page.

Variation

At any point in the lesson where communication breaks down due to a problem with an individual sound, open the interactive phonemic chart within the courseware.

Pron 6 Word stress

Level all
Interaction whole class
Aim To practise word stress.
Language focus word stress
Technology digital flipchart; infinite cloner tool

Before the class

Prepare a flipchart with ten words selected from a listening activity you are doing in the lesson. Select words where you think students will misplace the stress, such as words with several syllables. Create a small red square and click on *Infinite clone*.

Procedure

1 Open the flipchart and display the ten words. Ask students to say the first word and drag the red square over the main stressed syllable as an example. Tell students to look at the list and in pairs work out where they would put the word stress.

2 Invite a student out to drag the square over the stressed syllable in the next word. Ask students if they agree. If not, mark that word with a question mark.

3 Continue with the other words, asking students out in turn.

4 Open the audio script. Click on each sentence with the words you have selected. Students check their answers. Pause if necessary.

Follow up

Continue with the listening exercise in the coursebook. Students can transfer any new words into their Lexical Notebooks with the correct stress pattern marked.

 GAMES

Game 1   Connections

Level elementary
Interaction teams
Aim To review language from previous lessons through a quiz.
Language focus reviewing
Technology New Inside Out Digital (Elementary)

Before the class

Go to the Teacher's Area in the software and click on *Games*. In the *Games* menu, click on *Connections*. In the *Connections* editor area, select the words you wish to be included and click on the *Add words* symbol. You must add 25 words to play the game.

Procedure

1   Divide the group into two teams, red and blue. Explain the rules. The aim is to complete a connecting line of circles by guessing vocabulary items. Decide which team starts.

Figure 3.19 New Inside Out Digital (Elementary), Connections

2   Start the game. The team choose a letter. Click on the letter and a prompt appears. If the team answer correctly, award a point by clicking on the red or blue circle.

3   Continue until the first team completes a connecting line of circles. Announce the winner!

Variation

You can save the game and play it again. You can customise the activity by adding in your own words.

Thanks to the New Inside Out Digital Teacher's Guide for providing this activity.

Game 2 Racing

Level elementary
Interaction teams
Aim To answer quiz questions.
Language focus reviewing language
Technology New Inside Out Digital (Elementary)

Before the class

Decide how many teams you wish to play the game: two, three or four. Decide if you wish to play in race mode, or just in the conventional way, where the student scores are shown without graphics of runners and the animation. For *Racing* see figure 3.20. Go to the Teacher's Area in the software and click on *Games*. In the *Games* menu, click on *Racing*. In the *Racing* editor area, select the words you wish to be included and click on the *Add words* symbol.

Procedure

1   Set up the teams and explain that each group will receive a question and three possible answers. They should click on their chosen answer. If their answer is correct, click the + symbol to move their runner forward. You can check answers by clicking on the *Check* button.

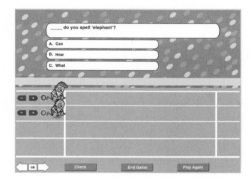

Figure 3.20 New Inside Out Digital (Elementary), Racing

2   Start the game. A member from team A comes out and selects an answer to the first question. The rest of the team can help!

3   Move on to team B. Continue until you reach the end of the game, or click on *End game* at any point – then the team closest to the finishing line is the winner.

Variation

This game is customisable. You can add in your own words to create the game. Use words which have come up in a lesson, or those which will appeal to members of your class.

Thanks to the New Inside Out Digital Teacher's Guide for providing this activity.

Game 3   Word scrambling

Level elementary
Interaction teams
Aim To play a language game where students re-order letters in order to complete words.
Language focus anagrams; fluency
Technology New Inside Out Digital (Elementary)

Before the class

Decide how many teams you wish to play the game: two, three or four. Go to the Teacher's Area in the software and click on *Games*. In the *Games* menu, click on *Word scrambling*. In the *Scrambling Editor* area, select the words you wish to be included and click on the *Add words* symbol.

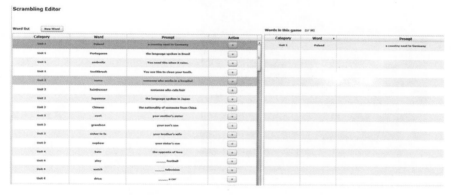

Figure 3.21 New Inside Out Digital (Elementary), Scrambling Editor

Procedure

1 Divide the group into teams and explain the rules. Each group will be given a word which has been scrambled. They should come out and unscramble the word. They can ask for a clue by clicking on *Clue*. Do a quick demonstration first.

2 Start the game. A member from the first team comes out and drags the letters into the correct position. The rest of their team can help if necessary.

3 Follow the same procedure with the second team / other teams. Continue until you reach the end of the game. Announce the winner!

Follow up

Students can check they have written any important words in their lexical notebooks.

Variation

You can save the game and play it again. You can customise the activity by adding in your own words to create the game.

Thanks to the New Inside Out Digital Teacher's Guide for providing this activity.

Game 4   Pelmanism

Level all
Interaction groups, whole class
Aim To review language through playing the memory game, pelmanism.
Language focus games are available for a range of lexical sets
Technology New Inside Out Digital (Elementary)

Before the class

Decide how many teams you wish to play the game.

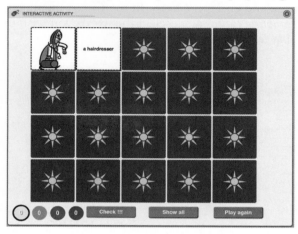

Figure 3.22 New Inside Out Digital Elementary, Pelmanism

Procedure

1   Open the activity by clicking on it.

2   Divide the class into teams. Check the students know the rules – they click on two cards, one pink (pictures) and one blue (words and phrases), and try to find matching pairs.

3   Ask a student to come out to the front and click on a pair of cards. Click *Check* to see if they are a matching pair. If so, the team receives a point. If not, the cards turn over again.

4   Proceed to the next team and continue as above until all the pairs are matched.

Comments

If students are struggling, click on *Reveal all* to show all the cards face up. If you click *Play again*, the same cards have different positions. Teachers can customise the game. Type in your own examples from previous lessons.

Game 5   Bridge builder race

Level pre-intermediate and above
Interaction groups
Aim To work as a group to construct sentences.
Language focus sentence building
Technology Macmillan English Campus, *Bridge Builder* Game

Before the class

On the Macmillan English Campus follow the path *Games, Word Games* and select one of the *Bridge Builder* levels (*Easy, Average* or *Difficult*). Then select one of the sentences and create a flipchart page with all the words vertically aligned forming the sentence. Restrict the words to move vertically only (select *ActivInspire Restrictors > Can Move > Vertically*) and jumble the words on the page.

Save the flipchart.

Procedure

1   Divide the class into groups of four or five students.

2   Show the flipchart page created before class and encourage students to go to the board to reorder the words to form the sentence. During the activity, guide students to notice sentence patterns.

3   Open the Macmillan English Campus and go to the activity previously selected for the group.

4   Select one of the groups and ask them to place themselves on a line on one of the sides of the board. Give the IWB pen to the first student on the line.

5   Start the activity and explain to students that they will have to build the sentence by placing the words in the correct order one student/word at a time as quickly as they can. After placing one word, the student should give the pen to the next student on the line.

6   Continue until the sentence has been built. During the process, the whole group can collaborate by suggesting which word should come next.

7   The group can then check the exercise and if it is not correct they start it again.

8   The next group then take their turn. The winning group is that which correctly builds its sentence in the shortest time.

Follow up

Students can create their own sentences on a flipchart page using the procedures described for the *Before the class* preparation and challenge the other students.

Activity contributed by Vilson Coimbra Oliveira Filho.

Case study: Teacher training

Jan works as a Director of Studies in a medium-sized language school in Portugal. It is part of a small chain of schools. The management made a decision to buy four interactive whiteboards for each centre and install them permanently in the largest classrooms. When Jan heard about the purchase, she was both excited and apprehensive. Her biggest fear was thinking about the teacher training sessions. Firstly, she herself was not very confident or competent in using IWBs. Moreover, some of the teachers were quite wary of technology, and were somewhat sceptical about purchasing these new whiteboards in the first place.

Everyone enjoyed the training session given by the IWB trainer from Promethean. He took the team through all the functions of the board. There was a lot to take in. The trainer made it seem easy, which was good, and some of the features were really great – the so-called 'wow' effect. However, during the hands-on training it was clear to most teachers that they had a long way to go until they felt confident.

Jan noticed that not all the teachers attended the demo, so the first thing she had to do was organise a 'repeat' session in-house. Luckily, Joe, the ADOS, had used IWBs before and was happy to deliver that. Jan realised two things at this stage. Firstly, that the IWB trainer had delivered an excellent session on mastering the technology, 'technology input', and that what the teachers now needed was 'pedagogical input': ideas on how to integrate the IWB seamlessly into their current teaching practice. Secondly, that what the school needed was an 'IWB champion'. Joe was happy to take on that role and so he planned out a training programme for the first term, since it was clear that the initial training, while very motivating and exciting, wasn't going to be nearly enough to get teachers up to speed.

Joe ran a series of lunchtime sessions as a kind of ideas-swap. This worked quite well, with teachers showing or describing something they had done using the IWB the week before. Again, not everyone could come, so Joe had the brilliant idea of setting up a training wiki. The first thing that meant was that if you missed the session, you could go to the wiki later and get the workshop notes as well as information on ideas which teachers had developed. Secondly, it meant that the other schools in the group could use the same platform.

Having the IWBs changed the school's working practices. For example, some teachers saved their lessons on the server. This meant teachers did not always have to prepare lessons from scratch. Also, this growing bank of lessons sometimes made things a bit easier for the substitute teacher covering lessons when someone was ill. On the practical side, Joe organised a sign-up sheet for booking the rooms with an IWB. He also started a system with a lockable drawer in each room and reminded teachers that they should NEVER take the pen away!

Last weekend, Jan ran a teacher training day for all the centres. She divided the staff into teams, matching confident IWB users with 'newbies'. The groups prepared materials and did mini-demos, which worked well. The main thing she noticed was that new teachers joining the school came into a positive IWB culture, as well as encountering an infrastructure comprised of support materials and the IWB training wiki. And of course, Joe's enthusiasm. . . .

Case study: Enhancing an e-lesson

What is an e-lesson? A one-page, 'print-and-go' pdf, available on the Macmillan website. The business English e-lesson usually addresses a relevant issue: a product recall, a recent CEO retirement, a new product launch. The accompanying teachers' notes include web-links and answers to the exercises. An e-lesson starts with a hook, contains a short text with a language exploitation exercise and finishes with a fluency activity. No preparation is necessary.

Lynne has been subscribing to the Macmillan e-lessons for a couple of years now. At first, she was happy to just download the lesson, print out the pdf and copy it for her students. She usually mentioned some of the websites suggested at the bottom of the teacher's notes page to her students, but she was never quite sure how to incorporate these hyperlinks more fully into her classes.

The school she works for recently acquired an interactive whiteboard. The big difference for Lynne in having the IWB was the permanent connection to the

Internet, which made her think about ways in which she could enhance the paper-based e-lesson with related activities and materials from the web.

Over the next few weeks, she experimented with incorporating short video clips. For example, in the lesson on Pecha Kucha, her students were able to watch examples of this style of timed presentation before preparing their own. When she did lessons based on a recent film, she showed the trailer to the film as a way of creating interest in the topic, pausing it in the middle to get students to guess the title. Since so many e-lessons deal with current news items, she would bring up the latest clip from a news website to see if a particular story had developed further. The students have really enjoyed some of the interactive visuals available on some news sites.

Among the other ideas she has tried are checking the results of any exercise on word frequency by using the Macmillan English Dictionary on-line in the class. She opens a new IWB page and embeds the website link in it before the class. She regularly splits the lesson in two. She sets a final homework task, such as preparing a short presentation, which students save to their memory sticks and bring in to the next lesson.

Lynne enjoys the fact that the In Company e-lesson and the Inside Out e-lesson archives are now searchable by date, level and topic. Her latest idea is to revisit some of her and the group's favourite lessons and ask students to work in groups to update the article, starting with a lesson on e-books.

4 CREATING AND ADAPTING YOUR OWN MATERIALS

INTRODUCTION

Many teachers love writing and creating their own materials. These materials range from text composed in word-processing software to recording and editing audio and video content. They include interactive exercises authored with programs like Hot Potatoes, which can generate digital materials such as gap-fills and mix-and-match exercises. The range of options for creating digital material has increased further with the tools available on the IWB.

There are five basic features you need to master in order to get started. These are:

1   Draw: drawing with the pen tools, and creating shapes such as circles, squares, ovals and rectangles.

2   Colour: using the colour fill, which can be used to change the background colour, the colour of text and the colour of the objects (such as squares, circles and rectangles) you create.

3   Order: placing objects on a page by 'layer'. This is exactly like the function 'bring to front' or 'send to back'. At a more sophisticated level, this may involve using several layers.

4   Lock: locking objects such as headers into place. This means that the objects cannot be moved around the IWB surface.

5   Group: grouping objects together. For example, making a magnifying glass involves locking together the handle and the lens so it becomes a single object.

Knowing how to use these functions allows the teacher to author impressive IWB content. For example, the teacher can create a drag-and-drop exercise where the answers are hidden by making them the same colour as the background; when they are dragged to a different part of the screen, they are revealed as if by magic.

It is possible to get to grips with these five skills fairly quickly. Similarly, it is relatively straightforward to import your own photographs, text and audio clips into a flipchart page. While it then takes a period of time to become quicker at creating materials and to build up your creative skills, the fact that you can re-use your material is a huge plus. Once you have made a mix-and-match exercise, you can easily customise the text. In addition, you can create material at home, save it to a memory stick and then bring it into the classroom for teaching.

All the activities in this section involve the teacher creating his or her own materials, using the tools within the IWB software package.

GRAMMAR

G1   Ordering items on a cline

Level beginner to intermediate (depending on the target language)
Interaction pairs
Aim To order adjectives on a cline.

Language focus *In the example:* adjectives of quality
Alternatives: adverbs of frequency, time periods (daily, weekly, monthly, etc), vehicles by size, adjectives describing temperature
Technology IWB software

Before the class

Use your whiteboard technology to create a page similar to figure 4.1 below.

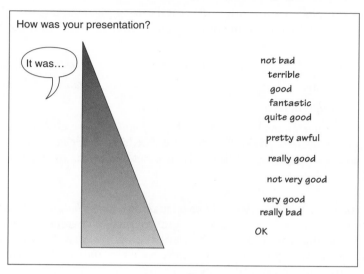

Figure 4.1 Items on a cline

The triangle is locked in place. The words on the right can be moved.

Procedure

1 Use the screen shade so that only the question is visible.

2 Put the students into pairs. Tell them to ask each other the question and make a note of each other's answer.

3 Elicit feedback by going round the group and find out these answers. If anyone responded 'OK', check to see whether they understood this to be a positive or negative response.

4 Reveal the rest of the page on the whiteboard. Ask the students to discuss in their pairs how they would organise the responses along the cline.

5 Get a volunteer to drag the words into position on the cline. If the class disagrees with this order, ask a second volunteer to make changes. Ask for and add any extra words/ phrases to the list.

6 Repeat steps 2 and 3 to find out if anyone has changed their response.

G2 Building sentences (word order)

Level elementary
Interaction small groups and whole class
Aim To drag words to build sentences with correct word order.

Language focus *In this example:* present simple for frequency
Alternatives: question forms, present perfect, conditional forms
Technology IWB software: clone tool

Before the class

Create a page with the questions *How often do you go on holiday? When do you go on holiday?*.

Lock the questions in place with room under each one to place an answer. Create the following words as individual, movable objects and scatter them around the bottom half of the page:

I	*go*	*on holiday*	*once*	*twice*
three times	*a year*	*usually*	*often*	*always*
sometimes	*in the summer*	*in the winter*		

Create three more similar pages but, instead of *go on holiday*, use *do homework, use the Internet, go shopping for clothes*. Make the movable words appropriate to the topics of these questions and the frequency of the activities. Set the words to clone.

Procedure

1   Display the first page. Ask the question *How often do you go on holiday?*. Elicit some answers then invite a student who has given a grammatically correct response to come to the board and drag the words to form their answer, eg *I go on holiday twice a year*. Repeat this with the second question, eg *I usually go in the summer*. Elicit the rules for positioning the words indicating frequency and time.

2   Display the next page with the question about homework. Divide the students into small groups and ask them to discuss their answers to the questions. Invite students to the board to drag the words to make their answers. Because the words are set to clone, each group can construct a sentence on the board. Give feedback and correction where necessary.

Follow up

Brainstorm other activities that are appropriate to your students on a clean page, eg *speak English, talk on the phone, visit the library, go on business trips, have meetings with your boss, write essays*. Divide the students into pairs and ask them to ask each other questions on these topics based on the models practised on the board.

G3   Daily routines

Level elementary
Interaction pairs and whole class
Aim To practise talking about daily routines by sequencing a set of pictures and matching verbs.
Language focus present simple for routines
Technology IWB software

Before the class

Create a page with a set of pictures showing the main events of an average day, eg getting up, taking a shower, having breakfast, going to work/school, having class or working in an office, going to lunch, going home, having dinner, going out to the cinema / watching television, going to bed.

You can get these pictures from the Internet, draw them yourself, use clipart or a combination of all three. Place them on the page in no particular order.

At the bottom of the page place the infinitive of the verb describing the action in each event, eg *get up, take, have* etc. Use the *Screen shade* or *Revealer* tool to hide these words.

Procedure

1　Display the pictures. Divide the students into pairs. Ask them to discuss and report back on what order they would put the pictures in to represent an average day.

2　Invite a student from one pair to come to the board and drag the pictures into the agreed order.

3　Reveal the verbs at the bottom of the page and ask the pairs to discuss and report back on which verb goes with which picture. Invite another student to drag the verbs into place.

4　Ask 'What time do you get up?' and elicit an answer from a student, eg 'I get up at half past seven.'. Ask a second student to ask the next question to a third, ie 'What time do you take a shower?'. Write the two questions and answers on the board.

5　Put the students into new pairs and ask them to ask and answer questions about each other's daily routine. Monitor and assist.

6　Ask for two or three volunteers to explain their partner's daily routine. Write some of the sentences next to the pictures on the board. Save and distribute the page.

Follow up

You can progress to other questions about daily routines, eg *What do you have for breakfast? How long does it take you to get to work? How do you get to school? Where do you have lunch?* and so on.

G4　The magnifier of truth verb activity

Level pre-intermediate
Interaction pairs
Aim To identify irregular verbs by dragging a revealing 'magnifier' over the terms.
Language focus irregular verbs
Technology all IWB software

Before the class

Draw a circle from the shapes tool and give it a white fill colour. Draw a small rectangle shape and attach it to the side of the circle so that it looks like a magnifying glass. Group the circle and rectangle together.

Write the following verbs on the page as separate items: *run, laugh, carry, charge, afford, listen, hold, teach, shoot, lick, seek, cut, light, guide, break.* Send all of the regular verbs to the back.

Procedure

1 Display the page and ask the students to work in pairs and to decide which of the verbs are regular and which are irregular.

2 When they have finished, conduct feedback. Ask students which verbs are regular and which are not and then move the magnifier over each verb to check. The irregular verbs will appear through the 'glass', whereas regular verbs will disappear, as if by magic.

3 Go through the endings of all the irregular verbs on the page.

G5   *-ing* or *-ed*?

Level pre-intermediate / intermediate
Interaction whole class, pair work
Aim To demonstrate via images the difference between *-ed* and *-ing* adjectives.
Language focus *-ed* and *-ing* adjectives
Technology IWB, images from the Internet

Before the class

Find images that illustrate *-ed* and *-ing* pairs of adjectives and prepare flipchart pages as follows:
Page 1: place an image illustrating an *-ed* adjective (eg *excited*) and write the corresponding pair of adjectives below (eg *excited* and *exciting*).
Page 2: place an image or images illustrating a pair of adjectives (eg someone who is *frightening* and someone who is *frightened*) and write the corresponding pair of adjectives below.
Page 3: show an image illustrating an *-ing* adjective (eg *boring*) and write the corresponding pair of adjectives below.

Procedure

1 Show the first flipchart page and ask the students to discuss, in pairs, which adjective describes the picture. Elicit an answer and discuss why the correct adjective is *-ed* and not *-ing*.

2 Show the second slide and have the students match the correct adjective to each person in the picture. Ask them to explain why, based on what they learnt from the previous picture.

3 Students again have to choose the correct adjective (this time with *-ing*) and explain why it is correct.

Follow up

Use the adjectives from the pictures to construct a speaking activity using questions such as *What is the most exciting thing you have ever done?* Students could also find pictures on the Internet and test each other.

Activity contributed by James Dunbar.

G6 Auxiliary verb noughts and crosses

Level pre-intermediate to intermediate
Interaction teams
Aim To add the correct modal verb to the sentence in a noughts and crosses game.
Language focus *In the example:* auxiliary verbs
Alternatives: question tags
Technology all IWB software

Before the class

Use the straight-line tool to create a noughts and crosses grid and then create a cross. Group the cross lines and clone it four times. Create a circle using the shapes tool and clone it four times.

Now, write the following eight sentences:

1 **Have** *you two met?*

2 **Is** *this the right place?*

3 **Do** *you like Greek food?*

4 **Are** *you enjoying yourself?*

5 **Have** *you already eaten?*

6 **Does** *this taste all right?*

7 **Are** *they having an argument?*

8 **Are** *we staying or leaving?*

Block out the auxiliary verbs with small squares and rectangles made with the shapes tool and cover all the questions, individually, with larger rectangles – give them a distinctive fill colour to make it easier for students to follow.

Procedure

1 Divide the class into two teams. Students can nominate which number question they'd like to answer. Delete the rectangle covering the question they have selected. Now, ask them which word is underneath the small rectangle. If they get it right, they get a chance to move a nought, or cross, into position on the grid.

2 Alternate between teams. The winning team will either have completed a run of three shapes or will have more of their shapes on the board.

G7 My life so far

Level pre-intermediate to intermediate
Interaction pairs and whole class
Aim To practise talking about events in your life.
Language focus past simple and present perfect
Technology IWB software

Before the class

Create several pages with the title *My life so far* at the top. Put a horizontal arrow pointing to the right and running across the centre of the page. At the far right end of the line put a small cross labelled *Now*. This version of the activity is aimed at working people or Business English students. Put this list of collocations at the bottom of the page: *be born, start school, finish school, start university, graduate from university, live in a town / city / country, move to a different town / city / country, join a company, work for a company, change jobs / departments / companies, get promoted.*

Use the screen shade / revealer tool to hide the time line and this list.

Procedure

1   Display the title of the page. Ask the students what period this covers, ie from when they were born up to and including now. Display the time line and explain they are going to talk about the main events of their lives so far.

2   Brainstorm the sorts of verbs they are likely to need to tell this story. Reveal the list at the bottom of the page and add any extra words that emerged in brainstorming.

3   Provide a model by talking about your own life. Use an IWB pen to make marks on the time line and write in the years. Drag the appropriate verbs into position. Make sure you include one or two sentences in the present perfect, eg *I've worked for … for … years* and *I've lived in … since …*

4   Put the students into pairs and ask them to come up with the questions for each of the sentences about your life, eg *Where were you born? When did you graduate from university? How long have you lived in … ?.*

5   Divide the class into pairs and ask them to find out about the life story of their partner. Tell them you do not expect them to talk about anything they regard as private.

6   Ask for two or three volunteers to tell the story of their life so far. Invite each one to come the board and use the pen and collocations in the same way you did in step 3. Encourage the rest of the class to ask more questions during these short presentations.

Follow up

Ask the students to produce a written version of their life stories as a homework task.

Variation

You can adapt the list of collocations to fit the types of students. For younger groups you can focus more on their school life and early-life experiences, eg *The first time I travelled abroad / I learned to ride a bicycle.* Business English students may prefer to skip the early biographical details and concentrate on *My career so far.*

Another variation is to have pictures instead of the collocations. The first step is to drag these into a reasonable sequence along the time line before putting words to them and then telling the stories.

G8   Time markers

Level pre-intermediate to intermediate
Interaction individual, whole class
Aim To decide if different time markers are used with the past simple or present perfect tenses.
Language focus past simple and present perfect
Technology digital flipcharts

Before the class

Prepare a flipchart with a diagram of two overlapping circles. Above one circle, write *Past simple*. Above the other, write *Present perfect*. Above the overlapping central area write *Both*.

Underneath the diagram type in the following list of time markers: *yesterday, three hours ago, for, since, recently, just, last week, this week, this morning, in 1999.*

Procedure

1 Open the flipchart. Ask the students to look at the time markers. Choose one at random and ask them to decide if it is used with the past simple or the present perfect or if it can be used with both. When the class reach a decision, drag the time marker into the correct circle.

2 Divide the class into pairs and ask them to do the same for the others.

3 Ask a student to come out to the whiteboard and tell them to drag a time marker to the correct place on the diagram. Ask for whole-class agreement.

4 Continue working through the time markers. Monitor and guide as necessary. Use the board to add any helpful diagrams or terms (eg *finished time* vs. *unfinished time*).

Follow up

Students write down an example sentence with each of the time markers. Print out the flipchart with the answers. This activity can be used diagnostically, so further work can be done on each tense as necessary.

Answers

Past simple: yesterday, three hours ago, in 1999, last week

Both: for, this morning

Present perfect: since, recently, just, this week

G9 Describing a process

Level intermediate
Interaction pairs and whole class
Aim To describe a process using the passive voice.
Language focus *In the example:* present simple passive
Alternatives: past simple passive, future passive
Technology IWB software

Before the class

Create a page with these sentences describing stages of a process, each within a box, and distributed at random around the page: *You leave the tea to brew for a few minutes. You put enough water for two cups into the kettle. You pour the boiling water into the teapot. You put two tea bags into the teapot. You stir the tea with a teaspoon. You pour a little bit of milk into two tea cups. You serve the tea to the guest. You switch on the kettle. You pour the tea into each cup.*

Procedure

1 Display the page. Give the students two or three minutes to read the information and think about what is being described, ie the process of making a cup of tea. If necessary, explain any key vocabulary, eg *brew, pour, teapot, kettle*.

2 Divide the class into pairs and ask the students to discuss the correct order of the stages.

3 Invite a volunteer from one pair to come to the board to drag the stages into order. Encourage discussion from the rest of the class if there is any disagreement. Once the correct order has been established, use the line tool to draw arrows between the stages. You could also write in sequencers at this stage, eg *first of all, next, after that, then*.

4 Explain how the passive voice is often used to describe processes in order to avoid repeating a name or pronoun and to change the focus of the sentence onto the object. As an example change the first stage to the passive, ie *Enough water for two cups is put into the kettle*.

5 Ask the pairs to change the other stages to the passive and to write down their answers. Monitor this stage and offer support.

6 Go round the pairs and elicit the passive form of each stage.

Follow up

Ask the pairs to think of a process they are familiar with and to prepare a short presentation of that process with each stage expressed using the passive voice, eg a technical process, a bureaucratic process, a recipe, and so on. Instead of a presentation, the pairs could prepare a page with the IWB software with the stages scrambled and invite the other students to put them into the correct order.

Variation

This activity could be extended to the past simple passive by beginning with a process that we used to use before moving on to the current process.

Answers

Enough water for two cups is put into the kettle. The kettle is switched on. Two tea bags are put into the teapot. The boiling water is poured into the teapot. The tea is left to brew for a few minutes. A little bit of milk is poured into two tea cups. The tea is poured into each cup. The tea is stirred with a teaspoon. The tea is served to the guest.

G10 Error sort

Level intermediate
Interaction pairs, groups
Aim To raise awareness of the kinds of errors students are making.
Language focus typical errors
Technology digital flipchart

Before the class

Open a digital flipchart. Fill it with a selection of 16 of the spoken language mistakes your learners made in a previous activity, lesson or series of lessons, eg

My father come from Berlin; It depends of the situation; So many peoples; I went to the UK before; How long you stay here?; I like laying on the beach; He's an account; She was feeling

relaxing; They must go in army; flied (fried); He live with me; informations; ad-VER-tising; to go in my country; tab (tap); This is [. . . . .] end of the first part.

Procedure

1 Tell students they are going to look at some errors and that they are going to group the mistakes into categories. Demonstrate this by dragging one mistake next to another similar mistake, eg *He live with me. My father come from Berlin.*

Tell students these are both grammar mistakes; the verb is missing the third person 's'.

2 Ask the students to discuss the words and phrases and decide on the errors.

3 Invite the students to come out one by one and drag similar mistakes together into clusters. Students should explain what kind of mistake it is in each example they move.

4 With the pen tool, draw a circle around a group of mistakes and give them a title. Tell students to study the clusters and give them a heading depending on what type of mistake has been made. Write up the suggested titles. Using a different colour, add any useful sub-headings in the grammar section such as *word order, tense, preposition.*

5 Ask students to tell you what they noticed, eg 'We make many more grammar mistakes than other kinds'; 'We make many more kinds of mistakes than just grammar'; 'We need to work on phonology'.

Follow up

Print out the list as a handout. Give students advice on how to tackle their ingrained errors, eg students can write down a list of the common mistakes that they make on a 'What I say vs. what I should say' sheet.

Typical clusters will include grammar, vocabulary, pronunciation, style / register.

G11 Matching conditionals

Level intermediate
Interaction pairs and whole class
Aim To match the correct halves of conditional sentences.
Language focus *In the example:* first and second conditional forms
Alternatives: other conditional forms
Technology IWB software

Before the class

Create a page with these half conditional sentences:

If my computer breaks,	*we'll get more business.*
If the economy improves,	*would you increase your order?*
If I won the lottery,	*we'd get more business.*
If I miss the train,	*we'll go to the park.*
If I were you,	*I'll buy a new one.*
If I gave you a discount,	*I'd never have to work again.*
When the rain stops,	*I'd take an umbrella.*
If I advertised more,	*I'll catch the next one.*

Procedure

1   Write these sentences on the board: *If my team wins the championship, I'll be really happy. If my team won the championship, I'd be really happy.* Elicit the difference in meaning between them and the rules for making first and second conditionals. Annotate the two sentences.

2   Display the page with the jumbled conditionals. Divide the class into pairs and give them time to discuss and match the halves.

3   Invite a student from one pair to come to the board and drag the second half of a sentence into position. Encourage feedback from the rest of the class. Invite the student to change their answer if necessary. Invite a second student to match another pair of sentence halves and so on.

Follow up

Allocate halves of the sentences to different pairs and ask them to create alternative condition or result clauses for them.

Variation

This activity can also be done with step 1 at the end. After the students have matched the sentence halves, use the examples to elicit the rules for first and second conditionals.

This activity can be done with any conditional form, individually or in combinations.

Answers

If my computer breaks, I'll buy a new one. If the economy improves, we'll get more business. If I won the lottery, I'd never have to work again. If I miss the train, I'll catch the next one. If I were you, I'd take an umbrella. If I gave you a discount, would you increase your order? When the rain stops, we'll go to the park. If I advertised more, we'd get more business.

G12   Reading the road signs

Level intermediate
Interaction whole class and pairs
Aim To practise explaining the meanings of road signs using modals of obligation.
Language focus *should, have to, mustn't*
Technology IWB software; Smart Notebook magic pen

Before the class

Use an image search engine to search for pictures of road signs. You can use several individual pictures or a ready-made montage. Paste the image onto a page. Use the magic pen to draw a circle about the size of one of the signs. This will cause all of the image to be shaded except for the space inside the circle.

Procedure

1   Display the page. Drag the 'magic' circle to reveal one of the road signs. Ask what the sign means, eg 'No entry'. Explain that you could also say: 'You mustn't enter this road.'.

2 Reveal two more examples in order to model the other two modal forms, eg *You have to give way to other drivers. You should drive carefully near a school.*

3 Continue to reveal other road signs and elicit what they mean and their explanations using *should, have to* and *mustn't.*

4 Divide the class into pairs and ask them to talk about the rules of the road in their country or countries. Invite students to report back.

Follow up

Reveal all the road signs. Divide the signs up between the pairs and ask them to write the explanations.

Variation

This activity can be done with other types of signs, especially if your students have not started driving yet. Try varying your search criteria when you are searching for suitable images. There are lots of images of funny signs on the Internet if you want a more light-hearted version of this activity for higher-level students.

G13 The future pie

Level intermediate
Interaction individual, whole class
Aim To review future forms.
Language focus future forms
Technology digital flipcharts

Before the class

Prepare a flipchart with a circle with six segments (see figure 4.2 below).

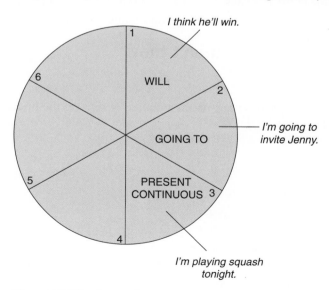

Figure 4.2 The future pie

Procedure

1 Open a blank flipchart page. Write next year in figures (eg *2012 / 2013*). Tell students to think of a sentence containing this time marker. Students come out and write their sentence on the whiteboard.

2 Ask students to peer correct the sentences. Make any changes necessary. Cluster the forms used. It is quite common for students to over-use the *will* form.

3 Move to the prepared flipchart. The circle – or 'pie' – represents all the future forms. Write the names of the forms used by students in each segment. Add an example sentence, and a description of the 'use' of the form and write these in on the chart, using different colours.

4 Tell students in pairs to discuss how they would complete any missing segments in the diagram.

5 Invite students out to complete the diagram, adding the form / use and also example sentences.

Follow up

Revisit flipchart 1 and elicit suggested changes to the original sentences, eg instead of *will*, use *going to*.

Variation

With higher-level students, add to the number of uses of *will* and add to the number of future forms on the chart, eg include the names of complex tenses (*future perfect* and *future perfect continuous*); input useful phases (*I expect to . . .*).

Suggested answers

1 *Will* (predictions) 2 *Going to* future (plans / intentions) 3 Present continuous (arrangements) 4 Present simple (schedules) 5 modals eg *can* 6 complex futures and other forms

G14   The question tags are right, aren't they?

Level intermediate
Interaction whole class
Aim To identify the correct question tags from a choice of two on the board.
Language focus question tags
Technology all IWB software

Before the class

On page 1, write the following:

*If the statement is **positive** the tag is **negative**.*
*If the statement is **negative** the tag is **positive**.*

On the next pages, write in the following pairs of sentences, one pair per page, linking the wrong answer to page 1 and the correct answer to the following page:

They wouldn't want to do that, wouldn't they?
They would say that, wouldn't they?

I've let the side down, haven't I?
He comes to work by bus, doesn't she?

He likes his coffee without milk, isn't it?
He's a professional actor, isn't he?

I haven't seen that film, haven't I?
They were here an hour ago, weren't they?

They don't believe you, do they?
She did call, did she?

He would say that, would he?
He would say that, wouldn't he?

You're not going to lose your job, are you?
You're not going to lose your job, aren't you?

Smart users can link objects to other pages by right-clicking the mouse on the object and then selecting *Link*. From here choose *Page in this File* and then the page number. Promethean users, right-click and select *Action Browser*. Then select *Other Page* and the page number from the space at the bottom. Hitachi Starboard users, select the object and from *Menu* choose *Edit Hyperlink*. In the window at the top of the box that is opened, select *Page in the Document*.

Procedure

1   Show the first pair of sentences and ask students which one they think is correct. Focus on the form of question tags, and in particular the fact that when the main clause is positive the tag is negative, and vice versa.

2   Ask students to come to the board, one at a time, to click on the right answers. If they are correct, they will move on to the next question. An incorrect answer takes them back to page 1. Keep your page selectors on display so that you can navigate quickly back to the page you were on to go back to the same question.

G15 Magic label gap-fill

Level intermediate to upper intermediate
Interaction individual, whole class
Aim To select the right adverbs to fill blanks in sentences.
Language focus *yet, still, already*
Technology all IWB software

Before the class

Write the sentence *It's a great book but I haven't finished it yet.* Before clicking out of the text box, select the word *yet* and change its colour to white, or whichever background colour you have chosen. Lock the whole sentence in place.

Now input the following sentences, changing the words in bold to match the background colour, before locking into place.

1   *I've **already** done my homework.*

2   *Are you **still** doing yours?*

3   *I haven't asked her what she wants for her birthday **yet**.*

4   *Have you made up your mind **yet**?*

5   *They **still** want to come along if that's okay.*

6   *David? He's **already** left.*

7 *They're **already** the biggest band in the UK and they haven't released an album **yet**.*

8 *I **still** don't think they're that good.*

Create a circle or rectangle from the shapes tool and fill it with a dark / primary colour (avoid yellow or anything too light). Make sure it is big enough to surround the words comfortably and send it to the back.

Procedure

1 Display the first sentence and ask students what the missing word is. When they guess it correctly, drag your coloured shape over the gap to reveal it.

2 Show the rest of the sentences and ask students to complete them.

3 Elicit answers and use the revealing object to confirm.

G16 Grammar matrix

Level intermediate and above
Interaction individual, whole class
Aim To ascertain students' own perceived level of grammatical knowledge and enjoyment of the area.
Language focus *In the example:* talking about grammar
Alternatives: talking about any of the language skills
Technology IWB software

Before the class

Create the following graphic on the flipchart.

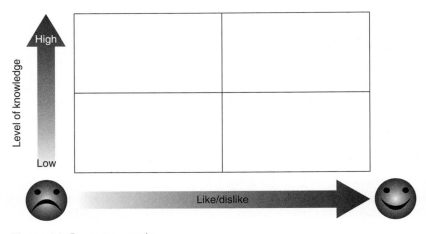

Figure 4.3 Grammar matrix

Procedure

1 Open the flipchart and explain the diagram, ie the horizontal axis shows how much you like grammar, ranging from low to high; the vertical axis shows your level of knowledge of grammar from low to high. If you don't know much and don't like grammar, you will be somewhere in this quadrant.

2 Ask students to talk to a partner about their level of knowledge of grammar and their attitude to grammar. Tell students to think about which quadrant they will write their name in, eg *I love grammar and I know a lot. I like grammar – but I don't know much. I don't like grammar BUT I know a lot about it. I don't like grammar AND I don't know much about it.*

3 Invite all the students to go out to the whiteboard and, using the pens, to write their name at an appropriate place on the diagram.

4 Debrief the activity. First, ask some students to explain the position of their name.

5 Draw circles around clusters of names situated in one section of the whiteboard. Elicit from the students what they have learnt about the class profile provided by the grammar matrix, eg 'About a third of students don't know very much about grammar.' 'Many students say they don't like grammar.'. Relate this information to the coming course, eg 'In our grammar lessons we'll be looking at some helpful rules / playing some grammar games.'.

Follow up

Save the flipchart and revisit this at the end of the course. Students can then come out and track their progress by drawing lines on the graphic.

G17 Conditional forms

Level upper intermediate
Interaction individual, whole class
Aim To review common conditional forms.
Language focus conditional forms
Technology digital flipcharts

Before the class

Prepare a flipchart with a grid with five rows and the following headings:

Type 0, Type 1, Type 2, Type 3 and *Mixed.*

Add the following prompts:

If | I | go | gone | will | would | have | drive | driven.

Procedure

1 Open a flipchart. Tell students that many grammar reference books describe five conditionals. This activity will review these forms. Ask them to work in pairs and create sentences which show each form.

2 Ask a student to come out and write a sentence in one of the rows. Get the others in the class to check it. Continue until all five conditional types are on the whiteboard. Monitor and correct as necessary.

3 Annotate the examples with contractions and negative forms, using different colour pens. Add any useful terms such as *possible, impossible, improbable.*

Variation

Write sentence halves for each conditional (see Suggested answers) so that students can match them.

Follow up

Students devise questions for the class using each of the conditional forms.

Suggested answers

Type zero: If I go there, I drive.

Type one: If I go there, I'll drive.

Type two: If I went there, I'd drive.

Type three: If I'd gone there, I would have driven.

Mixed: If I'd gone there, I'd be happy.

G18 Likely and unlikely language

Level upper intermediate
Interaction individual, whole class
Aim To raise awareness of 'non-standard' language.
Language focus non-standard grammar
Technology digital flipcharts

Before the class

Prepare a flipchart with a cline with the following points: *correct | likely | unlikely | incorrect* (see figure 4.4 below).

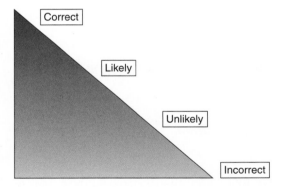

Figure 4.4 Likely and unlikely cline

Type in the following list of sentences and phrases which include mistakes, correct language and unlikely language which might be said in some instances:

40 persons; 40 people; We're at Tel Aviv; We're in Tel Aviv; If we would have done that, we wouldn't have survived; If we had done that, we wouldn't have survived; Did you do that already?; Have you done it yet?; If I was you . . .; If I were you . . .; Charles, you're not understanding me; Charles, you don't understand.

Procedure

1 Open the flipchart and display the first pair of phrases. Ask the students to decide if they are correct, incorrect or unlikely. Encourage discussion and then drag the phrases into the correct place on the cline.

2   Students discuss the sentences in pairs.

3   Ask a student to come out to the whiteboard and drag the next pair of sentences to the correct place on the cline. Ask for whole-class agreement. Encourage discussion by asking students to justify their answers if they disagree. Provide the suggested answer where necessary.

Follow up

Ask students to gather their own examples of non-standard sentences and bring them to class.

Suggested answers

40 persons [correct in narrow range of situations] / 40 people [correct]

We're at Tel Aviv. [incorrect / unlikely, eg said approaching airport from a plane]

We're in Tel Aviv. [correct]

If we would have done that, we wouldn't have survived. [US only / unlikely]

If we had done that, we wouldn't have survived. [correct]

Did you do that already? [US only / incorrect] Have you done it yet? [correct]

If I was you / If I were you [both correct, second more 'grammatical']

Charles, you're not understanding me. [unlikely] / Charles, you don't understand. [correct]

G19 Grammar jigsaw

Level upper intermediate and above
Interaction small groups
Aim To review tenses.
Language focus tenses
Technology IWB

Before the class

Create the following table on the flipchart. Allow enough room in each box for an example sentence and an explanation of use.

	SIMPLE	CONTINUOUS	PERFECT
PRESENT			
PAST			
FUTURE			

Make enough printed copies for your students.

Procedure

1 Open the flipchart and explain the table: 'We can imagine time as present, past and future. We have three types of tense in English. In this activity, we will complete a table with an overview of the tense system.'.

2 Ask students to help you complete the first box (present + simple) with an example sentence and an example of its use, eg:

> *Sentence: I live in Stratford.*
>
> *Use: simple statements of fact; generally true*

3 Put students into small groups to work together to complete the rest of the grid, using their printed copy.

4 Each group comes out in turn to complete one of the boxes, moving left to right, row by row. Use different colours for the example and the description of use. Ensure whole class agreement and peer correction. Monitor, input and correct as necessary.

5 Ask students which tenses are missing (present perfect continuous, past perfect continuous and future perfect continuous). For the sake of completeness elicit example sentences and descriptions of use for these tenses at the bottom of the flipchart, or on another flipchart. Finally, ask students to tell you how many tenses there are in English. Point out that there is a logic and a pattern to English grammar.

Follow up

Students can write personalised sentences with all the tenses.

Variation

Add suitable visuals in a different colour such as an eye looking backwards for *perfect*; a wavy line for *continuous*; time lines.

Comments

Most students will write an example with *will* in the future simple box. Point out that linguists maintain there is no future tense in English and that *will* is a modal verb. Put the *will* example in brackets and mention other future forms, such as the present continuous.

This activity can be used diagnostically with a new group to help decide some grammatical areas of weakness.

G20 Sequencing

Level all
Interaction individuals, pairs
Aim To put a series of events in order and describe the process using imperatives.
Language focus speaking skills, imperatives
Technology all IWB software

Before the class

Find a process that can be described using pictures as cues, eg cooking a curry. The more advanced the level, the more debate you want so that students have the opportunity to expand upon and justify their opinions.

Find pictures to represent the different stages, eg if describing making a curry, you can type *dry-fry spices* into an image search engine and you'll find a picture to represent this; likewise for *fry onions, browning chicken, add rice* and *boil rice*. High-quality photographs can be found online to show all of these procedures and indeed almost anything you would wish to describe.

Create a small, square box and clone it to the number of stages in the process you are describing, ie ten stages = ten boxes.

Number the boxes and place them in numerical order in a column at the left-hand side of the page. Use two columns if necessary.

Next, line up the images, in order, next to the boxes and tap on the top left box (No 1) and bring it to the front. Then, go to the image next to No 1 and bring that to the front.

Continue in this way until you have brought all of the boxes and images to the front. The last object brought to the front will be the image at the bottom of the screen next to the highest number.

Now lock all of the numbered boxes into place and jumble the order of the images.

The correct sequence of images will only be revealed when they ALL fit on top of the numbered lids.

Procedure

1 Show one of the images to the class and ask them to describe what they can see. Cover any key vocabulary.

2 Reveal all of the pictures and ask students to give you instructions as to where each should go. Encourage them to give orders, giving them the cues where needed (eg *put that one next to number three, move, drag, take that one away and … etc*).

3 When the final order has been established, ask students to work in pairs and describe the process.

4 Make a note of any new words at the side of the page, or if using Smart Version 10, activate the *Dual Page Display* mode and write them on the clean page.

5 Provide written practice by asking students to write the process down, in order, in their books.

VOCABULARY

V1 Fill the box labelling activity

Level beginner to pre-intermediate
Interaction individual, whole class
Aim To use cues to label a diagram.
Language focus *In the example:* kitchen vocabulary
Alternatives: town vocabulary, classroom items
Technology all IWB software

Before the class

Insert a picture of a kitchen onto your flipchart page. To create labels, draw a rectangle using the shapes tool and give it a white fill colour. Copy and paste the shape as many times as you will need it. Drag the labels next to the items you want to name and then click on the straight line / connector tool to link the labels directly with the various items. Lock everything on the page into place. At the top of the page, write the names of the items separately. Number the label boxes.

Procedure

1 Elicit from the students a few items typically found in a kitchen.

2 Display the page and ask students to work in pairs and to write down the names of the items labelled.

3 Drag down one word at a time and ask students which box they should go in. Leave wrong answers in place until all the words are in the boxes. At the end of the exercise, if there are any errors, move them to the right places.

Comment

This activity can be used to teach and not just to revise vocabulary, the visual cues giving all students a chance of participating whether they know the terms or not. It is not important whether they get the answers right at this stage. What is important is that they will have a better chance of remembering the terms because of the three-stage process you have taken them through.

V2 Rub and reveal vocabulary review

Level beginner to pre-intermediate
Interaction individual, whole class
Aim To review an earlier labelling activity.
Language focus *In this example:* kitchen vocabulary
Alternatives: town vocabulary, classroom items
Technology all IWB software

Before the class

Copy the page from activity V1 and, with the words in the right boxes, lock everything on the page into place. Then click on the pen tool, select a white font and scribble over the words in the rectangles.

Procedure

1 Display the page and ask students to write down the numbers and the item names next to them.

2 Using the eraser, rub away the white ink within the rectangles to reveal the answers.

V3 Prepositions of place toolkit

Level elementary
Interaction small groups and whole class
Aim To introduce and practise prepositions of place.
Language focus prepositions of place
Technology IWB software

Before the class

Create a page with a coloured square, a small coloured circle (small enough to fit inside the square) and then the following list of prepositions of place typed as individual, movable words:

in, on, next to, between, above, below, opposite, near, in front of, behind.

Set everything to clone.

Procedure

1   Display the page. Drag a square to an empty part of the page and drag a circle so that it sits inside the square. Ask the students 'Where is the circle?' and elicit the answer 'It's in the square.'. Drag the word *in* next to the shapes. Continue with the other prepositions. Elicit the questions and the answers.

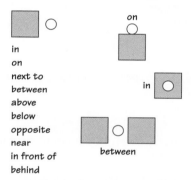

Figure 4.5 Prepositions of place toolkit

2   Select and delete all the completed combinations of shapes and prepositions and invite students to come to the board and drag the shapes and ask the questions. Alternatively, you can drag the preposition and invite a student to drag the combination of shapes appropriate to that preposition.

Follow up

Divide the students into pairs and ask them to ask and answer questions about the location of things around the room, eg 'Where is the computer?' 'It's next to the board.'. You can also do something similar using a photograph displayed on the board, eg a street scene.

Variation

Introduce a second, differently coloured square to make the sentences more complex, eg *The circle is next to the green square and below the red square.*

V4   Drawing and describing a room plan

Level elementary to pre-intermediate
Interaction pairs and whole class
Aim To create the plan of a room and describe it so that another student can draw it.
Language focus vocabulary for furniture and prepositions of place
Technology IWB software and line tool

Before the class

Create several blank pages in your IWB software. On the first page draw an example room plan as in figure 4.6.

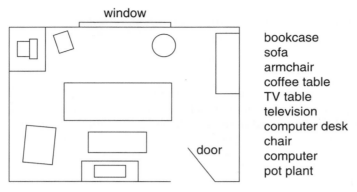

bookcase
sofa
armchair
coffee table
TV table
television
computer desk
chair
computer
pot plant

Figure 4.6 Example room plan

This activity is a good follow up to Chapter 4, V3 *Prepositions of place toolkit* and Chapter 1, V4 *Vocabulary groups word cloud*.

Procedure

1   As a whole class, brainstorm the type of furniture you would expect to find in a house. Write the words on the board.

2   Display the example floor plan. Divide the students into pairs and ask them to discuss how to label the plan. Invite a student to the board to drag the words into position.

3   Ask 'Where is the armchair?' ie 'It's in the corner next to the sofa.'. Go round the class inviting students to ask the class about the location of the remaining furniture.

4   Divide the class into pairs. Ask them to think of and draw a room in their house or their workplace, then describe that room to their partner. Monitor and provide assistance.

5   Ask for two volunteers from different pairs. One student describes their room while the other draws it onto a blank page. They can use the line tools or draw freehand using an IWB pen.

6   Continue with another two students until everyone has had an opportunity to draw or describe.

Follow up

Tell the students they have an unlimited budget and ask them to work in pairs and design their perfect room or office which they then describe for another student to draw on the board.

V5   Animal mapping

Level pre-intermediate
Interaction individual, whole class
Aim To navigate an information map to categorise and identify objects.
Language focus *In the example:* animals
Alternatives: sports, famous people
Technology all IWB software

Before the class

Use your shapes toolbox, straight line / connector tool and images to create the activity below.

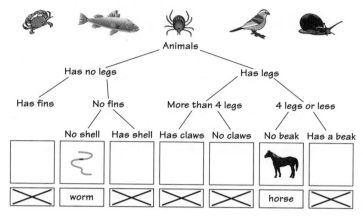

Figure 4.7 Animal mapping diagram

Note that two of the images have been dragged into place and that the boxes with crosses have been deleted to reveal the answers already written in. To begin the activity you will need all the lids in place on the bottom row and all the images lined up at the top.

Procedure

1 Ask students to study the diagram and to write down the names of the animals, in the order of the boxes they belong in at the bottom.

2 Ask individual students to come to the board and move an animal to the correct box. Reveal the answer by removing the lid on the box below.

3 Ask students to write sentences describing the animals, using the information on the board and adding any other information they know about the animals.

Answers

shark, worm, snail, crab, spider, horse, bird

V6 Countable or uncountable?

Level pre-intermediate
Interaction individual and groups
Aim To review the difference between countable and uncountable nouns.
Language focus countable and uncountable nouns
Technology IWB software

Before the class

Prepare a flipchart page. Draw two overlapping circles. Type *Countable* above the left circle and *Uncountable* above the right one. Above the overlapping central area type *Both*.

Type in the following set of words:

people, book, class, idèa, time, experience, furniture, coffee, information, luggage.

Procedure

1 Open the flipchart page. Tell students they must decide if the words on the whiteboard are countable, uncountable or both. Choose a word at random and ask the class to decide on the word category. When the class reach a decision, drag the word into the correct circle.

2 Divide the class into pairs and ask them to do the same with the other words.

3 Ask each student to come out in turn and drag the word to the correct place in the diagram. Invite students to provide an example. After each attempt, elicit whole-class agreement.

4 Ask students to write three questions using some of the words on the IWB. Provide prompts if necessary, eg *much, many, a lot of.*

5 Put students into pairs to ask each other questions. Monitor and correct as necessary.

Answers

Countable: people, book, class, idea

Both: time, experience

Uncountable: information, luggage, furniture, coffee

Note: we say 'a coffee' meaning 'a cup of coffee'

V7 It depends on (prepositions) 1

Level pre-intermediate
Interaction pairs and whole class
Aim To match dependent prepositions to verbs and adjectives.
Language focus *In the example:* dependent prepositions
Alternatives: phrasal verbs
Technology IWB software: clone tool and CD-ROM dictionary

Before the class

Create a page with the following words in two columns:

insist, interested, pay, responsible, focus, worried, care, pleased, know, excited.

Type a line of prepositions at the bottom of the page: *to, about, for, in, on, with.* The prepositions should be set to clone. They can also be in a different colour font to the other words.

Procedure

1 Write *listen* and *angry* on the board. Ask the students which prepositions usually follow these words, ie *to* and *about* or *with*. Look the two words up in a CD-ROM dictionary and show how the dictionary presents the combination of word and preposition. Explain that very often prepositions in English are part of fixed combinations with nouns or verbs or adjectives.

2 Display the page you created. Divide the class into pairs and ask them to decide which prepositions match the words. Tell them that some of the words can be followed by more than one of the prepositions. Encourage them to check in a dictionary.

3   Invite a student to come to the board and drag the prepositions to the verbs.
    Encourage feedback from the class if they do not agree. Invite a second student
    to do the same with the adjectives.

Follow up

Ask the pairs to create an example sentence for each of the verb + preposition and
adjective + preposition combinations. Again, encourage them to use a dictionary. Go round
the class and write some of the best examples on the board. Save and distribute this page.

Answers

insist **on**, interested **in**, pay **for**, responsible **for/to**, focus **on**, worried **about**, care **about/for**,
pleased **with/about**, know **about**, excited **about**

V8   It depends on (prepositions) 2

Level pre-intermediate
Interaction pairs and whole class
Aim To match verbs to dependent prepositions.
Language focus dependent prepositions in a business context
Technology IWB software and CD-ROM dictionary

Before the class

Create a page with this text:

*Good morning ladies and gentlemen. I'd like to _____ you all **for** coming.*

*Today I want to _____ you **about** our new computer network.*

*I've _____ my presentation **into** four main parts.*

*Firstly I'm going to _____ the benefits **of** the system to you.*

*Secondly I'll show you how we will _____ hackers **from** taking our data.*

*Thirdly I'll argue that we need to _____ more money **on** training.*

*And finally I want to show why we should _____ more **in** research and development.*

Below the text, type a line of verbs using a different colour: *prevent, divided, thank,
invest, explain, spend, tell.*

Procedure

1   Write this example on the board: *I _____ this book from Ben. He said I should read
    it.* Elicit the missing verb from the students, ie *borrowed*. Look the word up in the
    CD-ROM dictionary and show how the dictionary presents the combination of word
    and preposition. Explain that very often prepositions in English are part of fixed
    combinations with verbs although they are often separated from the verb by the object
    of the sentence.

2   Display the page you created. Divide the class into pairs and ask them to discuss how
    the verbs fit into the text. Encourage them to check in a dictionary.

3   Invite a student to come to the board and drag the verbs into the text. Encourage
    feedback from the class if they do not agree.

Follow up

Ask the pairs to create an example sentence for each of the verb + preposition combinations. Again, encourage them to use a dictionary. Go round the class and write some of the best examples on the board. Save and distribute this page.

Variation

This activity can also be used as an introduction to the language for opening a presentation.

Answers

In the correct order: thank, tell, divided, explain, prevent, spend, invest.

V9 Linking up collocations

Level pre-intermediate
Interaction pairs and whole class
Aim To match verbs to nouns to make collocations.
Language focus *In the example:* common business collocations
Alternatives: any sort of collocations, eg noun and noun, adjective and noun, and
   dependent prepositions
Technology Smart notebook, line tool and object animation

Before the class

Create a page as in figure 4.8. Use a bright colour for the arrows linking the verbs to the nouns. Make a white box that conceals the arrows. With the box selected, go to the *Object animation* menu and set the type to *Fade out*. This means that the arrows will be hidden until you click on the box which will fade out to reveal them.

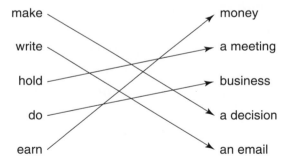

Figure 4.8 Page with the arrows visible

Procedure

1 Display the page and explain that each verb goes together with one of the nouns. Elicit an example from the students.

2 Divide the class into pairs and ask them to decide how the words match up.

3 Invite a student to come to the board and use an IWB pen to match up the words by drawing lines. Make sure they use a colour different to that of your arrows. If anyone disagrees with these answers, invite them to draw lines in another colour.

4 Use your finger to click on the white box which will fade away and reveal your arrows. Compare the arrows with the lines drawn by the students.

V10 *Make or do?*

Level pre-intermediate
Interaction small groups and whole class
Aim To form verb + nouns collocations with *make* or *do*.
Language focus common *make* or *do* collocations
Technology IWB software and CD-ROM dictionary

Before the class

Create a page with a two-column table with the headings *make* and *do*. Place this set of words at the bottom of the page:

a drink	*an exam*	*an effort*
a decision	*business*	*the washing up*
some damage	*progress*	*your homework*
a change	*a job*	*a noise*
some exercise	*an appointment*	*nothing*
a profit	*some shopping*	*an agreement*

Procedure

1   Write *a job* and *a mistake* on the board. Ask the students which one collocates with *make* and which one with *do*. Use the CD-ROM dictionary to look up each word and confirm the answers, ie *do a job* and *make a mistake*.

2   Display the page you created. Divide the class into small groups and give them time to discuss whether each noun goes with *make* or *do*. Encourage them to check in a dictionary.

3   Invite a student from one group to choose a noun and say which column it should go in. If everyone agrees, drag the word into the column. Continue until all the words are in the table.

Follow up

Ask the groups to personalise the collocations by creating example sentences for each one.

Answers

Make: a drink, an effort, a decision, progress, a change, a noise, an appointment, a profit, an agreement

Do: an exam, business, the washing up, some damage, your homework, a job, some exercise, nothing, some shopping

V11 Noun, verb or both?

Level pre-intermediate
Interaction individual and group
Aim To decide if a set of business-related words are nouns, verbs or both.
Language focus business language
Technology flipchart

Before the class

Prepare a flipchart. Draw two overlapping circles. Type *Verbs* above the left circle and *Nouns* above the right one. Above the overlapping central area type *Both*.

Type in the following words as individual, movable items:

invest, risk, fund, target, aim, goal, sell, sale, fall, lose, loss, graph.

Procedure

1   Open the flipchart. Tell students they must decide if the words on the whiteboard are verbs, nouns or both. Choose one at random and ask the class to decide on the word class. When the class reach a decision, drag the word into the correct circle.

2   Divide the class into pairs and ask them to decide on the other words.

3   Ask each student to come out in turn and drag a word to the correct place in the diagram. After each attempt, elicit whole-class agreement.

Follow up

Students in groups create sentences for the words in the central area, one where the word is used as a noun and one where the word is used as a verb.

Answers

Nouns: goal, sale, loss, graph

Verbs: invest, sell, fall, lose

Both: risk, target, aim, fund

V12   Re-ordering a dialogue

Level pre-intermediate
Interaction pairs and whole class
Aim To re-order and practise a short dialogue.
Language focus *In this example:* language for asking for a product in a shop
Alternatives: greetings and introductions, business phone calls, simple small talk situations
Technology IWB software

Before the class

Create a page with each line of the following conversation within a box, and placed along the left or right edge of the page. The numbers given here show the correct order and should not be included on the page.

Just a moment, I'll see what we have in stock.	(5)
You're welcome. Goodbye.	(11)
What type of phone is it?	(3)
Thank you.	(6)
That's a good idea. Thanks for your help.	(10)
Goodbye.	(12)
Good morning, how can I help you?	(1)
I'm sorry, we don't have a charger for that phone at the moment.	(7)

It's a Nokia 2800. (4)

Do you know another shop that might have it? (8)

Good morning. I need a new charger for my phone. (2)

You could try the mobile phone shop in the mall. (9)

Procedure

1 Display the page. Give the students two or three minutes to read the lines from the dialogue. Ask where the conversation is happening and why, ie in a mobile phone shop; the customer wants to buy a new charger for her phone.

2 Go through each line and ask if it is said by the shop assistant or the customer. Reposition the shop assistant's lines on the left of the page and the customer's on the right.

3 Divide the class into pairs and ask them to discuss and decide on the correct order of the lines.

4 Ask for a volunteer to come to the board and put the lines into the correct order. Encourage the other students to comment if they do not agree.

5 Ask two students to read the dialogue. Monitor and give feedback on pronunciation. Repeat with two more students until everyone in the class has had a turn.

6 Ask the pairs to practise the dialogue. Tell them they can vary the product and the request if they wish.

Follow up

You can review and practise this dialogue at a later stage in the course using the procedure in Chapter 4, S8 *Hiding half a dialogue*.

V13 Verb identifier

Level pre-intermediate
Interaction individual
Aim To come up with verb forms based on a given noun.
Language focus verbs and nouns
Technology all IWB software

Before the class

Write the following words and sentences on the board:

*That woman is a police **inspector**.*	*inspect*
*Jane is a very bad **loser**.*	*lose*
*Michelangelo was a great **painter**.*	*paint*
*Stephen Hawking is a great **thinker**.*	*think*
*Bob's always wanted to be an **actor**.*	*act*
*He's a very experienced **sailor**.*	*sail*
*The city is full of tourists and other **visitors**.*	*visit*
*Pavarotti was a great **singer**.*	*sing*
*Mozart was a brilliant **composer**.*	*compose*
*My dad's a terrible **driver**.*	*drive*

Lock the words onto the page. Access the pen colour settings and choose a white font. Scribble over the words that are emboldened in the example.

Procedure

1 Show the class the first sentence and elicit the noun of the given verb.

2 Put the students into pairs and ask them to decide on the verb forms of the other nouns.

3 Reveal the answers by using the eraser to rub away the white ink.

V14 *Do, play or go?*

Level pre-intermediate to intermediate
Interaction pairs
Aim To identify the correct verb in a phrase.
Language focus sport vocabulary
Technology all IWB software

Before the class

Write the following phrases, in columns, on the page:

Do judo, Play football, Play the guitar, Play the piano, Go skiing, Play chess, Do karate, Go walking, Play tennis, Go cycling, Go climbing, Go blackberry picking, Do knitting, Do crosswords, Play Scrabble.

Change the font colour for each verb, *Do, Play, Go,* to match the background. Now make a small magnifying glass shape by grouping a circle and a rectangle, and give the circle a dark fill colour that will reveal the hidden words. Don't fill the rectangle as it can reveal answers without you wishing to.

Send the magnifying tool to the back.

Procedure

1 Show the list of phrases and ask students to work in pairs and decide which verb collocates with each item.

2 When they have finished, elicit answers and reveal the answers on the board by holding the magnifying glass over the hidden words. Get students to mark their own work.

V15 **Backs to the interactive board**

Level intermediate and above
Interaction groups
Aim To describe words that their team mates must guess.
Language focus speaking
Technology all IWB software

Before the class

Type 100 or so words on the board. Ensure that the words you include vary in the level of difficulty.

Now, stack all of the words on top of one another at the top left-hand side of the page.

Procedure

1 Ask a pair or group of students to come to the front of the class and ask all but one of them to sit facing the class with their backs to the board. The remaining student will stand facing their team mates and the board behind them.

Ask a student from another group to come to the board. Activate the clock and set it to count down from two minutes.

2 At the word *go*, the student at the board must drag down a word from the jumble of words at the top of the screen. The student facing the board must describe the word to their team mates. When they name the word correctly, the student at the board drags another word into the middle of the screen. Each team must guess as many as they can in the allotted two minutes.

NB: Students can pass, in which case the word must be placed at the bottom of the page. Award three points for a correct answer and take away one point for each pass. If the opposition student who drags the words into place wastes time, penalise their team.

V16 Blended words

Level intermediate
Interaction individual
Aim To present and practise a set of 'portmanteau' words.
Language focus vocabulary
Technology IWB software, writing tool

Before the class

Prepare a flipchart with the words below displayed randomly. Use red and green.

Red: *motor car, smoke, web, break, brief, romantic, emotion, fact, Internet.*

Green: *etiquette, comedy, fog, log, fiction, icon, hotel, case, fast.*

Procedure

1 Open the flipchart. Elicit from students the term 'portmanteau word'. Drag the words *motor car* and *hotel* next to each other and write the newly created word *motel*. Draw attention to the meaning of the word. Ask the students to look at the whiteboard and make as many such words as they can in just one minute.

2 Invite students out in turn to drag one word next to its partner. They write in the newly created word. Get whole class-agreement.

3 Continue until students have completed all the words.

4 Students in pairs should select five new words and create sentences with them which illustrate meaning. They read out their sentences leaving a blank, and the others in the class shout out the missing word.

Follow up

Students can note any new words in their lexical notebooks. To continue work in this area, students work in two teams to brainstorm five more portmanteau words. They can use dictionaries, or the Internet. They come to the IWB and write them up. The other team can come out and write underneath the two original individual words.

Variation

For stage 1, read out definitions of the portmanteau words, eg 'an economic situation in which prices rise continuously, unemployment is high, and many businesses are not making money'. The first student to put up their hand comes out and attempts to create the portmanteau word (*stagflation*).

Answers

motel, smog, blog, breakfast, briefcase, romcom, emoticon, faction, netiquette

V17 Common phrasal verbs

Level intermediate
Interaction pairs, whole class
Aim To match phrasal verbs with their collocations and then to decide on their meaning.
Language focus phrasal verbs
Technology IWB flipchart

Before the class

Prepare four flipchart pages with mind-maps as in figure 4.9.

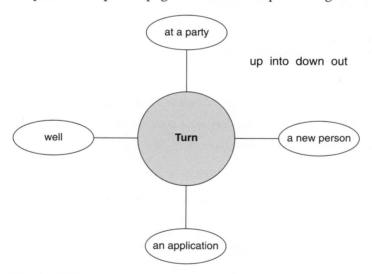

Figure 4.9 Phrasal verbs mind-map

Page 1:

Type *Turn* in the centre circle, then type the following phrases in the outside circles: *at a party, a new person, an application, well.*

Across the top type the following individual words: *up, into, down, out.*

Page 2:

Type *Look* in the centre circle, then type the following phrases in the outside circles: *a word, a crime, a baby, something lost.*

Across the top type the following individual words: *up, after, into, for.*

Page 3:

Type *Take* in the centre circle, then type the following phrases in the outside circles: *notes, my father, yoga, a company.*

Across the top type the following individual words: *down, after, up, over.*

Page 4:

Type *Go* in the centre circle, then type the following phrases in the outside circles: *become bad, try and get, continue, check.*

Across the top type the following individual words: *off, for, on, over.*

Procedure

1 Open the first flipchart page and ask students to work in groups to decide where the particles go to complete four phrasal verbs.

2 Students in turn come out and drag the words to the correct small circle. Get whole class agreement. Add examples with the pens. Ask students to think of other ways of expressing the meaning, eg *turn up = arrive unexpectedly.*

3 Complete the verbs on the other three pages.

Follow up

Students use their dictionaries to find another new phrasal verb for each mind-map. They come out and add them to the diagrams. They could also add example sentences for all the phrasal verbs. At the end of the activity, students note down any new words in their lexical notebooks.

Answers

Turn: up (at a party); into (a new person); down (an application); out (well)

Look: up (a word); into (a crime); after (a baby); for (something lost)

Take: down (notes); after (my father); up (yoga); over (a company)

Go: off (become bad); for (try and get); on (continue); over (check)

V18 Frequency of connectors

Level intermediate
Interaction pairs and whole class
Aim To decide on the order of the most common connectors used in writing.
Language focus common connectors
Technology IWB software, *Infinite clone* tool

Before the class

Prepare a flipchart page with the ten connectors below. Click on each word with the *Infinite clone* tool.

Therefore; However; Then; Finally; First, second etc; Thus; On the other hand; Also; For example; In addition

Prepare a second flipchart page with the answer (see below).

Procedure

1   Write the word *connector* on a blank flipchart page and elicit some common connectors from the students. Write them up. Move to the first prepared flipchart page and compare the students' ideas with this list of the top ten most common connectors in English.

2   Divide the class into small groups. Tell students they should decide on the order of frequency of these common connectors in English.

3   Invite a student from a group to drag the words into a possible order. Invite the next group to do the same, placing their list next to the first list. Continue with the remaining groups.

4   Reveal the correct order on the next flipchart and ask if there are any surprises.

Answers

| 1 However | 2 First, second etc | 3 Thus | 4 Also | 5 For example |
| 6 In addition | 7 Finally | 8 Therefore | 9 On the other hand | 10 Then |

Thanks to Academic writing for Graduate students (Swales and Feak 1994) for the original data.

V19   Opposites

Level intermediate
Interaction individual and group
Aim To practise common prefixes.
Language focus vocabulary
Technology flipchart, *Infinite clone* tool

Before the class

Prepare a flipchart with the following prefixes and words. Use the *Infinite clone* tool to reproduce the prefixes.

Im, Un, In, Il, dis

mature, moral, comfortable, fortunate, forgivable, literate, logical, human, reliable, agree, satisfied, accurate

Procedure

1   Open the flipchart. Ask students in pairs to give an example of the opposite of each word (eg *mature – young*). Encourage examples which do not use a prefix.

2   Check students know the term *prefix*. Ask them to look at the whiteboard and in pairs decide on the opposite of each adjective which uses a prefix.

3   Invite students out in turn to drag a prefix to the front of each word. Do a whole-class check after each word. Monitor and correct as necessary.

4   Continue until students have completed all the words correctly.

Answers

immature, immoral, uncomfortable, unfortunate, unforgivable, illiterate, illogical, inhuman, unreliable, disagree, dissatisfied, inaccurate

V20   Review of phrasal verbs types

Level intermediate
Interaction pairs and whole class
Aim To present different types of phrasal verbs.
Language focus phrasal verbs
Technology flipchart

Before the class

Prepare a flipchart page with four columns with the following headings:

Type 1: intransitive

Type 2: transitive + separable

Type 3: transitive + inseparable

Type 4: three-part

In the bottom half of the page type the following phrasal verbs:

look out, look after, look up, look up to, get up, count on, pick up, stand up for.

Procedure

1   Put students into pairs and ask them to decide which type of phrasal verb each of the ones shown on the IWB is. Give them a time limit to do this in.

2   When the time limit is up, ask students in turn to come out and drag the words to the correct column. Get whole-class agreement.

3   Annotate any on-screen examples with the pen tool in order to clarify which verbs are separable (eg I picked her up at the airport, I picked my mum up) and which verbs are inseparable (eg I looked after her, I looked after my mum). Ask students to produce sentences with some of these phrasal verbs and add them to the IWB.

Follow up

Divide the students into two groups. Students use their dictionaries to find four more phrasal verbs and come out and add them to the types of phrasal verbs.

Answers

Type 1: look out, get up

Type 2: look up, pick up

Type 3: look after, count on

Type 4: look up to, stand up for

V21   Unhealthy anagrams

Level intermediate
Interaction small groups and whole class
Aim To solve anagrams in a context.
Language focus *In the example:* illness and injury
Alternatives: clothing, personality traits, weather, food
Technology IWB software and CD-ROM dictionary

Before the class

Create a set of pages with one of these sentences on each:

*I don't feel well. I think I've caught a **dclo**.*

*I fell off my bike and **kroeb** my arm.*

*I've got a terrible **dahehace**. Do you have an aspirin?*

*You should go and see a **trocod**.*

*He **drujine** his leg playing football.*

*I have to take these **battles** three times a day.*

*Her holiday was a disaster. On the first day, she caught a tropical **aseedis**.*

*That looks serious. You should go to the **stophail**.*

Each of the anagrams needs to be made from individual letters which can be moved to reconstruct the correct word and should be in a different colour from the rest of the text.

Create a final page with all the sentences and the correct answers.

Procedure

1   Ask the class to brainstorm words linked to illness and injury. This activity works best if it is a review of a previous lesson focusing on this lexis. Write the words and collocations on the board.

2   Divide the class into small groups and explain the game: one of the words in each sentence has its letters jumbled up. The students have one minute to discuss what they think the word is. When the time is up, the first group to put up their hands get the first go at solving the anagram and a point if they are correct.

3   Set a timer for one minute and reveal the first sentence. If the first group to answer does not solve the anagram correctly, invite the next group to answer. Continue through the remainder of the sentences.

Follow up

Divide the group into pairs and ask them to use some of the words to talk about any minor illness or injury they or friends and family have experienced.

Variation

This activity can be made slightly easier for lower level students by locking some of the letters in the correct positions. These letters should be in a different colour to the others.

Answers

cold, broke, headache, doctor, injured, tablets, disease, hospital

V22   What's in a word?

Level intermediate and above
Interaction pairs, whole class
Aim To select and describe a picture which expresses a connotation of a given word.
Language focus connotation
Technology images from a photosharing website and memory sticks

Before the class

Go to an online source of photographs where students can search for and download images.

Create a flipchart with the title: *Communication*. Choose a positive picture and a negative one to represent the word. Paste them into the flipchart.

Write two cards, one for each group (A and B) with the following five words on it: *faith, strength, commitment, relaxing, challenge.*

Procedure

1 Open the flipchart page you created and reveal only the word *Communication*. What images come to mind? Elicit responses. Show students the two photographs. Remind them of the word *connotation*, ie the feelings associated with a word, and that often words have different meanings for different people.

2 Divide the class into two groups. Issue each group with a card with five words on it. Tell the students to discuss each word and then discuss the connotations of each word.

3 Students access the Internet and select a photograph which illustrates an aspect of their word which they have discussed, then download and save the image onto a memory stick.

4 With the help of a student from Group A, create a flipchart page for each word and import the five images to the appropriate pages. Do the same for Group B, importing each image to the appropriate page, so that each page has one word and two images.

5 Run through the flipchart pages, bringing up each word and the two juxtaposed images. Students in each group explain the rationale for each photograph to students in the other group.

Variations

1 Set the discussion and search task for homework. In the next lesson, import the students' chosen images.

2 Give groups of students one word each. They have to select two images to show radically different interpretations of the same word.

Comment

This activity works especially well with imaginative groups. It is inspired by a series of adverts created by the HSBC bank where words are illustrated by two pictures, each illustrating a different aspect of the same word. The power of the advertisement comes from the juxtaposition of the images and the radically differing interpretations of the words.

V23 Collocations of *argument*

Level upper intermediate
Interaction groups, whole class
Aim To present alternative collocations of the noun *argument*.
Language focus collocations
Technology flipchart

Before the class

Prepare three flipchart pages, as follows:

Page 1, type in the following text:

Argument = row
Argument = set of reasons used for persuading others

Page 2, type in the heading *Adjective + Argument*.

Create a five-column grid and type in five column headings, as follows:

Strong reasons used for persuading others, Most important, Sensible and well-argued, Based on incorrect facts, About a particular subject.

Lock the grid and headings into position, and type the following words individually under the grid, so they are each movable:

compelling, convincing, valid, central, core, main, cogent, plausible, coherent, fallacious, flawed, spurious, ethical, political, philosophical.

Page 3, type in the heading *Verb + An argument*.

Create a five-column grid and type in five column headings, as follows:

Suggest or use an argument, Think of or develop an argument, Not accept an argument, Make an argument weaker, Make an argument stronger.

Lock the grid and headings into position, and type the following words under the grid:

articulate, outline, put forward, construct, develop, hone, rebut, refute, dismiss, contradict, undermine, demolish, endorse, substantiate, strengthen.

Procedure

1 Open flipchart page 1. Remind students that *argument* has more than one meaning. This lesson will focus on the second meaning.

2 Go to flipchart page 2. Ask students to work in pairs and as quickly as possible, decide where each word might go. As an example, drag *main* to the column headed *Most important*. Students complete the grid.

3 Do the same for flipchart page 3. As an example, drag *develop* to the column headed *Think of or develop an argument*.

Follow up

Students record the most important of the examples in the Lexical Notebooks. This activity is a good way to introduce learners to the Collocations Dictionary (Macmillan).

Variation

Print the headings and words out and cut these up. Students do the exercises as a sorting task and then the teacher uses the IWB as above to check their answers.

Answers

Page 2:

Strong reasons used for persuading others: compelling, convincing, valid

Most important: central, core, main

Sensible and well-argued: cogent, plausible, coherent

Based on incorrect facts: fallacious, flawed, spurious

About a particular subject: ethical, political, philosophical

Page 3:

Suggest or use an argument: articulate, outline, put forward

Think of or develop an argument: construct, develop, hone

Not accept an argument: rebut, refute, dismiss

Make an argument weaker: contradict, undermine, demolish

Make an argument stronger: endorse, substantiate, strengthen

Activity based on the Collocations Dictionary (Macmillan).

V24 Idioms jumble

Level upper intermediate
Interaction pairs, whole class
Aim To match beginnings and endings to form idioms related to Business English.
Language focus idioms
Technology flipchart

Before the class

Type the beginnings and endings of a selection of idioms into a flipchart, as follows, and mix up the endings. Use two colours.

Don't pass	*the buck.*	*That's writing*	*a blank cheque.*
Don't jump	*on the bandwagon.*	*They moved*	*the goalposts.*
Don't talk	*shop.*	*They went*	*to the wall.*

Procedure

1 Show students the first half of one of the idioms and ask them if they can supply the second half.

2 Remind students what an idiom is. Remind them that it is useful to recognise these when used by native speakers.

3 Open the flipchart and ask students to match the halves of the phrases together to create some business idioms.

4 Ask students to come out in turn and drag phrases together to create idioms. Monitor and correct if necessary. See if the students can explain the idiom.

5 Ask students to work in pairs to say if any of these idioms exist in their own language.

Follow up

Students search an Internet website to find another business idiom which they can ask other students to guess.

Variation

With general English classes, use some relatively common idioms, eg

You can take a horse to water but you can't make it drink. I wouldn't touch it with a bargepole. Take it with a pinch of salt. That's pot calling the kettle black. You're pulling my leg. You can't have your cake and eat it.

V25 Phrasal verb equivalents

Level upper intermediate
Interaction pairs, whole class
Aim To match a number of phrasal verbs related to Business English with their single-word equivalents.
Language focus *In the example:* phrasal verbs related to Business English
Alternatives: any group of phrasal verbs
Technology IWB software

Before the class

Write the following words in random order on a flipchart, using red and green:

Red words: *acquire, dismiss, resign, diversify, liquidate, organise, profit, recover.*

Green words: *take on, lay off, stand down, branch out, wind up, set up, cash in, bounce back.*

Procedure

1 Tell students that many phrasal verbs have one-word equivalents. Open the flipchart and elicit the meaning of one of the phrasal verbs from students.

2 Put students into pairs. Tell them they should match the red words with their equivalent phrasal verb in green.

3 Students in turn come out and drag a red word to its equivalent. Get the class to agree.

4   Continue until all the words are matched. Monitor, help and correct as necessary. Remind students that these equivalents are only approximations and that they are not always interchangeable. The meaning of one word may be more limited than the other; there is often a difference in register.

Follow up

Divide the students into two groups. One group creates a short story using five of the red words, the other using the green words. Students exchange texts and read each other's stories, checking for accuracy and appropriateness. At the end of the activity, students note down any new words in their lexical notebooks.

Comment

This activity is a good way to draw attention to the final section of the Phrasal Verbs Plus Dictionary (Macmillan), which lists phrasal verbs and their single-word equivalents.

Answers

acquire – take on, dismiss – lay off, resign – stand down, diversify – branch out, liquidate – wind up, organise – set up, profit – cash in, recover – bounce back

V26   Prefixes

Level upper intermediate
Interaction individual and group
Aim To present and practise a set of prefixes.
Language focus vocabulary
Technology digital flipchart, timer (optional)

Before the class

Prepare a flipchart page with the following prefixes displayed randomly:

anti, auto, bi, inter, micro, mono, over, poly, post, pre, pseudo, semi, sub, ultra.

Then type the following meanings in a different colour:

after, against, before, between or among, extremely, false, half or partial, many, of or by oneself, one or single, small, too much, two, under.

Procedure

1   Open the flipchart. Write up the ending of some words which take the same prefix, eg *-marine, -zero, -stitute.* Ask students to supply the missing prefix, ie *sub.* Using this example, check students undertand the term *prefix.* In these examples, the prefix has the meaning of *under* or *below.* Tell them they will be matching a set of prefixes with their meanings. Ask them to look at the prepared flipchart page for a few minutes.

2   Invite students out in turn to drag a prefix to the correct meaning. Do a whole-class check after each word. Continue until students have completed all the words correctly.

3   Ask students to work in pairs or small groups and brainstorm as many common words as they can with the prefixes in three minutes. Provide an example, eg *automatic.* Students then write one gapped sentence for each prefix in the list.

4   Students read their gapped sentences to another partner who guesses the missing word.

Variation

Students can use dictionaries in step 3 to find four new words for each prefix.

Answers

anti – against, auto – of or by oneself, bi – two, inter – between or among, micro – small, mono – one or single, over – too much, poly – many, post – after, pre – before, pseudo – false, semi – half or partial, sub – under, ultra – extremely

V27 Idioms of time and money

Level upper intermediate to advanced
Interaction pairs and whole class
Aim To introduce and practise a set of idiomatic phrases.
Language focus idioms of time and money
Technology IWB software and CD-ROM dictionary

Before the class

Create a page with two headings, *Time* and *Money*, at the top of the page, then the following phrases distributed at random in the bottom half of the page:

every now and then, behind the times, in no time, in the long run, for the time being, out of the blue, in the red, What a rip off!, flat broke, cut corners, money talks, cost an arm and a leg.

Procedure

1 Write the following sentence on the board: *I can't afford to come out tonight because my new mobile phone cost an arm and a leg.* Elicit the meaning from students and clarify that the students know what an idiom is and when they are used, ie a fixed expression mostly used in informal contexts.

2 Display the page with the idioms. Divide the class into pairs and give them a short time to discuss which of the phrases are idioms about time and which about money. Invite a student to come to the board and drag the idioms into position under the two headings. Invite a discussion about whether this is the correct answer.

3 Ask half the pairs to discuss what they think the time idioms mean and half to discuss the money idioms. Ask the pairs to report back. Use the CD-ROM dictionary to check and confirm their answers.

4 Distribute the idioms amongst the pairs and ask them to think of situations in which they could imagine using those expressions. Ask the pairs to report back.

Follow up

Write the idioms on cards. Distribute these at random to students. Ask the students in pairs to roleplay some simple situations, eg buying a new phone, asking for advice about getting a new car, telling a story about a trip to a retaurant, but including the idioms on their cards in the conversation at an appropriate moment.

Answers

Time: every now and then, behind the times, in no time, in the long run, for the time being, out of the blue

Money: in the red, What a rip off!, flat broke, cut corners, money talks, cost an arm and a leg

LISTENING

L1 Listening for numbers

Level pre-intermediate
Interaction pairs and whole class
Aim To listen to and identify the correct numerical information given in a short radio report.
Language focus numbers
Technology IWB software and online news service

Before the class

Go to the website of a television or radio news broadcaster and identify a short audio or video report that will be of interest to your students and which contains several numbers and dates, eg the earnings of a celebrity, company profits, box office takings.

Create a whiteboard page with a set of multiple-choice questions. Each question should refer to one of the numbers in the report. Provide three very similar answers to each question, including the correct one. If you have time, make a complete transcript of the report. Create a headline that describes the story or take this from the website.

Procedure

1 Write the headline of the report on the board and ask the students if any of them remember the story and what it was about. If no one does, ask them to predict what they think it might be about.

2 Play the report and elicit the main idea.

3 Display the page with the information. Explain they need to listen and catch the correct figure for each piece of information.

4 Play the audio again. Divide the students into pairs and ask them to discuss the answers. If necessary, play the audio a third time.

5 Invite a student to come to the board and draw a circle around the correct answer for the first piece of information. Encourage any discussion about whether this is the correct answer. Repeat with other students marking the other figures. If you have a transcript, display it now and play the audio again.

Variation

With higher level students, do not include the numbers on the whiteboard page. The task then becomes that of giving the most accurate rendering of each figure.

L2 Putting events into order

Level intermediate
Interaction pairs and whole class
Aim To listen to and identify the sequence of events in a news report.
Language focus listening for key events
Technology IWB software and online news service

Before the class

Go to the website of a television or radio news broadcaster and identify a short audio or video report that will be of interest to your students. Some broadcasters allow you to download and save the report but in other cases the reports are only on the website for a limited period. Part of a podcast is a good alternative if you wish to use the report several times, refer back to it or share it with your students.

Make a note of the main events of the story being described in the report, write these as statements in the present simple then create a whiteboard page listing these events but in the sequence they are mentioned in the report. This is not usually exactly the same as the original chronological sequence. Place these on the right side of the page.

On the left side, create a vertical line labelled, from the top: *Past, Present, Future*. If you have time, make a complete transcript of the report. Create a headline that describes the story or take this from the website.

Procedure

1   Write the headline of the report on the board and ask the students if they know the story and what it is about. If no one does, ask them to predict what they think it might be about.

2   Explain that you are going to play a short radio report about the story and that they should listen for the main idea. Play the report and elicit the main idea.

3   Display the page with the jumbled events of the story. Give the students a short time to read them. Explain they are going to listen again and put the events into the order in which they occur in the past, present and future.

4   Play the audio again. Divide the students into pairs and ask them to discuss the order of the events. If necessary, play the audio a third time.

5   Invite a student to come to the board and drag the events into order. Encourage any discussion about whether this is the correct answer. Display the transcript and play the audio again. Ask the students whether they want to make any further changes to the order on the board.

Follow up

As a grammar activity, higher-level groups can be asked to change the sentences (which are all in the present simple) into the grammatical forms used in the original report.

READING

R1 Heads or tails

Level any
Interaction whole class
Aim To decide whether statements are true or false.
Language focus reading
Technology all technology

Before the class

Write the heading *True or False* then write down 10–15 statements on the board. Some of these statements must be grammatically correct, the rest should contain errors.

Write the answer *true* or *false* at the end of each sentence but cover with white ink to hide the words.

Activate the screen shade / revealer and reveal only the heading.

Procedure

1 Tell students that they must decide if each of the statements they are about to read is true or false. If true, they are to put their hands on their heads. If they think the statement is false they must put their hands on their hips (hence, *heads or tails*).

2 Ask them to stand.

3 Draw the shade down to reveal the first statement. When all students have their hands either on their heads or hips, wipe away the white ink at the end of the sentence to reveal the answer. All those with the incorrect answers must sit down.

4 Keep revealing the statements until one person remains standing, or the end of the exercise.

Follow up

Get groups of students to write their own questions. This can be done as homework or by 'carouselling' – groups of up to five students typing in their statements on the computer in the class (remember to deactivate the projector connection whilst doing this).

R2 Text organisation

Level pre-intermediate and above
Interaction small groups
Aim To sort words from a reading text.
Language focus vocabulary, preparation for reading
Technology IWB software, reading text from the courseware or another source

Before the class

Select a text to use in the class. Type 12–20 words from the text into the flipchart. Include a good number of nouns and key-words. Copy this flipchart page enough times for each group in the class.

Procedure

1 Divide the class into small groups and explain that they are going to sort some words into groups.

2 Open the flipchart page and tell students they should first of all check they understand the words. They should work together and explain any unknown words to the other members of the group.

3 Each group should then decide which words are related in some way and categorise them, eg by word class or in sense groups.

4 Invite a student to come out to the flipchart and drag related words together. When the student has finished, ask them to circle each cluster of words and then explain why they have grouped them like this. Invite comments from the other groups.

5 Move to the next flipchart page and ask a student from the next group to repeat step 4. Continue until all the groups have presented their word groupings.

Follow up

Issue the text and ask students to scan it and underline the words from the exercise. Ask students if they were surprised by anything, such as the way a word is actually used in the text. Continue with intensive reading of the text.

R3 Collocation search

Level intermediate and above
Interaction individual and whole class
Aim To form collocations from given words in order to prepare for a text.
Language focus *In the example:* environment vocabulary
Alternatives: music in the digital age, executive stress
Technology IWB software

Before the class

Select a text to use in the class, eg a text about global warming, and identify a number of collocations from the text. Type both parts of each collocation into the flipchart, using a different colour for the first and second word, eg *Kyoto Protocol, global warming, greenhouse gases, climate change, heat wave, scientific model.*

Split up the collocations and jumble the individual words on the page.

Procedure

1 Tell students the topic of the text, eg *global warming.* Ask students to brainstorm individual words they think will be used in the text. Open the flipchart and show students the words. Drag *global* to *warming* and tell students these words form a strong collocation. Ask them to work in pairs to match the words to create the other collocations.

2 Invite a student to come out to the flipchart and drag a word to its partner. Check with the group. Continue until all the words are matched. Monitor and help if necessary during the task.

3 Ask students to see if they can add a word or phrase before or after the collocations, eg *sign the Kyoto Protocol, prevent climate change.*

Follow up

Issue the text and ask students to scan it and underline the collocations. Continue with further pre-reading work such as checking what comes before the collocations.

R4 Reading gap-fill

Level all
Interaction individual, whole class
Aim To fill gaps in a text using given words.
Language focus reading, understanding vocabulary and context
Technology all IWB software

Before the class

Load the text you wish to use onto a flipchart page and lock the text into place on the page.

Using the IWB pen tool cover over the words you wish to focus on in a white font.

Type the hidden words, separately from each other, and store them at the side of the page.

Procedure

1 Display the heading of the text and ask students to discuss what they think it is going to be about.

2 Print off the page and hand out one copy to each student. Ask the students to fill in the blanks using the words placed at the side of the page.

3 When they have finished, ask students to come to the board, one at a time, to drag a word from the side into the right place.

4 Ask the class if they agree or disagree with the choices and to explain their reasons.

5 Ask students to make the necessary corrections to their own work as they go through the exercise.

SPEAKING

S1 Planning a town

Level elementary to intermediate
Interaction pairs and whole class
Aim To brainstorm typical features of a town then use those to plan a small town.
Language focus vocabulary for features of a town, language for expressing opinions, agreeing and disagreeing
Technology IWB software

Before the class

Create a page with a grid background. Draw a wiggly blue line across one corner of the page and a small oval in another corner. Lock these items in place.

Procedure

1 Divide the students into pairs and ask them to brainstorm the things that they would expect to find in a small town, eg *school, shops, houses, roads*.

2 Display the page. Explain that the blue line is a river and the oval is a small mountain but all the other land is flat and fertile. Tell the students that they are going to build a small town in this location.

3 Ask the pairs to report back. Draw and label small boxes to represent the things that they are suggesting should be in the town. Put these boxes on one side of the page in no particular order.

4 Appoint one student to chair the discussion and one student to move the items around the map on the board. For lower levels chair the discussion yourself. Set a time limit for the discussion, monitor and provide feedback and correction where necessary.

Follow up

Save the resulting plan. Make a copy but make some changes. Explain to the students that your second plan is the town ten years later. This provides you with the basis to introduce or practise the present perfect to talk about what has changed.

Variation

An alternative to going directly into the whole-class discussion is to distribute printed versions of the empty map to pairs or small groups and give the students time to discuss before they reach a group decision on the board.

S2 Doodles

Level elementary to intermediate
Interaction pairs and whole class
Aim To talk about a doodle and then tell a story.
Language focus *I think it looks like . . .*
Technology IWB software

Before the class

With lower levels you can create five or six pages, each with a doodle or rough sketch that already looks a little like something. It should be something that can be interpreted in different ways, not a clear picture. With higher levels you can skip this option and begin with blank pages.

Figure 4.10 A doodle that suggests a bird

Figure 4.11 A doodle that suggests a boot

Figure 4.12 A doodle that suggests a car

Procedure

1 If you have already created some doodles, display the first one. If not, draw something on a blank page. Ask the students what they think it looks like. Invite a volunteer to come to the board to add details to the doodle and to explain what they think it looks like.

2 Display your next doodle, or invite a student to the board to draw one. Divide the students into pairs and give them time to discuss what they think they can see in the doodle. Invite a student to add to the doodle and explain what they think it looks like. If you have a large class, make three or four copies of the doodle then allow several students to add to and identify what they have drawn.

3 Once you have used all the pre-prepared doodles or have created about ten pictures, ask the pairs to discuss and think of a short story that links the things created from the doodle.

4 Invite some of the pairs to tell their stories, using the pictures created from the doodles to illustrate them.

Follow up

The pairs can write up their stories as homework.

S3 Identity parade

Level pre-intermediate to intermediate
Interaction small groups
Aim To describe people's features to identify characters.
Language focus vocabulary for descriptions
Technology all IWB software

Before the class

Import a range of faces onto a page; use around 12, arrange them in two rows of six and label them with names.

Procedure

1 In pairs, ask students to select four names, and write them down in order.

2 Tell students that a notorious gang have been robbing banks in the city and that they have spotted the gang making a getaway from their latest heist. Put the pairs together to make groups of four and explain that each pair is to take it in turns giving the other pair, the 'police officers', descriptions of the gang.

3 When the first pair have given all their descriptions, they swap roles and become the police, thus taking details of the other pair's descriptions.

4 At the end of the activity the pairs reveal their findings to each other.

S4 Mini topics

Level pre-intermediate and above
Interaction small groups
Aim To practise spontaneous conversation about general small talk topics.
Language focus small talk topics
Technology IWB software

Before the class

Create a page with a 3 × 3 table. Type one of these topics into each of the cells of the table then apply the shade to each cell to hide the word:

the weather, my home town, my hobbies, travel, food and drink, sport, movies, fashion, current affairs.

Procedure

1 If you have a large class, divide the students into small groups of three or four. Explain that they are going to make small talk about a subject given to them at random.

2 Invite a student to come to the board and click on one of the cells to remove the shade. Tell the students that this is their first topic.

3 Allow the conversations to continue for a fixed period of time, depending on the level of the students and whether you are using this activity as a warmer or major component of the lesson.

4 When the time is up, interrupt the conversation and invite another student to choose the next topic.

5 Repeat steps 3 and 4 until all the topics are used up.

S5 The balloon debate

Level pre-intermediate and above
Interaction small groups
Aim To practise debating skills and language.
Language focus language of agreeing and disagreeing
Technology IWB software

Before the class

Choose six celebrities who are currently in the news or have been mentioned in previous lessons.

Insert images of them into a flipchart page, and cover each image with a square drawn with the shapes tool. Give each square a different fill colour. Next, select each square, then *Object animation* and *Fade out*. When clicked, the square will disappear to reveal the image of the celebrity beneath.

Procedure

1 With lower levels start by checking vocabulary such as *balloon* and *celebrity* and *debate*. Then introduce the concept that a balloon containing six celebrities is sinking and so some celebrities must be thrown out to stop it from crashing to the ground. The students will now have to defend one of these celebrities and say why the others should be thrown out of the balloon.

2 Divide students into pairs and ask each pair to choose a colour from those on the flipchart. Click the coloured square to reveal the celebrity they are going to defend. Check that everybody knows who each celebrity is.

3 Give the students some time to come up with ideas why they should save their celebrity.

4 Each pair then presents their argument both for their own celebrity and against the others – the others are allowed to reply to these arguments and state why they agree / disagree. The class must vote at the end to decide who stays and who goes.

Variation

Instead of people you could use books, films or other objects relative to the topic of your lessons.

Activity contributed by Kirsty Greig.

S6 The discussion bucket

Level pre-intermediate and above
Interaction small groups
Aim To give opinions and explain reasons why these opinions are held.
Language focus language of opinion, reason and example
Technology IWB software

Before the class

Produce a flipchart in which a picture of a large container (eg a bucket or a top hat) is placed on the top layer of the flipchart and locked in place. Type single words or phrases, eg *childhood, golf, doing homework, going on holiday,* onto the flipchart, place them on the middle layer and 'hide' them behind the container. This is a great opportunity to recycle vocabulary from recent lessons. In the top left and top right of the flipchart, place a 'love' and 'hate' symbol or emoticon, or just write the words. Save the flipchart.

Procedure

1 Pull out a word or phrase from the container and place it under the 'love' symbol. Ask the group for reasons why somebody might love the item.

2 Next, move it over so that it is under the 'hate' symbol and elicit reasons for this.

3 Explain to the class that they are going to have to talk for one minute about why they love or hate certain topics. Divide students into groups of three and assign each student a letter within each group (A, B and C).

4 Select a new topic from the container. Student A in each group speaks for one minute, explaining why they love the topic using the opinion–reason–example model, which should have been demonstrated and / or pre-taught in a previous lesson.

5 Use the IWB clock to time the minute.

6 After student A has finished, student B takes over by explaining why he/she hates the topic.

7 During both minutes, student C listens for both positive uses of language and for mistakes. He/She then gives feedback to students A and B. This feedback should help to improve performance the next time they attempt the activity.

8 Roles are rotated for the next topic: student B loves the topic, student C hates the topic and student A listens and gives feedback.

Variation

Record the students using a digital dictaphone, so that they can hear themselves attempting the exercise. These recordings can be used in the following lesson's feedback or even sent to their email accounts so that they can listen to them many times.

Activity contributed by Brian Finch.

S7 Completing a dialogue

Level intermediate
Interaction pairs and whole class
Aim To customise and practise a shopping dialogue.
Language focus *In this example:* language for buying clothes
Alternatives: language for buying shoes, mobile phones, computers
Technology IWB software

Before the class

Create a flipchart page with these questions:

1 *What was the last item of clothing you bought?*

2 *What will the next one be?*

3 *How do you usually pay?*

4 *What factors do you take into consideration when buying clothes?*

Then create a second page with the start and end of a dialogue between a shop assistant (A) and shopper (B):

A: *Good morning. Can I help you?*

B: *Hello. Yes, I'm looking for . . .*

. . .

A: *So, that's _____ in total.*

B: *Here you are.*

A: *Thank you.*

B: *Thanks for your help.*

A: *You're welcome. Goodbye.*

Procedure

1 Display the page with the questions. Tell the students that they are going to discuss the questions with each other. Focus on question 4. Ask the students what kind of factors might be considered, eg style, colour, materials, size, price, label or brand, season.

2 Divide the students into pairs and give them time to ask and answer the questions. Ask the students to report back. Make a note of some of the answers.

3 Display the page with the start and end of the dialogue between the shop assistant and shopper. Explain that the class is going to complete the dialogue. Ask the pairs to think about what sort of questions the shopper would ask. Display the first page again with the information collected in step 2.

4   Ask the students to report back with their questions, eg *Do you have this in a smaller size? Do you have anything in cotton? Do you have this in yellow? Can I try it on?*. Correct them if necessary and write these on a blank page.

5   Choose one of the answers to question 2, ie the next item of clothing someone plans to buy. At this stage, it is best to make it something unisex such as a pair of jeans or a T-shirt. Ask the students to choose the first question the shopper would ask. Copy this to the dialogue and ask for an appropriate answer. Continue until the shopper has all the information they need to decide to buy the item. Choose a payment method from the answers to question 3 and use this to complete the dialogue.

6   Choose two volunteers to read the completed dialogue.

7   Re-organise the pairs and ask them to use the dialogue to role-play the purchase of their answer to question 1 or 2. The pairs should take it in turns to play the shop assistant and the shopper.

Follow up

Save the completed dialogue for a review later in the course or to modify for similar situations.

Variation

Students could also record their dialogues for future reference.

S8   Hiding half a dialogue

Level intermediate
Interaction pairs and whole class
Aim To practise a shopping dialogue.
Language focus *In this example:* language for buying clothes
Alternatives: language for buying shoes, mobile phones, computers
Technology IWB software: screen shade/revealer tool

Before the class

If you have already done activity S7, *Completing a dialogue,* then re-use the dialogue created there. Otherwise, any short exchange between two people that will fit onto a single page can be used. The dialogue needs to be laid out so that the lines of one speaker are on the right-hand side of the page and those of the other are on the left-hand side.

Procedure

1   Display the page with the dialogue. Ask two volunteers to read the parts of the shop assistant and the shopper. Give any necessary feedback on pronunciation and ask two more students to read it again.

2   Use the screen shade/revealer to hide the part of the shop assistant. Ask two more students to perform the role play. Encourage the whole class to help the student playing the hidden role if they cannot remember the next line.

3   Repeat step 2 with the other side of the dialogue and another two students.

4 Divide the students into pairs and ask them to practise the role play with first one side hidden, then the other. Tell them that, when they are playing the shopper, they can choose what item of clothing they wish to buy.

5 Ask for two volunteers to perform the role play with the entire text hidden.

Follow up

If you are doing this as a follow up to S7, *Completing a dialogue,* and you recorded the students' dialogue, record them again and give them an opportunity to compare the two recordings.

Variation

Hide the start or the end of the dialogue or increasing proportions of it from the start or from the end.

S9 Digital camera conversations

Level intermediate and above
Interaction pairs
Aim To write the script for a short video clip using visual clues.
Language focus any
Technology digital camera

Before the class

Record a short piece of video using a standard digital camera on *video* setting. This could range from unplanned, unscripted and unrehearsed 'eavesdropped' type videos, surreptitiously recorded in the teachers' room or cafeteria (check you have permission to use them!) through to carefully scripted videos acted by willing colleagues.

Download the clip from the camera onto a computer. Most computers will do this automatically without the need for the software which came with the camera.

Play the video and pause at a suitable moment. Use the Promethean camera tool to take a photo of this still frame. Paste this photo into a blank flipchart, then position and resize before setting it as an object which, once clicked, will play the associated embedded video.

Procedure

1 Divide the class into pairs and explain that they are going to hear the audio from a video, and they must predict and speculate about the scene, setting and characters. Hide the picture and play the sound only.

2 Elicit ideas from the pairs.

3 Turn off the sound and now play the video. The scene, setting and characters are clear but the dialogue must be guessed.

4 Next, ask students to write a new script (serious or comic) and then read it as a voice over as the video plays on screen. Alternatively, the new script can be recorded and then 'dubbed' over the video.

Activity contributed by Brian Finch.

S10 Food link discussion

Level intermediate and above
Interaction whole class
Aim To use a linking activity to discuss food.
Language focus food and diet
Technology all IWB software

Before the class

Insert images to represent the following food groups: protein, fibre, carbohydrates and fats. If you have chosen several pictures for each item, group them together and then position the four groups on the page, equidistantly apart. Now, type in a few sentences about each food group on separate, consecutive pages. Right-click on one of the pictures, select *Link* and then *Page in this file*. Select the actual page you want to link the picture to and repeat the process for the other three pictures.

Now cover each set of images with a square drawn with the shapes tool. Give the squares a fill colour and then type in the collective terms on top, ie *Protein, Carbohydrates*, etc.

Procedure

1 Ask students what kinds of foods you would find in each box. Click the squares and delete them to reveal the images after a general consensus has been agreed, allowing any differences of opinion to stand.

2 Put students in pairs and ask them to discuss what they know about each food group.

3 Conduct whole-class feedback and when you are satisfied that the subject has been given time to develop as fully as you would like, click on each image to link to information about each food group. See if there are any differences in the written account and students' opinions.

S11 Literary definitions

Level intermediate
Interaction whole class
Aim To read clues and guess which novel is being described.
Language focus general knowledge
Technology all IWB software

Before the class

Write the following four clues on the board, leaving a space between each one:
Which novel:

was first published in 1843 by Chapman and Hall?

takes place in late-December?

tells the story of a mean old man who eventually changes his ways?

features the ghosts of Christmas past, present and future?

Now, draw a rectangle around the first clue, give it a white fill colour and clone the rectangle four times, placing the shapes over the remaining clues.

Procedure

1 Ask students to write down their names on a small piece of paper and tell them they're going to take part in a quiz.

2 Reveal the first clue by tapping on the rectangle and deleting it. If you are writing your own questions this first clue should be broad, making it very difficult to get the answer right at this stage. Any students who think they know the answer must write it underneath their name, fold up the piece of paper and hand it over to you. You will put any suggestions in a pile on your desk. Students submitting an answer at this stage cannot take any further part in the quiz but if they get it right, they will get 10 points.

3 Now, reveal the second clue and follow the same procedure. Again, any students wishing to answer must write their answer underneath their name and hand it over to you. You will put these answers in a second pile next to the first pile. Anyone getting it right at this stage will get 8 points.

4 Go through all of the clues. Anyone making a guess at the last clue stands to win 2 points.

5 Tell them the answer at the end: *A Christmas Carol,* by Charles Dickens.

Follow up

Ask students to write their own descriptions of books or films.

S12 Who's coming to dinner?

Level intermediate and above
Interaction small groups and whole class
Aim To discuss who to invite to an imaginary dinner party and decide on the seating plan.
Language focus expressing opinions and agreeing and disagreeing
Technology IWB software

Before the class

Create a page with a long, narrow rectangle shape across the centre of the page (the table) with four small squares along each side and one at either end (the chairs). Leave plenty of space around the edges for the names.

Procedure

1 Display the page. Tell the students that this is a dining table laid out for a dinner party for ten guests. Explain that they are going to decide who to invite and where everyone should sit. Explain that these guests can be anyone from any time in history. Remind them that the art of organising a good dinner party is to have lots of interesting guests.

2 Divide the students into three or four small groups. Ask them to discuss and nominate five people to be invited. Give plenty of time for this discussion.

3 Ask a representative from each group to write the names of their five nominees on the board. Remove any duplicates.

4 Organise a vote for each of the nominees. Move the names of the successful invitees to the top of the page and erase all the others.

5 Reconvene the groups and ask them to discuss and decide on a seating plan. They should also choose members of their group to present and defend their proposal.

6   Invite one of the groups to drag the names into position around the table and explain their thinking. Allow the spokespeople of the other groups to agree and disagree with the seating of each person and to give their reasons why. You can moderate this discussion yourself or nominate a student to take the chair. Allow the debate to continue until a seating plan has been agreed.

Follow up

You could retain the list of names of the invitees and use them in a balloon debate in a later class. In a balloon debate students have to represent one of the people in order to argue why they should not be thrown out of a rapidly sinking hot air balloon.

S13   The ideal colleague

Level upper intermediate
Interaction individual, group, whole class
Aim To raise awareness of individual preferences and similarities in cultural preferences.
Language focus vocabulary; speaking
Technology IWB software

Before the class

Prepare a flipchart page with the following adjectives:

humorous, willing to compromise, modest, honest, diplomatic, confrontational, conservative, respectful, talkative, volatile, reserved, patient, punctual, extrovert, reliable, direct.

Copy the content to a series of flipchart pages, matching the number of countries represented in the class.

Procedure

1   Open the flipchart and show students the list of words. They should work together to check they know the meaning of the words. They can use their dictionaries. Invite students to come out in turn to annotate the unknown words.

2   Tell students to write down the six adjectives they would use to describe their ideal colleague.

3   Ask students to form groups with others from the same country where possible (ie in multilingual classes). They should compare their lists, find any words that are included in more than one list and count the number of times they appear.

4   Ask students from one group to go out to the front and write the name of their country at the top of a flipchart. They then highlight any words / phrases which occur in more than one list in their group, with the number of occurrences in brackets.

5   Continue until all the countries have fed back.

6   Conduct a feedback session, examining what this shows about culture in the workplace in different countries. Many values are the same across cultures, although countries also retain some individual traits and preferences.

Variation

Ask General English students to think about their ideal friend.

Comment

This activity is designed for use with multilingual classes where there is more than one student from each country. It can still be used with students from the same country as there will be similarities and differences in the results. This activity could start a cultural-awareness training seminar.

S14 Uncertainty avoidance

Level upper-intermediate and above
Interaction individual, whole class
Aim To present one dimension of culture: uncertainty avoidance.
Language focus cross-cultural terminology
Technology IWB software

Before the class

Prepare a series of flipchart pages as follows:

Page 1:

Draw a horizontal line with an arrow head at each end. At one end, write *Risk taker*. At the other end, *Risk avoider*.

Page 2:

Title: *Uncertainty avoidance*

Definition: the extent to which people in a country are comfortable with levels of uncertainty

Descriptions: High = people plan carefully to minimise uncertainty / Low = people are more relaxed and comfortable with uncertainty

Page 3:

Title: *Uncertainty avoidance*

Draw a horizontal line with an arrow head at each end. At one end, write *High*. At the other end, *Low*.

Procedure

1   Give students a minute to think about how they would describe themselves: as a risk taker or a risk avoider? Open the flipchart and ask students to come out and write their name at an appropriate point on the line.

2   Ask students to work with a partner to discuss and compare the points on the line they wrote their name. They can give examples such as the type of shares they would buy, the types of sports they like and holidays they take.

3   Move to the next slide and explain the concept of 'uncertainty avoidance'. Put students into nationality groups. They then discuss and agree on where their country lies on the scale. Ask a student from each group to mark the position of their country on the line, inviting student comments and reactions.

Follow up

Continue the lesson with further work on uncertainty avoidance, such as a role play activity from In Company Upper Intermediate, or exploring other dimensions of culture in a similar way.

Variation

This activity can be easily adapted to work with other dimensions of culture, such as whether countries are more masculine or feminine, individualist or collectivist.

S15 The power of persuasion

Level advanced
Interaction small groups and pairs
Aim To indicate opinions and try to persuade others to change theirs.
Language focus language for opinions and persuading
Technology IWB software

Before the class

Create four pages, each with a double-headed, horizontal arrow with one end labelled *Strongly agree* and the other end *Strongly disagree*. Make a number of different coloured Xs, one per person in the group.

At the top of each page put one of these topics:

Private education is always better than education funded by the state.

The single currency is vital for the future economic success of Europe.

Violent films and computer games cause criminal behaviour.

Government health systems should not treat people who suffer from life-style illnesses.

Procedure

1   Display the page with the first topic. Invite the students to come to the board and drag an X onto the line to represent their opinion. For larger classes it may be necessary for the students to put their initials next to the X if there are not enough colours.

2   Tell the students they are going to try and persuade someone with an opinion different from theirs to change their mind. Divide the class into two groups: those whose Xs are closer to the *agree* end and those who are closer to the *disagree* end. Give them time to compare their ideas and opinions and decide how they will try to persuade the students in the other group.

3   Put the students into pairs based on the position of their X on the line, eg put someone who strongly disagrees with someone who agrees but has put their X closer to the centre.

4   Give the pairs ten minutes to discuss and try to persuade each other. When the time is up, allow anyone who wants to re-position their X to do so.

5   Move on to the next sentence.

Follow up

If writing is an important component of the course, ask the students to write an essay on the arguments for and against one of the statements.

Variation

If you know in advance that the students are very interested in one of these topics, you can extend step 2 to include research time. The students use the Internet to find information and figures to support their positions and strengthen their arguments.

WRITING

W1 Paragraph writing

Level intermediate
Interaction pairs, whole class
Aim To put sentences into the correct order to form a coherent paragraph.
Language focus writing a paragraph
Technology IWB software

Before the class

Prepare five flipchart pages, as follows:

Page 1: at the top of the page type the heading *Parts of a paragraph*. Then below type the following categories:

Topic sentence

Example / Explanation / Definition / Information / Restatement

Concluding sentence

Pages 2 and 3:

Type the following sentences:

Global warming continues to top the scientific agenda.

There is, however, disagreement on whether the Earth's temperature is really rising.

Many statistics on climate change, for example, are contradictory.

A similar variance can be seen in data connected with rising sea-levels.

As we examine the data sets, whether climate change does or does not exist remains inconclusive.

Copy and paste the sentences onto a third page, then jumble the sentences on page 2.

Pages 4 and 5:

Type the following sentences:

The UK prison population has risen dramatically in recent months.

The latest figures, for example, show high levels of over-crowding in jails.

Is it not high time to seek effective alternatives?

After all, community service is more beneficial to society as a whole.

Which leads to the central issue: are we simply trying to punish prisoners, or are we trying to ensure they can rejoin society?

Copy and paste the sentences onto page 5, then jumble the sentences on page 4.

Procedure

1 Open the first page of the flipchart and tell students they will be looking at how to construct a good paragraph. Ask students how they think a paragraph should be structured (it usually looks at one particular topic or central idea; it helps the reader if the topic sentence is first; the concluding sentence often re-phrases the idea of the topic sentence).

2 Move to the second flipchart page. Ask students to read the sentences and re-order them to create a good paragraph.

3 Ask students to come out and re-order the sentences. Elicit whole-class agreement. Move on to page 3 in order to check the answer. Elicit and write on the function of each sentence from the descriptions on page 1.

4 Follow the same procedure for pages 4 and 5.

Follow up

Students work together to produce their own paragraphs. Provide a suitable topic area or areas, eg write a paragraph for or against capital punishment.

Suggested answers

Page 2: Topic sentence, restatement + information, concluding sentence

Page 4: Topic sentence, example + information, concluding sentence

W2 Abbreviations and symbols in note-taking

Level intermediate and above
Interaction individual and whole class
Aim To present a number of abbreviations used in note-taking.
Language focus abbreviations
Technology IWB software

Before the class

Prepare a flipchart with a selection of abbreviations and symbols, as follows:

e.g.   etc.   i.e.   viz.   N.B.   re.   c.   vs.   v.v.   cf   >   <   →   ≠   ~   ∴

Procedure

1 As an introduction, write the words *abbreviation* and *symbol* on the flipchart. Ask students to give an example of each and tell you when these are used, eg in a lecture, taking notes in a meeting, secretarial short-hand, in a code, in maths, making notes on a long text. Remind students they need to use abbreviations in their academic life as students.

2 Move to the prepared flipchart. Tell students to study the whiteboard and in pairs, see if they can work out what the abbreviations and symbols mean.

3   Ask students to come out in turn and write the meaning next to the abbreviation. Input as necessary and continue until all the symbols have been completed.

4   Students copy down any useful abbreviations.

Follow up

Ask students to use the abbreviations in the next set of notes they take. Re-visit the flipchart as a quiz.

Answers

Abbreviations

e.g. – for example [exemplum gratis]; etc. – and so on / [et cetera]; i.e. – that is [id est]; viz. – namely [videlict]; N.B. – the information that follows is important [nota bene]; re. – referring to; c. – about [circa]; vs. – versus; v.v. – vice versa; cf. – compared [confer]

Symbols

> is greater than; < is less than; → causes; ≠ is not equal to; ~ about; ∴ therefore

W3   Effective note-taking

Level intermediate and above
Interaction individual, whole class
Aim To present a set of tips for effective note-taking.
Language focus note-taking
Technology IWB software

Before the class

Prepare a series of flipchart pages as follows:

Page 1: draw a horizontal line with an arrow head at each end. At one end, write *Good note-taker*. At the other end, *Poor note-taker*.

Page 2: leave blank

Page 3: type the heading *Ten tips for effective note-taking*, then type the following text:

1   *Title / lecturer or author's name / date*

2   *Use numbers (1,2,3)*

3   *Use headings*

4   *Underline*

5   *Use abbreviations (abbrvs.)*

6   *Use symbols*

7   *Use diagrams*

8   *Use colours*

9   *Legible*

10 *Usable / useful*

Procedure

1 As an introduction, ask students to think about whether they produce a good set of notes or if they are poor at note-taking. Open the flipchart and ask students to come out and place a cross at an appropriate point on the line.

2 In small groups, ask students to brainstorm five or more tips for effective note-taking.

3 Ask students to come out in turn and write up their ideas on page two of the flipchart.

4 Move to the next chart to compare your answers. Annotate the answer, eg elicit common ways of abbreviating words (*prob = problem*).

5 Open a blank flipchart page and describe three different ways of taking notes, using the whiteboard to illustrate each approach, as follows:

a) linear notes

b) diagrammatic notes

c) mind-map

Follow up

Give students a note-taking task, eg taking notes from a lecture or a text.

W4 Compiling a bibliography

Level intermediate and above
Interaction group, individual
Aim To order students' surnames for a bibliography.
Language focus compiling bibliographies
Technology IWB software

Procedure

1 As the students come into the class, tell them to go to the keyboard and type in their surname, followed by their initials. They may need an example, so provide one yourself, eg *Sharma, P. K.*

2 Tell the students that they should now alphabetise the names on the whiteboard. Ask someone to come out and drag their name to a suitable space somewhere on the flipchart.

3 Invite the next student to come out and drag their name above or below the first name.

4 Continue until all the students have come out and the exercise is complete. Encourage the students to help the person at the front if necessary. Monitor the activity.

5 Check the complete list. Remember it is an academic convention you will need to follow.

W5 Process writing

Level intermediate and above
Interaction groups, whole class
Aim To present the concept of process writing; to start a course on writing.
Language focus writing
Technology IWB software

Before the class

Prepare two flipchart pages.

Flipchart page 1 has the following words on it in jumbled order, on the left:

publish, rough draft, final proof read, brainstorm, edit, second draft, review.

On the right, write the words in their correct sequence (see answers below), lock the words into position and cover them with a large white square. Send the words to the back.

Create the following simple diagram on flipchart page 2:

Figure 4.13 Process writing

Procedure

1   Elicit from students what they understand by the term 'process writing'. As an introduction, remind students that for many students, writing is the most difficult of the four language skills. One way to improve this skill is to see writing more as a continuous process of drafting and re-writing, rather than a one-off writing activity. State the lesson aim. Open flipchart page 1 and tell students to read the stages.

2   Ask someone to come out and drag the stages of process writing into an acceptable order. Elicit feedback and agreement from the students.

3   Delete the white square to confirm the answer. Use the pen to add in any other useful steps or vocabulary, eg *research* (after *brainstorm*), *speedwriting* (next to *rough draft*), *peer review* (before *final proof read*).

4   Move to page 2. Tell students that writing is cyclical, with constant revisions and edits.

Follow up

Students should copy down the correct answer. The students then produce a short piece of writing on a suitable topic following these steps.

Answers

brainstorming, rough draft, review, edit, second draft, final proof reading, publish

W6 Paraphrasing

Level upper intermediate
Interaction pairs, whole class
Aim To present paraphrasing.
Language focus paraphrasing
Technology IWB software

Before the class

Prepare a series of flipchart pages as follows:

Page 1:

Type the heading *Paraphrasing* and the following text:

What? Changing text so it is different from the source

Why? to avoid plagiarism

How? change vocabulary | word class (V→N) | word order

Page 2:

Insert a four-sentence text you wish students to paraphrase, eg

Blended learning means different things to different people. One definition is the combination of classroom teaching with on-line teaching. For some, it is the best of both worlds; for others, it is the worst of both worlds. This workshop examines the benefits and constraints of a blended approach to language learning.

Pages 3–6:

Cut and paste one sentence from the text on page 2 (see example above) onto each blank page 3–6.

Procedure

1 Open the flipchart and present the 'what', 'why' and 'how' of paraphrasing on page 1.

2 Show the text to paraphrase on page 2. Divide the class into four small groups. Ask each group to paraphrase a different sentence.

3 Move to page 3. Students from the first group go out and write up their paraphrase underneath the original sentence from the text. Invite comments from the other groups and amend as necessary.

4 Continue until the text has been completely re-written. Use a word count feature to see if the paraphrase is shorter, longer or the same number of words.

W7 Spelling bee: text-to-board

Level any
Interaction individual
Aim To practise spelling.
Language focus spelling
Technology learner response devices

Before the class

Prepare a list of the ten words you wish your students to practise, eg

accommodation, achieve, beginning, clothes, definitely, develop, necessary, unfortunately, recommend, separate.

Procedure

1 Issue students with their learner response device and check they know how to use it.

Figure 4.14 Promethean ActiVote: Learner response device

2 Dictate the first word and tell students to spell it on their device. Show them that by clicking *Enter* their word is sent to the whiteboard. Do a quick practice to check that the devices are working.

3 Dictate the words and let students spell each word and 'text' it to the whiteboard. You can see how many students are correct and incorrect.

Follow up

Ask students to transfer any words they find problematic to their lexical notebooks. Do the same test again in order for the students to see any progress in the scores.

PRONUNCIATION

Pron 1 Past forms *-ed* endings

Level elementary to pre-intermediate
Interaction pairs and whole class
Aim To sort regular verbs by the pronunciation of their past form *-ed* endings.
Language focus common regular verbs
Technology IWB software

Before the class

Create a page with the following sentences:

I started learning Italian three years ago.

We changed trains in London.

I finished reading that book last night.

Create a second page with a three-column table. Head the columns: /ɪd/ /d/ and /t/. Type these verbs as separate, movable items at the bottom of the page:

answer, arrive, ask, call, close, collect, cook, dance, drop, expect, happen, include, increase, invite, listen, move, raise, remember, select, talk, travel, visit, wait, want, watch.

Procedure

1 Ask for a volunteer to read the first sentence. Draw the students' attention to the pronunciation of the *-ed* ending of *started*. Underline the ending with an IWB pen and label it /ɪd/. Ask for a second volunteer to read the next sentence. If they do not pronounce *changed* correctly, give them a second opportunity, then ask the rest of the class for the correct pronunciation. Model it yourself. Mark and label it /d/. Repeat for the final sentence with the /t/ ending of *finished*.

2 Clarify that the students understand that there are three different pronunciations of *-ed* depending on the sound at the end of the infinitive.

3 Display the page with the table and list of verbs. Divide the students into pairs and give them time to decide which verbs go into which column.

4 Invite a volunteer to come to the board, drag a word into a column and say the past form. Ask the rest of the class whether they agree or not. If necessary, give the student a second chance to classify the verb. Continue to invite students to the board until all the words have been put into the correct columns.

Follow up

Ask the pairs to choose eight or ten verbs from the list and use them in a short oral report on something they did last week. Each pair then gives their report to the class. Give feedback on their pronunciation of the verbs.

Answers

/ɪd/	/d/	/t/
collect	answer	ask
expect	arrive	cook
include	call	dance
invite	change	drop
select	close	finish
start	happen	increase
visit	listen	remember
wait	move	talk
want	raise	watch
	travel	

Pron 2   Phonetic symbols – identify a word

Level pre-intermediate
Interaction teams and whole class
Aim To identify a word from its phonetic spelling.
Language focus words that are difficult to pronounce, using phonetic symbols
Technology IWB software, clone tool and CD-ROM dictionary

Before the class

This activity can be used as a follow up to activity Pron 1 in Chapter 1.

Create a page with the phonetic symbols (see figure 4.15). Apply the clone tool to each symbol.

Create two handouts with the following words:

Handout A: *late, daughter, shoes, cheap, through, work, music.*

Handout B: *light, bought, choice, ship, month, talk, skiing.*

Procedure

1   Display the phonetic symbols. Review each one to check your students remember the sounds they represent. Drag the appropriate symbols to the centre of the board to spell out / ˈraɪtɪŋ /. Ask the students to identify the word, ie *writing.* See figure 4.15.

Consonants

p b t d k g f v θ ð s z
ʃ ʒ h x tʃ dʒ m n ŋ w r l j

Vowels and diphthongs

ɪ e æ ɒ ʌ ʊ ə i u iː aː ɔː
eɪ əʊ ɔɪ ɪə aʊ ʊə eə

/r aɪ t ɪ ŋ/ *writing*

Figure 4.15 Dragging phonetic symbols to write the pronunciation of *writing*

2   Divide the class into two teams. Give each team one of the lists of words. Ask them to discuss and write out the words using the phonetic symbols. Monitor and assist.

3   A student from team A goes to the board and drags the symbols to write the first word on the team's list. Team B have a short time to discuss what they think the word is. If they are right, they get a point. If not, team A gets a point.

4   A student from team B uses the symbols to write a word for team A to identify. Continue until both sets of words have been completed. If the students are not sure, use your CD-ROM dictionary to model the pronunciation and show how the phonetics are written.

Follow up

This activity can be done regularly to review any words that have presented pronunciation issues during the course.

Variation

Pairs of students could also test each other by producing a short list for homework to use in the next lesson.

Answers

late / leɪt /   light / laɪt /

daughter / ˈdɔːtə(r) /   bought / bɔːt /

shoes / ʃuːz /   choice / tʃɔɪs /

cheap / tʃiːp /   ship / ʃɪp /

through / θruː /   month / mʌnθ /

work / wɜː(r)k /   talk / tɔːk /

music / ˈmjuːzɪk /   skiing / ˈskiːɪŋ /

These answers are all British English pronunciation. Whether you include the /r/ sound in *daughter* and *work* depends on your accent.

Pron 3   Phonetic symbols – write a word

Level pre-intermediate
Interaction teams and whole class
Aim To listen to and write words using the phonetic symbols.
Language focus pairs of words which cause pronunciation difficulties
Technology IWB software, clone tool and CD-ROM dictionary

Before the class

This activity can be used as a follow-up to introducing the students to the phonetic symbols in Pron 1 in Chapter 1.

Create a page with the phonetic symbols as in the previous activity. Clone or copy the page five times.

Use this list of words: *hair, here, bought, boat, chair, share, close (adj), close (v), feel, fill.*

Procedure

1   Display the first of the pages with the phonetic symbols. Say the word *three*. Drag the symbols to spell the word in the centre of the board, ie / θriː /. Now say *tree*. Ask a volunteer to come to the board and use the symbols to spell the word, / triː /.

2   Divide the class into teams. Explain that they are going to hear ten words. They will have time to discuss each one before someone tries to spell the word on the board using the phonetic symbols.

3   Read the first word on the list, ie *hair*. Give the teams a minute to discuss then ask for a volunteer to come to the board and spell the word. Read the second word, ie *here* and repeat the procedure. Go to the next page and continue with the next pair of words. If you want to have a competitive element to the activity, award points for success.

4   Continue until the end of the list. If the students are not sure, use your CD-ROM dictionary to model the pronunciation and show how the phonetics are written.

Answers

hair / heə(r) /	here / hɪə(r) /
bought / bɔːt /	boat / bəʊt /
chair / tʃeə(r) /	share / ʃeə(r) /
close (adj) / kləʊs /	close (v) / kləʊz /
feel / fiːl /	fill / fɪl /

These answers are all British English pronunciation. Whether you include the /r/ sound depends on your accent.

Pron 4   Linking sounds

Level pre-intermediate to intermediate
Interaction whole class
Aim To raise awareness of linking sounds between words.
Language focus linking sounds
Technology IWB software, clone tool

Before the class

Find a picture of an elephant and paste it onto a flipchart page. Apply the clone tool to this picture.

Procedure

1   Display the picture and ask the students what it is. When they answer, write *nelephant* next to the picture. Say 'a nelephant' and ask the students to repeat.

2   Drag two pictures into place below the first and explain that these are *welephants*. Drill the students in saying *tu welephants*.

3   Write *an elephant* and *two elephants* next to the pictures and draw arrows and the phonetic symbols /n/ and /w/ to show how the linking sound is carried from the end of *an* and *two* and is attached to the start of the next word.

4   Drag more pictures onto the screen and elicit and drill *three yelephants*, *four relephants*, and *fi velephants*.

Follow up

Divide the students into pairs and ask them to think of more words beginning with vowel sounds that also require linking sounds in the same way, eg *apple, egg, octopus, onion*.

Pron 5   Phonetic symbols – change a symbol

Level pre-intermediate to intermediate
Interaction teams and whole class
Aim To change one word into another by changing the phonetic symbols one at a time.
Language focus *In the example:* single-syllable minimal pairs
Technology IWB software, clone tool and CD-ROM dictionary

Before the class

This activity can be used as a follow up to introducing the students to the phonemic symbols in Pron 1 in Chapter 1 and Pron 2 in Chapter 4.

Create a page with the phonetic symbols as in the previous activity. Clone or copy the page several times.

Procedure

1 Display the first page with the phonetic symbols. Say the word *three*. Drag the symbols to spell the word in the centre of the board, ie / θriː /. Write *three* in the top right corner of the page. Ask the students what happens if you change the /θ/ symbol to /t/, ie the word becomes *tree*. Do this and write *tree* under *three*. Continue by changing /t/ to /f/ (*free*), the vowel to /aɪ/ *(fry)*, and the first sound to /d/ *(dry)*.

2 Divide the students into teams, go to the next page with the phonetic symbols and drag the symbols for the word *car*, ie / kɑː(r) /. Ask a volunteer to identify the word and write it in the top right corner. Explain that the game is to change from one word to another by changing one sound in the word at a time. Allow the teams time to discuss possible changes then invite a student from the first team to change the word, eg to / keə(r) / (*care*) or / bɑː(r) / (*bar*). If they are successful award a point, if not, invite the next team to try. Once a team is successful, give more discussion time then invite the next team to modify the new word to make another. Continue until no team can think of any changes. If you have time, go to the next page and start with a new word.

Pron 6 Homographs

Level intermediate
Interaction pairs and whole class
Aim To decide on the correct pronunciation of homographs.
Language focus homographs
Technology IWB software, digital version of the phonemic chart

Before the class

Prepare a flipchart with the following words: *lead, wind, row, tear, read.*

Procedure

1 Write two sentences on the flipchart: *I read it yesterday* and *I don't usually read much.* Ask students to say each sentence. Draw attention to the two different ways of pronouncing the verb form. Tell students they will be researching words with more than one pronunciation.

2 Open the interactive phonemic chart and click to play the alternative sounds for *read.*

3 Tell students to work in pairs and to write two sentences with each of the other four words, using their dictionaries. During this stage, tell students they can come out and check the sounds using the phonemic chart.

4 Invite students to come out in turn and write their two sentences. They then read their sentences aloud to the group. Monitor and correct as necessary.

Variation

With higher-level groups, ask students to work without dictionaries.

Pron 7 Practising vowel sounds with limericks

Level intermediate
Interaction pairs and whole class
Aim To practise vowel sounds by looking at rhymes instead of spellings.
Language focus vowel sounds
Technology IWB software

Before the class

Type the following three limericks on separate flipchart pages. For the second and third create each line as a separate object that can be moved around the page and jumble up the lines.

Page 1:

There once was a man with a boat

Which he bought with a twenty pound note

He sailed over the water

With his wife and his daughter

That's the end 'cos that's all that I wrote

Page 2:

A foolish young man named Ted

Never listened when all his friends said

'Don't try to ski

Round both sides of a tree'

Ted tried it, and now Ted is dead

Page 3:

In every hotel where I've stayed

I've slept there for free, and not paid

When they call for the law

I'm, quick, out the back door

So, the policemen, I always evade

Procedure

1 Display the first limerick. Explain that it is a five-line, humorous poem in which the first, second and final lines rhyme and the third and fourth lines rhyme. Explain that rhymes usually occur when words have the same vowel sound and number of syllables.

2 Display the second limerick and explain that the lines are out of order. Elicit the pronunciation of the words at the end of each line, ie *Ted, said, ski, tree, dead*, and which ones have the same vowel sounds. If necessary, use a CD-ROM dictionary to look up the words and provide a pronunciation model. Draw the students' attention to the differences in spelling of words with the same vowel sounds.

3 Divide the students into pairs and give them a few minutes to try and put the lines into the correct order. Invite a student to come to the board and drag the lines of the limerick into position. Once the correct order has been established, read the limerick to demonstrate the rhythm and how the rhyming words fit together.

4 Display the third limerick and ask the pairs to discuss the vowel sounds. Ask the pairs to report back, then repeat step 3.

Follow up

The rhythm of a limerick when you say it is important. This depends on which words are stressed in each line. Say the first limerick and ask the students to identify which words are stressed. Invite a student to the board to underline the words. Invite other students to read the limerick, stressing the underlined words. Provide a model for the other limericks and ask the pairs to determine the stressed words.

Pron 8 Stress patterns: nouns and verbs

Level intermediate
Interaction whole class
Aim To raise awareness of patterns of word stress in verbs and nouns.
Language focus word stress
Technology IWB software

Before the class

Prepare a flipchart page with the following eight words:

export, import, record, transfer, produce, report, object, subject.

Procedure

1 Tell the students that these words are stressed differently when they are said as a noun and as a verb. Write two sentences, one with the word as a verb and one as a noun, eg *He was transferred to Real Madrid. / The money was a bank transfer.* Elicit the stress on the words *transferred* and *transfer* and the reason. Divide the class into two groups. Ask students in each group to write a sentence with each word used either as a noun or as a verb.

2 Ask group 1 to read their sentences out. Ask someone from group 2 out to the whiteboard. After each sentence, the listener writes *V* or *N* and marks the stress pattern. Check back with the speaker if they are correct or not. Continue until all the words have been done.

3 Change groups and repeat the activity.

4 Encourage students to transfer the words into their lexical notebooks with the correct stress pattern marked.

Pron 9 Word stress in word families

Level intermediate
Interaction pairs and whole class
Aim To mark the word stress of words in word families.
Language focus *In the example:* word stress for families based on *photograph* and *electric*
Alternatives: word families based on *production, economy, variation*
Technology IWB software, clone tool and CD-ROM dictionary

Before the class

Create a flipchart page with these two sentences:

My father is a keen _____, he takes his camera everywhere.

Natalia takes so many _____when she's on holiday but they all show the same thing.

Then create a page with these two lists of words:

photograph	*electric*
photography	*electricity*
photographic	*electrical*
photographer	*electrician*
photographically	*electrically*
	electrification

Create a coloured box, the right size to position above a single syllable in each word. Set this box to clone.

Procedure

1   Display the page with the gapped sentences and ask the students to suggest words to complete them, ie *photographer* and *photographs*. Explain that these words are part of a word family. Brainstorm the rest of the word family for *photograph* and the entire family for *electric*. If necessary, allow the students to look in dictionaries to find the words.

2   Display the page with the word families. Explain that, even though words are from the same family, they may not have the same stress pattern. Elicit the pronunciation of *photograph*. Ask which syllable is stressed, ie **pho**tograph and drag a coloured box into position above that syllable. Play the model from a CD-ROM dictionary and draw the students' attention to how the word stress is indicated by the stress mark before the stressed syllable, ie / ˈfəʊtəˌgrɑːf /. In this example, draw the students' attention to the secondary stress.

3   Divide the class into pairs and ask the students to decide on the correct word stress for each word.

4   Invite a volunteer to come to the board. Ask the student to drag a box into place on the next word and to say the word to demonstrate the stress. Encourage feedback from the rest of the class if there is any disagreement. If there is any uncertainty, play the pronunciation model from your CD-ROM dictionary. Repeat with different students for the remaining words.

Answers

photograph	e**lec**tric
photo**gra**phy	elec**tri**city
photo**gra**phic	e**lec**trical
pho**to**grapher	elec**tri**cian
photo**gra**phically	electrifi**ca**tion

Pron 10 Silent letters

Level upper intermediate
Interaction individual and group
Aim To practise spelling words with silent letters / to familiarise students with the phonemic script in dictionary entries.
Language focus vocabulary
Technology IWB software, eraser tool

Before the class

Prepare a flipchart with the following words displayed randomly:

honest, comb, palm, gnome, knee, salmon, psyche, pneumonia, autumn, island, doorknob, fasten.

Procedure

1 Open the flipchart. Tell students there is one 'silent' letter in each word. Ask students to look at the first word, *honest*, and decide which is the silent letter. They should use their dictionaries to decide, individually or in pairs.

2 Invite students out in turn to highlight or erase the silent letter. Do a whole-class check after each word. Ask students to pronounce the word.

3 Continue until students have completed all the words correctly.

4 Ask students to record any useful spellings in their lexical notebooks. Give the same list as a spelling test later on in the course.

Answers

honest, com**b**, pa**l**m, **g**nome, **k**nee, sa**l**mon, **p**syche, **p**neumonia, autum**n**, i**s**land, door**k**nob, fas**t**en

Pron 11 Sound linking

Level upper intermediate
Interaction whole class
Aim To practise sound linking in connected speech.
Language focus pronunciation
Technology IWB software

Before the class

Prepare a flipchart as follows, with a wide space between the words on each line:

1 serious   *accident*

2 exact   *opposite*

3 warm   *breeze*

4 starting   *tomorrow*

5 half   *full*

6 some   *milk*

7 car	*engine*
8 pure	*oxygen*
9 who	*is*
10 go	*away*
11 see	*it*
12 completely	*empty*

Procedure

1 Remind students that in connected and fast speech, words are often linked together. Sometimes a new sound is formed. This activity will focus on some of these sound changes.

2 Conduct a drill of the words *serious* and *accident*, *exact* and *opposite* individually. Drag the sets of words together and then link the words with the symbol . Using the highlighter, point out that the first word ends with a consonant and the second starts with a vowel. Say them together quickly to show they are linked smoothly: *seriou / saccident; exa / ctopposite* and conduct a drill so that students practise saying these words quickly.

3 Do the same for each pair of words (see the answers below).

4 Ask the students to write a short dialogue with five of the phrases. They should then mark the sound linking and practise their dialogue in pairs before reading it to the whole class.

Answers

1–2: consonant sound at the end of a word is linked smoothly to a vowel at the start of the next

3–4: when a word ends in a consonant and the next one starts with a consonant, there is no break; sometimes the first sound changes slightly to make it easier to move to the second consonant

5–6: when a word ending in a consonant is followed by a word with the same consonant, one lengthened consonant sound is made

7–8: intrusive 'r'

9–10: intrusive 'w'

11–12: intrusive 'j'

GAMES

Game 1 Travel game

Level intermediate
Interaction small groups then teams
Aim To create and play a game to practise a series of travel problem situations.
Language focus language for travel situations
Technology IWB software

Before the class

Create a page with a grid like the one in figure 4.16. Create several different coloured circles as playing pieces, one per team. If your software has an interactive dice, add one to the page as well.

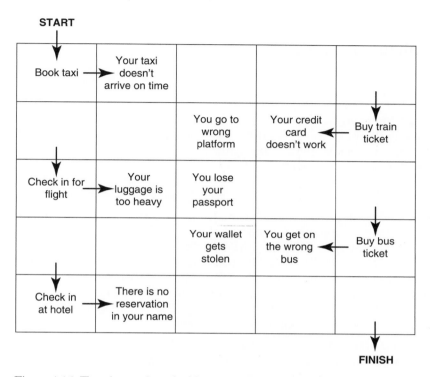

Figure 4.16 Travel game board with some problems already written in

Procedure

1 Display the page. Divide the students into small groups and ask them to brainstorm as many problems as they can imagine associated with travelling and staying at a hotel. If they cannot think of any, suggest they consider difficulties with timetables, losing things and the problems of finding your way around an unfamiliar place, as well as issues relating to fellow passengers.

2 Ask the students to report back. Add the problems to the empty squares on the game board. If you do not have enough problems to fill all the squares, add: *buy souvenirs, ask for tourist information for a good weather / bad weather day.*

3 Divide the class into teams. The first team rolls the dice and moves their playing piece the appropriate number of squares on the board. Read out the problem or situation on that square. Ask the team to nominate a member to be the traveller. Choose a student from another team to be the other person in the situations. Ask them to role play the situation that arises from the problem. Provide any necessary feedback.

4 Continue the game. Make sure that everyone has an opportunity to take part in a role play. If a situation comes up more than once make sure different students take part. The game can finish when one team reaches the end or continue until every team has reached the end.

Variation

This game can be used as a follow up to a first conditional review. After you have collected the problems brainstormed in step 1, tell the students to imagine they are going on a trip and ask them to decide what they will do if they encounter these problems. Then you can put the problems onto the board and play the game.

Game 2 Kooshball challenge

Level all
Interaction teams
Aim To review recently studied structures.
Language focus any
Technology IWB Notebook software and Kooshball to be thrown at the IWB
    Warning – please do not use **any other** objects to throw at the IWB as they may
    cause damage to the board.

Before the class

Think of a series of questions which could be used to form a revision quiz for your class, and insert each question on a flipchart page (you could also use any previously prepared Gallery activities such as a Keyword Match or a Word Guess to form a question). Insert each question on a flipchart page. On the first page of the flipchart insert a number of shapes of different colours. Link each of the individual shapes to one of the pages with the questions. To do this, right-click on a shape and choose *Link* from the menu that appears. When the *Insert link* window appears, click on the *Page in this file* option, and use the page titles which will appear to allocate a page.

On each page you have created, add a shape which links back to the first page, as outlined above. This will enable you to return to the first page after each question. (See figure 4.17).

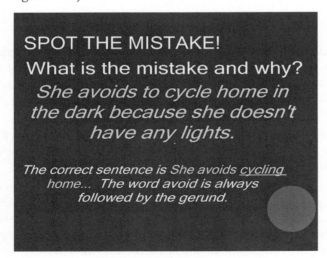

Figure 4.17 An example of a question used in the Kooshball Challenge

If you want to increase 'competitiveness', add an extra slide (linked to the first slide) where you can write the team scores.

Procedure

1 Divide the class into teams of three or four and briefly demonstrate the game. Ask a student to throw the Kooshball at one of the shapes on the first flipchart page. This will take them to a quiz question which they have to answer. Decide whether the student who throws the ball has to answer the question, or whether the students in the team are allowed to confer.

2 Decide which team will go first, and give the Kooshball to a member of the first team, who should throw the Kooshball at the board and answer the question which appears. Sometimes the Kooshball will not activate the link: if this happens, click on the circle closest to where the Kooshball hit the board. If they answer correctly, they are awarded a point. If not, the question is passed to the other teams to answer. Click on the shape to return to the first page before the next team takes a turn.

3 Repeat step 2 until each team or a student from each team has answered a question, or all of the questions have been answered. The team with the most correct answers wins!

Follow up

Students can be asked to study in greater depth areas which proved to be problematic, or lessons can be prepared for future study.

Activity contributed by Jo Timerick.

LEARNING TO LEARN

L2L1 Talking about myself!

Level elementary
Interaction group and individual
Aim To guess the relevance of words for an individual in order to learn something about them.
Language focus speaking
Technology IWB software, digital camera

Before the class

Prepare a digital flipchart page with adjectives and nouns connected with you, eg names of family / where you grew up / birthplace / your pet's name etc.

If possible, include photos of people and places.

Procedure

1 Open the flipchart and tell students that the words and pictures are all important to you. Ask them to guess the significance of things on the flipchart. 'Is that your daughter?' 'Were you born there?'

2 When you have finished, take a digital photo of each student in the class.

3 Students work alone to write down five things about themselves. While they do this, copy the photos into a new flipchart page.

4 Students go out in turn and add the words around their picture. They explain their descriptive words to the class. Encourage questions.

Follow up

Re-visit the flipchart and erase the annotations. Find out if everyone in the class remembers the students' names and something about them.

L2L2 Alphabetise it!

Level pre-intermediate
Interaction small groups
Aim To practise putting words in alphabetical order, in order to improve dictionary skills.
Language focus scanning for specific letters
Technology IWB software, timer

Before the class

Prepare a series of four flipcharts, one per group. Choose ten words at random from a monolingual dictionary page and type them onto the first flipchart, eg *miscellaneous, misfit, misguided, miracle, misbehave, mischief, mislead, misinform, misery, misjudge.*

Ensure the words are out of sequence. Repeat the process with a different set of words for the other three flipcharts.

Procedure

1   Divide the class into four groups. Tell the students they will see eight words and they need to drag them into alphabetical order. As soon as they finish, they should stop the timer. Ask group 1 to come out to the whiteboard and re-order their words. Start the timer. Note down the time.

2   Do the same with the other three groups. See which group was the fastest!

Follow up

Remind groups that they need to look up words in their monolingual dictionaries. This activity can be used as a warmer or cooler.

L2L3 Language skills evaluation

Level pre-intermediate and above
Interaction individual and group
Aim To introduce students to the language skills course.
Language focus speaking
Technology IWB software, *Infinite clone* tool

Before the class

Prepare a flipchart with four letters on it: *L, R, S, W.* Click on each letter and click on the *Infinite cloner.*

Procedure

1   Remind students that in language teaching we often refer to the four language skills of listening, reading, speaking and writing. Two skills are receptive, two are productive. Tell students that they will compare their strengths and weaknesses in the four language skills and compare them with other students in the class.

2 Ask students to take out a piece of paper and write down the four letters in a vertical line, with their weakest skill at the top, and their strongest skill at the bottom.

3 Invite students out to the IWB in turn to click on each letter and drag it into their own order. Students write their name under each list.

4 When students have finished, circle or highlight any patterns you notice. Point out that in any class, there are differences in strengths and weaknesses. Discuss how you will use the results to modify the course: eg 'We will have a class reader as a lot of students have problems with the skill of reading.'.

Variation

With larger groups, students work in small groups to compare their answers first. They can then come to the IWB to highlight significant patterns by dragging out any of the letters (L, R, S, W) and annotating them with the number of students who found this skill particularly difficult / easy.

L2L4 Effective vocabulary storage and retrieval

Level intermediate and above
Interaction group, individual
Aim To discuss which ideas for storing new vocabulary are the most effective.
Language focus vocabulary learning
Technology IWB software, the Internet

Before the class

Prepare a flipchart with eight circles on it and the following text in the circles:

1 *in a list with a translation next to them*

2 *in my alphabetical notebook*

3 *in a diagram, such as a 'word tree' or a mind-map*

4 *on index-cards, with a translation on the back*

5 *in an Excel spreadsheet*

6 *in a lexical notebook*

7 *in an electronic notebook on the Macmillan English Campus*

8 *in the notebook I bring to class.*

At the top of the flipchart page, draw a line. At one end of the line, write *effective* and at the other, *ineffective*. Above the line, type the sentence starter: *I write down my new words …*

If possible, on the next flipchart page, create a hyperlink to the electronic notebook on Macmillan English Campus or the student's MPO (Macmillan Practice Online).

Procedure

1 Open the flipchart. Tell students they are going to look at a number of ways in which students record the new vocabulary that comes up in class. Demonstrate or explain any terms or systems which students may be unfamiliar with. For example, draw a word tree diagram; click on the hyperlink to show the vocabulary storage tool on the Macmillan English Campus.

2   Students work in pairs to discuss whether they think these systems are effective or ineffective.

3   Ask individual students to come out and drag the circles to the left or right of the chart, depending on whether they think they are good ideas for storing vocabulary or not. Encourage whole-class discussion.

4   Find out if students use any other systems. If so, write students' ideas on the flipchart. Tell students that although there is no one 'right way', clearly some systems are better than others.

Variation

With higher-level groups, do step 4 as a brainstorm / lead-in.

L2L5   Knowing a word

Level intermediate and above
Interaction pairs and whole group
Aim 'To brainstorm ideas about what we 'know' about a word.
Language focus vocabulary learning
Technology IWB software

Before the class

Prepare a diagram on the flipchart: draw a circle and type the words *Knowing a word* in the centre, then add eight short spokes coming out.

Procedure

1   As an introduction, ask students to think of one or two words which were new for them in recent lessons and write them on the flipchart below the diagram. Tell students that they will be looking at what we know about a word, such as the meaning. Write *meaning* on the flipchart against one of the spokes.

2   Ask students in pairs to write down anything else they know about the word, such as how to spell it.

3   Elicit students' ideas and add them to the diagram. Modify students' ideas as necessary. For example, use a different colour to add things which are useful to know.

4   When students have finished, add anything missing from the diagram (see Suggested answers).

Follow up

Elicit from students the implications of writing down new words, ie writing down a word with a translation is not enough for many words. This is good exercise to begin a lesson on exchanging ideas on how to store vocabulary (see L2L3 in Chapter 1) or word frequency (see V15 in Chapter 1).

Suggested answers

meaning / how to use it / forms, eg adj v adv / pronunciation (including word-stress) / spelling / collocations, eg verb–noun, adjective–noun, noun–noun / Connotation / Register (formal, informal, colloquial)

Useful to know

synonyms / antonyms / etymology / frequency

L2L6 Pre-task checklist

Level intermediate and above
Interaction pairs and whole class
Aim To establish objectives before performing a speaking task.
Language focus language for telephone calls
Technology IWB software

Before the class

This activity can be used as the first stage in a lesson to practise telephoning language, for example as a business skill. The final stage could be the *Post-task checklist* activity which follows this one. Create a page with the following sentences:

Who am I calling?

How well do I know them?

Why am I calling them?

What information do I need to give?

What information do I expect to receive?

What difficulties might I face?

Then clone the page so that you have as many pages as you have pairs of students or telephone role plays you plan to conduct. This activity works best on Business English courses since these generally involve people who are familiar with the idea of setting objectives as part of a strategy for improvement.

The telephone call role plays themselves can be simple situations such as leaving a message, giving or receiving information, making a complaint, making a booking etc, or they can be provided by the students themselves to fit with their specific needs.

Procedure

1 Explain to the students that they are going to practise making short telephone calls in pairs. However, before doing this, they are going to prepare and think about the type of language and communication issues they might face.

2 Choose a pair of students to make the first call. Choose a situation and outline it to them.

3 Display the checklist on the board, discuss it with the group, filling in the answers as you go. Use two colours to represent the points of view of the two students participating in the role play, eg for the first question, there may be two answers: *a customer, a supplier*. Discuss the consequences for the language the students will need to use, eg will it be more or less formal?

4 For the last question, ask the students to focus on possible language and communication issues, eg not understanding something, needing to repeat or spell something.

5 Once the checklist has been completed, invite the first pair of students to role play the situation.

6　If the next pair does the same role play, you can use the completed checklist again. If the situation is different, fill in a new one.

Follow up

Save these pages so that you can repeat the role plays in a subsequent lesson.

Variation

With some minor modification, this type of checklist can be used as preparation for most discrete speaking tasks. In a Business English context it could be adapted for presentations, and meetings or negotiations role plays.

L2L7　Post-task checklist

Level intermediate and above
Interaction pairs and whole class
Aim To measure and discuss performance after a speaking task.
Language focus language for telephone calls
Technology IWB software

Before the class

This activity can be used as the third stage in a lesson to practise telephoning language, for example, as a business skill. The first stage could be the *Pre-task checklist* activity L2L6 which precedes this one. Create a page with the following items and then clone it so that you have as many pages as you have students or telephone role plays you plan to conduct:

How well did I achieve my objective?

How well did I use the standard telephone phrases?

How well did I understand the other person?

How well did the other person understand me?

How happy am I with my overall performance?

What do I need to do to improve my performance?

This activity works best on Business English courses since these generally involve people who are familiar with the idea of measuring performance in order to plan a strategy for improvement.

Procedure

1 After the students have completed the telephone role play, if you did activity L2L7, display the pre-task checklist to remind the students of the objective of the call; otherwise, display the post-task checklist you created on the board.

2 Invite two students to the board and ask them to draw an X on each of the scales in answer to the questions and explain why. Make sure they use different colours. The first time people do this they will tend to underestimate their performance. If you feel they are being unfair on themselves, say why and encourage them to place their Xs in a more appropriate position.

3 Discuss the last question on the basis of the position of the students' Xs on the scales. If it is a small group and your students are comfortable with peer feedback, encourage other members of the group to provide input as well. As a result of this discussion, add some notes at the bottom of the page, eg *need to speak more slowly, ask for repetition.*

4 Repeat the role play, or another role play with a second pair of students then repeat steps 2 and 3 for those students.

5 If there is time, ask each pair to repeat the role plays and then return to their checklist and invite them to re-position their markers on the scales.

Follow up

Save these pages and repeat the role plays in a subsequent lesson. Again, invite the students to reassess their performance and mark it on the scales.

Variation

With some minor modification, this type of checklist can be used as a follow-up to most discrete speaking tasks. In a Business English context it could be adapted to assess students' performance after presentations, and meetings or negotiations role plays.

L2L8 Speaking vs. writing

Level intermediate and above
Interaction groups, whole class
Aim To present the difference between the two skills of speaking and writing / to introduce students to the writing component of their language course.
Language focus writing
Technology IWB software

Before the class

Prepare a digital flipchart with two headings: *Speaking* and *Writing* and lock these words into position.

Then type in the following words and phrases in a column down the centre of the page. Each phrase should be in a separate text box so it can be dragged to the correct column.

mistakes tolerated | mistakes not tolerated

two-way | one-way

informal | formal

unfinished sentences | completed sentences

pronunciation important

punctuation important

spelling important

contractions used | contractions avoided

intangible | tangible

Procedure

1 Tell students that they are going to look at the differences between the language skill of speaking and the skill of writing. Open the flipchart and ask students to look at the first two phrases. Tell them that in speaking, the listener is tolerant of mistakes which don't cause a breakdown in communication, such as *I'm born in Spain*; drag the phrase *mistakes tolerated* to the *Speaking* column. In writing, the reader is not tolerant of mistakes. Drag the phrase *mistakes not tolerated* to the writing column.

2 Tell students they should read the phrases and decide which column they should go to. Students discuss in pairs.

3 Invite students out to the front in turn to drag the phrases to the correct column. Monitor and help as necessary with vocabulary and examples.

4 When the activity has been completed ask students what implications this has for their writing, eg they should spend more time on a document / do a proof read / be aware of more formal expressions / use a spell-checker etc.

Follow up

Move on to a writing task. Print out the flipcharts if required.

Variation

With strong groups, only provide one example. Put students into pairs or small groups and ask them to brainstorm further differences. Invite students out to the front to write up their ideas in each column. Have the above ideas on a second flipchart to show at the end of the activity so students can compare their ideas to yours.

Answers

Speaking:

mistakes tolerated, two-way, ie speaker and listener, informal, unfinished sentences, pronunciation important, contractions used, intangible

Writing:

mistakes not tolerated, one-way, formal, completed sentences, punctuation important, spelling important, contractions avoided, tangible

Case study: The experimental teaching space

Kumar works at a UK university. The university recently established the Teaching Grid service, an initiative to provide accessible, collaborative support for all staff involved in teaching or training. In the library is an area known as the Experimental Teaching Space. Teachers are encouraged to use this area to experiment with new ways of using technology, including the use of IWBs. There is a space for teachers to practise, containing three large Smart Boards. Next to this area is a teaching room with two LCD boards – heralding the next generation of touch-screen IWBs. There are movable panels, and the seats here can be arranged flexibly, allowing for a range of different layouts.

Apart from the IWBs, there is a range of cutting-edge tools available to teachers, such as a document visualiser, which looks like an overhead projector: if you place a coin, artefact, document or realia on the surface, it can be projected onto the IWB screen – great for science subjects. There is also a tabletop sympodium. This lectern is designed to sit on top of a desk, and features all the interactive functions and annotation capabilities of a Smart Board. It can be used at an angle, and can effectively become a horizontal IWB screen, which could benefit anyone with problems standing at the IWB. Best of all, support staff are available to help you use the tools.

To teach in the Experimental Teaching Space, Kumar first had to complete a form, available on the university website, outlining what was new about the proposed lesson. He decided to use the *Personal Response System* (PRS), an electronic voting system, and booked his class in. Before the lesson, he called in to the room and was shown how to use the devices by one of the Experimental Teaching Space support staff. He received a useful handout outlining the various steps: firstly preparing a presentation, then issuing the devices to the learners.

On the day of the lesson, Kumar was pleased to know the support staff were available in case things went wrong. This effectively took away a lot of the worry about using the devices for the first time. He was struck by how easy it was to use the devices. The so-called 'clickers' came in a box, and he distributed one to each student. Voting itself was easy. Kumar had asked his students to generate the questions beforehand. He asked students to vote, and the results were displayed on the screen. During the lesson, the technology did freeze up, and needed to be reset. This was done by the support staff while Kumar continued teaching the class. Afterwards, he wrote a short report on the lesson, reporting that the students certainly enjoyed the experience. They also said they were happy that voting was anonymous, and this helped some of them be more honest than if they had to raise their hands to vote!

Kumar continues to have a few reservations about the Experimental Teaching Space. In his busy schedule, there was quite a lot of additional paperwork to book the space, draw up a proposal and do the write-up. On the other hand, his motivation was high to try something new, and the presence of the support staff was crucial in enabling him to leave his comfort zone. In itself, Kumar deemed this is a good thing in terms of teacher development. Writing up the session for other staff did enable colleagues to benefit from his experience.

Overall, Kumar feels happy that the university is making such new technology available for personal development as well as providing support, since it increases the chance that he will eventually embed the technology into his educational practice.

Case study: Project work

Anthony teaches multi-national groups at a language school in London. His classes are based on a standard coursebook used by all the students and supported in the classroom by an IWB set-up running the courseware for that book. Although he is expected to follow the book, Anthony does have some freedom to occasionally organise projects for his students that stray from this routine. In the past, these projects have tended to require the students to research and report back on something in one of London's tourist destinations such as museums or galleries. Recently, however, one of Anthony's class groups contained a significant number of longer-term students who had already done several such projects.

He decided to use the students and their curiosity about each other's countries and cultures as a resource and couple this with their tendency to use the Internet as a research tool. He divided the students into several small project groups. Each group contained three or four students of different nationalities. He then listed every nationality represented in the class on the board and by drawing lots, the groups chose which one they would focus on. The entire class then agreed to the range of topics to be covered. These included things such as customs and traditions, food and drink, and attitudes towards the family, time and work, and avoided topics that could be regarded as sensitive.

The first part of the task was for the groups to use their experience and knowledge, coupled with research, to prepare and give a presentation to the rest of the class about the country they had chosen and its culture. These presentations were spread over several days. Most of the groups ran their presentations via the IWB. They then took questions from their audience.

After the presentations, Anthony introduced the second stage of the project. He asked the project groups to prepare a short quiz for the rest of the class based on the content of their presentation. In order to standardise this, he created a quiz template using the IWB software. This had spaces for ten questions – five on each of two pages. The answers were to be written on the page first, then each one covered by a moveable box on which the question was written. He placed a pre-set timer on both pages. He showed the students how to use this template then distributed it on memory sticks to each project group. This stage proved to be the most problematic as the students were unfamiliar with the software and could only use it on the handful of computers in the school's self-access centre. Anthony had to postpone the date of the quizzes in order to give time for him to help some of the groups build their IWB page. Eventually this was achieved and all the quizzes were copied to the classroom computer.

About two weeks after the last of the presentations, each group took it in turns to administer their quiz to the rest of the students in the class. Anthony kept score and handed out small prizes to the winning group. Many students cited this project as a highlight of their course when they gave feedback on their last day in the school.